An Educator's Guide to
INDEPENDENT SCHOOLS

David M. Brown
B.A., LL.B.

Aurora Professional Press
a division of Canada Law Book Inc.
240 Edward Street, Aurora, Ontario

© **CANADA LAW BOOK INC., 1998**
Printed in Canada

All rights reserved. No part of this book may be reproduced in any form by any photographic, electronic, mechanical or other means, or used in any information storage and retrieval system, without the written permission of the publisher.

The paper used in this publication meets the minimum requirements of American National Standards for Information Sciences — Permanence of Paper for Printed Library Materials, ANSI Z39.48-1992.

Cover Photograph :
Charles Thatcher/Tony Stone Images

Canadian Cataloguing in Publication Data

Brown, David M.
  An educator's guide to independent schools

Includes bibliographical references and index.
ISBN 0-88804-261-2

1. Private schools — Law and legislation — Ontario. I. Title

LC51.2.O5B76 1998   344.713'072   C98-931705-6

To My Parents
Alan and Marion Brown

Foreword

The legal environment for independent schools is changing rapidly in Ontario. The courts are intruding into "private" school operations at an accelerated pace and the level of government control over public schools is rising. Teachers, parents and students are resorting to more litigation in order to improve educational accountability in Canada. Thus it is very difficult for those charged with governing and administering an independent school to avoid a direct brush with the law even in areas such as income tax receipts or student discipline.

As a result of this changing environment, education law should be considered a necessary component of administrative training programs for independent schools. This excellent book will be part of any such course of study. This is the first book in its field that deals extensively with the court cases arising from independent school issues. More than that, it deals with all the practical, everyday problems of setting up an independent school.

A study of education law has very practical merits as well as long term theoretic benefits which will improve the effectiveness of school management. Law is the most practical of disciplines when in the service of sound virtue. In the realm of education, that is the right to educate in accordance with one's own conscience.

> English law respecting the freedom of the individual has been built up from the procedure of the Courts: and . . . contains within it the fundamental principle that, where there is any conflict between the freedom of the individual and any other rights or interests, then no matter how great or powerful those others may be, the freedom of the humblest citizen shall prevail over it . . . The freedom of the individual, which is so dear to us, has to be balanced with his duty; for, to be sure every one owes a duty to the society of which he forms part . . . What matters in England is that each man should be free to develop his own personality to the full: and the only duties which should restrict this freedom are those which are necessary to enable everyone else to do the same . . . In these lectures I hope to show how the English law has kept in the past the balance between individual freedom and social duty: and how it should keep the balance in the social revolution of today.[1]

---

[1] Sir Alfred Denning, *Freedom Under the Law* (London: Stevens & Sons Ltd., 1949) at pp. 4-5.

In my experience, independent school administrators often borrow the public school legal model embodied in the *Education Act*. Many do not have information about other sources of law which govern private organizations such as independent schools. The *Education Act* has very limited relevance to independent schools. This book will provide the necessary information and legal principles to explain why this is so.

My own quest for educational justice has led to a number of court cases recorded in this book, and to a mission to expand and improve education law so as to create a new school sector in Ontario. In the past there was little by way of published literature for independent schools. Mr. Brown has provided a very significant service for independent schools by collecting all the necessary legal information on a wide range of problems in one volume. The book is written in a direct and lucid style with all the practical details that administrators need and it is completely up to date. The author brings to his legal expertise a measure of realism derived from his experience in dealing with officials at the Ministry of Education and Training as well as from his own background as a parent of children in independent schools.

The range of legal issues is necessarily broad, since independent schools cannot afford a staff of specialized legal advisors. Independent school administrators will be well served with this handy reference which provides basic information and helpful appendices. It will result in improved educational decision-making, clarify the legal position of independent schools and thus improve education in Ontario.

I strongly recommend this book to principals, superintendents, school board and ministry officials, lawyers, members of Parliament and all thoughtful parents. It is the book many of us have been waiting for. May it serve to strengthen educational choice and accountability in Ontario education.

Ancaster, Ontario   Adrian Guldemond
June, 1998   Executive Director
                           Ontario Alliance of Christian School Societies

Preface

Since my first professional contact with independent schools nearly ten years ago, I have come to marvel at their diversity and richness. In an age marked by an increasing centralization of educational decision-making in the hands of provincial governments, independent schools offer parents a broad range of alternatives for the education of their children.

This book seeks to fill a gap in the existing literature on education law. While several fine guides to Ontario education law have been written in recent years, most refer to independent schools only in passing, confining their treatment to a few paragraphs. In this book I have sought to review in detail the various areas of the law which touch upon the creation and operation of independent schools. These schools confront a host of corporate governance and financing issues not encountered by their public system counterparts and also maintain a significantly different relationship with the Ministry of Education and Training. I have tried to describe the legal framework in which Ontario independent schools operate in order to provide a practical understanding of the law to those engaged in their administration.

Given the wide variety of independent schools which operate in the province, it has been a difficult task to write a book which addresses the legal issues faced both by an Upper Canada College and a school of 20 children operating in a church basement. While such diversity necessitates a certain amount of generalization in describing the law, at the end of the day, both the big and the small operate in the same legal environment.

A book such as this is never written in isolation; many people have generously responded to my requests for information and advice. I must express my deep gratitude to Dr. Adrian Guldemond, Executive Director of the Ontario Alliance of Christian Schools Societies, for his stimulating discussion and thoughtful insights over the past ten years on many of the issues facing independent schools. Robert Taylor kindly reviewed portions of the manuscript from the perspective of a parent who has been instrumental in establishing two independent schools in Toronto. My partner, Alison Youngman, gave wise advice on issues relating to corporate governance.

I especially wish to thank my secretary, Jean Lew Lum, for her patience and assistance, without which this book could not have been written.

I am grateful to Howard Davidson of Aurora Professional Press for his initial faith in the project and his guidance these past nine months.

To my wife, Claudia, my critical editor and advisor, no words of thanks are sufficient to satisfy my debt to her. I wish to thank my sons, Ian, Patrick and Brendan, for allowing me the time to write this book.

I have attempted to state the law as of May, 1998. I have used the terms "independent school" and "private school" interchangeably. Since the term "independent school" more accurately captures the essence of such schools, I have favoured its use except when dealing with specific provisions of the *Education Act* which still use the older term, "private school".

Notwithstanding the kind advice and guidance of others, any errors in this book are mine alone.

Etobicoke, Ontario
May, 1998   David M. Brown

Table of Contents

	PAGE
Foreword	v
Preface	vii

1 The History and Legal Position of Independent Schools in Ontario ... 1

A Brief History of Independent Schools in Ontario	1
The Constitutional Position of Independent Schools in Ontario	4
The Different Approaches to Independent Schools Across Canada	7
An Overview of Ontario Legislation	9

2 Establishing the Independent School: Corporate Issues ... 13

Possible Legal Forms for an Independent School	13
The Procedure for Incorporating a Non-Share Corporation	15
Corporate Governance — Drafting the By-laws	20
Annual Corporate Filings	32
Personal Liability of Members and Directors of a Non-Share Corporation	33
The Independent School as a Registered Charity	35
Municipal Approvals for an Independent School	38

3 Dealing with the Ministry of Education ... 41

The Notice of Intention to Operate	41

September Statistical Filing 45
Inspections of Independent Schools by the Ministry of Education and
    Training 45
Inspected Independent Secondary Schools 47
Can an Independent School Operate Home Campuses? 54

4 The Contract of Instruction 57

The Contractual Relationship between Parent and School 57
The Legal Capacity of the Parties 58
The Documents Constituting the Contract of Instruction 58
Returning Students 62
Refunds of Tuition 63
Human Rights Considerations for Admissions 63

5 Financial and Operational Issues 67

Absence of Government Funding 67
Sources of Revenue 69
Taxation of Revenue 69
Tuition as a Charitable Donation 70
Other Charitable Donations 75
Receipts for Charitable Donations 77
Tuition as an Employee "Fringe Benefit" 78
Expenditures 78
Interest Rates on Overdue Student Accounts 80
Books and Records 80
Filings 81
Municipal Taxes 82
Insurance 84
Co-operation Agreements with School Boards 86

6 Programs of Study 87

Overview 87
Elementary Schools 88
Independent Secondary Schools which do not grant Ontario Diplomas . 89
Inspected Independent Secondary Schools 90

What does "Satisfactory Instruction" Mean?	92
Textbooks	96
Province-wide Tests	97
Special Education	99
School Health Programs and Services	100
School Year and Holidays	100
Course Hours	101
Religious Education Credits	101

7 Principals and Teachers 103

The Role of Principals and Teachers	103
Application of the Education Act to Independent School Teachers and Principals	105
Principals	107
Qualifications of Teachers	109
Teachers' Contracts of Employment	112
Codes of Conduct	117
Non-teaching Staff: Codes of Conduct	124

8 Student Records 127

General Requirements	127
Ontario Student Transcript	128
Report Cards	129
Ontario Education Numbers	129
Confidentiality of and Access to Student Records	130
Defamatory Statements in Student Records	133

9 Student Discipline 135

The Legal Source of the Power to Discipline	135
Reasonableness of Disciplinary Rules: In Loco Parentis	136
Procedural Fairness in Discipline	138
Remedy for Breach of the Principles of Fairness	141
Search and Seizure	142
Use of Reasonable Force for Corrective Purposes	142
Restricting Access to School Premises	144

10 Liability for Student Injuries 145

General Principles of Negligence 145
Liability of a School for Negligent Acts of its Teachers 152
The Legal Effect of Consent Forms and Releases 153
Contributory Negligence 154
Occupiers' Liability Act 154

11 Miscellaneous Statutory Obligations 157

Immunization of Students 157
Child and Family Services Act 159
Occupational Health and Safety Act 162
Fire Code 166

Appendices 167

Appendix "A" Relevant sections of the Ontario Education Act 167
Appendix "B" Associations of Independent Schools in Ontario 170
Appendix "C" Applications for Incorporation (Sample Objects of
    Existing Independent Schools) 172
Appendix "D" Applications for Incorporation (Special Provisions of
    Existing Independent Schools) 175
Appendix "E" Notice of Intention to Operate a Private School 181
Appendix "F" September Report, 1997 — Private School 182
Appendix "G" Private School Manual: Information for Inspected
    Private Secondary Schools, August, 1997 (excerpts) 183
Appendix "H" Private School Inspection Report 189
Appendix "I" Revenue Canada Information Circular 75-23 190

Index 193

1

The History and Legal Position of Independent Schools in Ontario

Independent schools have played an important role in Ontario's education system since pre-Confederation times. At the present time, approximately 80,000 students out of Ontario's total school population of 2.1 million students attend independent schools. Recent years have witnessed a significant increase in the number and importance of independent schools as parents look for alternatives to the programs of study offered in public and separate schools. While the legal framework governing Ontario's independent schools has remained largely unchanged for many years, many misconceptions still exist about the requirements which Ontario law imposes on the operation of independent schools. The purpose of this book is to explain the law in Ontario as it affects independent schools in a way that will assist those who are interested in establishing, or are currently operating, an independent school. It will also identify the legitimate demands which the Ministry of Education and Training and other government agencies may make on them.

A BRIEF HISTORY OF INDEPENDENT SCHOOLS IN ONTARIO

In 1984, the Ontario government set up a commission of inquiry into private schools for the purpose of considering whether the province should grant some public funding to independent schools. The commission of inquiry was carried out by Mr. Bernard Shapiro, and his 1985 report, *The Report of the Commission on Private Schools in Ontario*, quickly became known as the Shapiro Report.[1] While the question of public funding of independent schools formed the focus of the Shapiro Report, the report also nicely summarized their history in Ontario.[2]

---

[1] (Toronto: Ministry of Education, 1985).
[2] See "A History of Private Schools in Ontario" by Robert Stamp, Appendix G to *The Report of the Commission on Private Schools in Ontario* (1985).

The Shapiro Report identified four phases in the development of Ontario's independent schools. During the first phase in the late 18th and early 19th centuries, when Ontario's public school system was not yet in place, independent schools were "schools of necessity". Since the province was not involved in education, families who desired schooling for their children turned to the private sector.[3] While modest steps to create a public school system began around 1816, and then expanded as the years went by, as late as the early 1840s the number of schools not receiving any government funding roughly equaled the number of those that did.[4] That situation ended in the 1850s when legislation allowed local municipalities to finance common schools through property assessment. By the time of Confederation, with public schools readily available and accessible, independent schools as "schools of necessity" waned and then died.[5]

Thus began the transition to independent schools as "schools of privilege". Upper Canada College had been founded in 1829 primarily to educate the children of the higher classes. The second-half of the 19th century saw the founding of many of the great private boarding schools of Ontario which joined Upper Canada College as the schools of the elite — Trinity College School (1862), Bishop Strachan School (1867), Ridley College (1889), Albert College (1857) and Havergal College (1894). Most of the independent schools founded in the late 19th century resulted from initiatives by various religious groups, with the high Anglicans, low church Anglicans, non-conformist denominations and Roman Catholic groups establishing schools to provide sectarian-based instruction to the sons or daughters of their own flocks.[6]

The third period of development of Ontario's independent schools, during the first-half of the 20th century, saw the emergence of "schools of innovation". Independent entrepreneurs began to replace religious denominations as the initiators of new private schools. These non-sectarian schools differed from the previous denominational schools by including more urban-based day schools and catering to a new generation of rising urban professional and commercial families.[7] Many of these new independent schools initiated pedagogical reforms and promoted programs of study considered experimental in their day. By the early 1950s, however, Ontario's independent schools had sunk into a kind of lethargy. As described in the Shapiro Report:

> The general public seemed more indifferent than openly hostile, but it was almost a damning kind of indifference. "In the image of middle class equality that Canadians have with their society," wrote sociologist John Porter, "the pri-

---

[3] *Ibid.*, at p. 195.
[4] *Ibid.*, at p. 196.
[5] *Ibid.*, at p. 196.
[6] *Ibid.*, at p. 197.
[7] *Ibid.*, at p. 199.

vate school does not belong. It is something associated with the aristocratic societies of Europe and is rarely thought of as being a significant feature of Canadian Life."[8]

All of that was to change in the 1960s, the beginning of the fourth stage of development of Ontario's independent schools which the Shapiro Report described as the period of "schools of protest". From the 134 independent schools operating in Ontario in 1947-48, the number rose to 242 in 1969-70, 335 in 1977-79, and to 551 by 1984. By 1983, 83,463 pupils attended independent schools, of whom approximately 30,000 were students attending the senior grades of Roman Catholic high schools which did not then receive public funding.

With the passage in 1985 of Bill 30, which extended public funding to the senior grades of Roman Catholic separate schools, most of the students attending private Catholic schools moved into the publicly funded sector. Yet this enrolment loss of close to 30,000 students was quickly filled by the creation of new independent schools in the late 1980s and early 1990s, so that by the 1995-96 school year, 80,340 students were enrolled in 560 independent schools.[9] Of these schools, 305 were elementary schools, 57 secondary schools and 160 combined elementary and secondary schools; 38 schools were ungraded.

The independent schools which have emerged since the 1960s have aptly been described as "schools of protest".[10] Several large religious communities, particularly the Christian-Reformed and Jewish communities, rejecting the increased secularization of the province's public schools, established large numbers of independent elementary and high schools to serve their communities. Parents who became disenchanted with the courses of study offered in public schools opted to send their children to independent schools which provided alternative structures and programs of study.[11] In more recent years, a growing concern about the quality of the academic program offered by public and separate schools and the lack of student discipline in those schools, has prompted an increasing number of parents to search out an alternative education in independent schools, whether denominational or non-sectarian. As concluded by the Shapiro Report:

> Whatever the motives in their founding, whatever influences they had on public education, Ontario's private schools had assumed a significance in the early 1980's that could not have been predicted a generation earlier. Their religious diversity reflected the multi-cultural nature of the province; their philosophic diversity mirrored Ontario's secular pluralism. Proponents of public education had

---

[8] *Ibid.*, at p. 200.
[9] *Quick Facts: Ontario Schools, 1995-96*, Ontario Ministry of Education and Training (www.edu.gov.on.ca/eng/document/brochure/quickfac/facts97e.html).
[10] Shapiro Report, at p. 201.
[11] *Ibid.*, at p. 202.

long hoped to accommodate such diversity within the state-supported school system. But an increasing minority of students and parents had chosen the private sector. By this time the private schools of Ontario could no longer be classified exclusively as schools of necessity, or schools of privilege, or schools of protest. Like their public school counterparts, they had become the schools of diversity. Like their public school counterparts, they had become schools of Ontario.[12]

THE CONSTITUTIONAL POSITION OF INDEPENDENT SCHOOLS IN ONTARIO

The supreme law of our country is the Constitution of Canada. Section 93 of the *Constitution Act, 1867*, gives to each province the authority to make laws in respect of education. In certain provinces this legislative power is subject to the restriction that the province cannot pass laws which infringe on denominational rights guaranteed to specific minorities at the time of Confederation. Pursuant to this constitutional power over education, all the provinces of Canada have passed comprehensive legislation setting up and operating a system of funded public schools. Although most provincial education legislation also allows parents to choose to send their children to independent schools, the *Constitution Act 1867*, does not specifically refer to independent schools nor to a right of parents to send their children to schools outside the public school system.

When the Canadian Constitution was enlarged in 1982 by the enactment of the *Canadian Charter of Rights and Freedoms* (the "Charter") the foundation was laid to fashion a constitutional claim by parents to a right to send their children to independent schools. Although the Charter makes no reference to such schools, or for that matter to education, a series of cases decided by the Supreme Court of Canada under the Charter has moved the law a long way towards recognizing a constitutional right of parents to send their children to independent schools.

The first case decided by the Supreme Court of Canada, *R. v. Jones*,[13] involved a situation which the trial judge described as a stand-off between "a stiff-necked parson and a stiff-necked education establishment, both demanding the other make the first move in the inquiry to determine whether the children are receiving efficient instruction outside the public or separate school system".[14] The pastor, Mr. Jones, ran a private school in Alberta called the Western Baptist Academy which operated in the basement of his church. The *Alberta School Act* permitted a child to be excused from attendance at a public school if a government inspector certified that the pupil was under efficient

---
[12] *Ibid.*, at p. 205.
[13] (1986), 31 D.L.R. (4th) 569, [1986] 2 S.C.R. 284.
[14] *Supra*, at p. 291.

instruction at home or elsewhere, or if the pupil was attending a private school approved under Alberta's *Department of Education Act*. The pastor refused to apply for approval of his academy as a private school, taking the position that to request permission from the state to do what he was authorized by God to do would violate his religious convictions. Nor would the pastor request that government officials inspect his school to certify that the pupils were receiving efficient instruction. Although the pastor had no objection to the school authorities inspecting his academy and testing his pupils to ascertain their level of achievement, he asserted that his religious convictions prevented him from making the first move by submitting a request to the school authorities. For their part, the Department of Education and the local school board declined to send inspectors to the pastor's school unless they first received a formal request from the pastor. The stand-off between the pastor and school authorities finally was broken when the pastor was charged with truancy. Although the pastor was acquitted at trial, the Alberta Court of Appeal reversed the judgment and entered convictions, and the Supreme Court of Canada dismissed the pastor's appeal.

In dismissing the pastor's appeal, the Supreme Court of Canada made it quite clear that a province is obliged to make room in its system of education for those who wish to educate their children at home or in independent schools, especially if the parents are motivated by religious convictions. On this point Justice LaForest wrote:

> How far the province could go in imposing conditions on the way the [pastor] provides instruction, if he had applied for registration of his academy as a private school or for certification of the efficiency of his instructions, I need not enter into. *Certainly a reasonable accommodation would have to be made in dealing with this issue to ensure that provincial interests in the quality of education were met in a way that did not unduly encroach on the religious convictions of the [pastor].* In determining whether pupils are under "efficient instruction", it would be necessary to delicately and sensitively weigh the competing interests so as to respect, as much as possible, the religious convictions of the [pastor] as guaranteed by the *Charter*. *Those who administer the province's educational requirements may not do so in a manner that unreasonably infringes on the right of parents to teach their children in accordance with their religious convictions. The interference must be demonstrably justified.*[15]

In the *Jones* case, the Supreme Court concluded that requiring a person who gives instruction at home or elsewhere to obtain certification of that instruction as efficient was a justifiable requirement, as was the need to apply to the appropriate authorities for certification that such instruction complied with provincial standards of efficiency. The court regarded both requirements as minimal or peripheral intrusions on religion.[16]

---

[15] *Supra*, at p. 298 (emphasis added).
[16] *Supra*, at p. 299.

Then, in a 1995 decision, *B. (R.) v. Children's Aid Society of Metropolitan Toronto*,[17] the Supreme Court of Canada went one step further and recognized the right of parents to educate their children according to their religious beliefs as an integral element of the guarantee of freedom of religion contained in section 2(a) of the Charter. In the *B. (R.)* case, Justice LaForest, speaking for the majority, stated:

> It seems to me that the right of parents to rear their children according to their religious beliefs, including that of choosing medical and other treatments, is an equally fundamental aspect of freedom of religion.[18]

Justices Iacobucci and Major stated:

> The parents of Sheena are constitutionally entitled to manifest their beliefs and practise their religion, as is their daughter. That constitutional freedom includes the right to educate and rear their child in the tenets of their faith. In effect, until the child reaches an age where she can make an independent decision regarding her own religious beliefs, her parents may decide on her religion for her and raise her in accordance with that religion.[19]

One year later, in *Adler v. Ontario*,[20] the Supreme Court of Canada considered a claim brought by Jewish and Christian-Reformed parents, who sent their children to religious independent schools, that the failure of the Ontario provincial government to provide some public funding to such schools violated their rights of freedom of religion and equality guaranteed by the Charter. The Supreme Court rejected the parents' claim, holding that the Constitution of Canada does not oblige a province to fund independent religious schools, although provinces were free to fund such schools if they wished.

Although the right of parents to send their children to independent schools was not squarely at issue in the *Adler* case, several of the judges took the opportunity to affirm that such a constitutional right exists. In his judgment, Justice Sopinka wrote:

> There is no disputing the fact that the appellants enjoy a fundamental constitutional right to send their children to the religious school of their choice. This Court has recently reiterated that parents have the right to educate their children in the religion of their choice. In *B.(R.) v. Children's Aid Society of Metropolitan Toronto*, [1995] 1 S.C.R. 315, LaForest J., writing for the majority, made the following statement, at p. 382:
>
> > "It seems to me that the right of parents to rear their children according to their religious beliefs, including that of choosing medical or other treatments, is an equally fundamental aspect of freedom of religion."

---

[17] (1995), 122 D.L.R. (4th) 1, [1995] 1 S.C.R. 315.
[18] *Supra*, at p. 382, para. 105.
[19] *Supra*, at pp. 434-5, para. 223.
[20] (1996), 140 D.L.R. (4th) 385, [1996] 3 S.C.R. 609.

The appellants cannot, however, complain that the Ontario *Education Act* prevents them from exercising this aspect of their freedom of religion since it allows for the provision of education within a religious school or at home. The statute does not compel the appellants to act in any way that infringes their freedom of religion.[21]

Justice McLachlin also appeared to recognize the existence of such a right, although in a more indirect way. She wrote:

If the *Education Act* . . . required all children to go to either secular or Roman Catholic schools, it would impinge on the religious freedom of those whose beliefs require non-Roman Catholic religious education. The *Education Act* does not do this. Section 21 excuses children from school attendance if they are receiving satisfactory instruction elsewhere. Parents whose beliefs do not permit them to educate their children in the secular or Roman Catholic school systems are free to educate their children in other schools or at home. The requirement of mandatory education therefore does not conflict with the constitutional right of parents to educate their children as their religion dictates.[22]

This recognition by the Supreme Court of Canada of a constitutional right of parents to secure an education for their children outside the government-established school systems conforms with a similar right found in several international human rights conventions.[23]

THE DIFFERENT APPROACHES TO INDEPENDENT SCHOOLS ACROSS CANADA

Independent schools exist in most Canadian provinces. Provincial legislatures have adopted different approaches in setting up the legal frameworks within which independent schools operate. Several provinces have enacted legislation or regulations specifically governing independent schools — British Columbia,[24] Alberta[25] and Quebec[26] are the most notable examples. These Acts, and in some cases their accompanying regulations or subordinate legislation, generally establish the minimum standards which independent schools must meet, as well as the reporting requirements owed by an independent school to

---

[21] *Supra*, at pp. 699-700, para. 171.
[22] *Supra*, at p. 711, para. 196.
[23] For example, Article 18 of the *International Covenant on Civil and Political Rights*, 1966, 999 U.N.T.S. 171, provides in subsection 4:
"The states parties to the present covenant undertake to have respect for the liberty of parents and, when applicable, legal guardians to ensure the religious and moral education of their children in conformity with their own convictions."
[24] *Independent School Act*, R.S.B.C. 1996, c. 216.
[25] *Department of Education Act*, R.S.A. 1980, c. D-17, s. 10 and the regulations made thereunder.
[26] *An Act Respecting Private Education*, R.S.Q. 1977, c. E-9.

the provincial ministry of education. Each of these provinces also provides varying levels of public funding to independent schools, with the amount of funding usually representing a percentage of the per pupil student grant provided to public schools in the province.

Ontario has taken a different approach from most other provinces by not passing specific legislation for independent schools. Instead, a few sections of the Ontario *Education Act*[27] deal with independent schools. The advantage of this approach lies in its simplicity — the Ontario *Education Act* imposes very few requirements on independent schools, providing them with great latitude and flexibility in their operations and in the programs of study which they may offer their students. Ontario's flexibility, however, comes with a high price tag. Alone among the major Canadian provinces, Ontario does not provide any public funding to independent schools. As mentioned, an effort by Jewish and Christian parents in 1996 to persuade the Supreme Court of Canada that Ontario was constitutionally obliged to fund independent schools was not successful.[28]

Efforts over the years to persuade the Ontario government to provide some indirect support to independent schools through public school boards have also failed. In 1976, a tentative agreement was reached between the Associated Hebrew Schools of Toronto and the North York Public School Board to implement a pilot program under which the junior high school grades of the Associated Hebrew Schools would be integrated into the North York Public School system. The proposal envisaged that the students in the integrated schools would all participate in mandatory Hebrew religious education. The Minister of Education objected to this aspect of the proposal and strongly resisted a court application made by the North York Board of Education for approval of the project. The court rejected the proposed plan on the basis that the *Education Act* did not permit mandatory religious education in any schools under the auspices of a public school board.[29]

Ten years later the Shapiro Report proposed the recognition of a new category of school, an "associated school", which would be an independent school which had reached an agreement with the local school board to operate in association with that board. Associated schools would be a hybrid, preserving some autonomy in their program of study, while agreeing to report to the school board in exchange for access to government funding.[30] The Ontario government never acted on the recommendation to create associated schools.

---

[27] R.S.O. 1990, c. E.2.
[28] *Adler, supra*, footnote 20.
[29] *Board of Education for Borough of North York v. Ministry of Education* (1978), 19 O.R. (2d) 547, 6 M.P.L.R. 249 (H.C.J.).
[30] Shapiro Report, at pp. 53-7.

AN OVERVIEW OF ONTARIO LEGISLATION

While the specific legal issues relating to the establishment and operation of an independent school in Ontario will be discussed in the chapters which follow, given the simplicity of Ontario's legislation, it is appropriate at this stage to identify those provisions of the *Education Act* which relate to independent schools.

An examination of the Ontario *Education Act* must start with the definition of the word "school". As used in the *Education Act*, the word "school" essentially refers to schools under the jurisdiction of a district board of education — *i.e.*, an English-speaking public district board, a French-speaking public district board, an English-speaking Roman Catholic board and a French-speaking Roman Catholic board. Independent schools are not included in the definition of "school" in the *Education Act*. This point is central to a proper understanding of the Act. The overwhelming number of obligations and duties created and imposed by the *Education Act* are on "schools" or "boards", not on independent schools. When reading the Act, this point must always be kept in mind.

In the *Education Act*, independent schools are termed "private schools" which are defined as follows:

> "private school" means an institution at which instruction is provided at any time between the hours of 9 a.m. and 4 p.m. on any school day for five or more pupils who are of or over compulsory school age in any of the subjects of the elementary or secondary school courses of study and that is not a school as defined in this section;[31]

In other words, under the *Education Act*, an independent or private school possesses the following characteristics:

(a) a private school is not a "school" as defined in section 1 of the Act;
(b) a private school is an institution;
(c) a private school must provide instruction to five or more pupils;
(d) the instruction must be provided any time between the hours of 9:00 a.m. and 4:00 p.m. on any school day; and
(e) the instruction must be in any of the subjects of the elementary or secondary school courses of study.

Armed with these basic definitions, the three major sections of the Act affecting independent schools can now be considered.

Ontario's education system rests on a fundamental principle — parents are compelled by law to secure an education for their children who are of compulsory school age. Section 21(1) of the Act requires every child 6 to 15

---

[31] *Education Act*, s. 1(1).

years of age to attend an elementary or secondary "school" on every school day — that is, to attend a public or Roman Catholic elementary or secondary school. Section 30(1) of the Act provides that a parent or guardian of a child of compulsory school age who neglects to cause the child to attend "school" is guilty of an offence and, on conviction, liable to a fine of not more than $200.

These compulsory attendance provisions of the Act contain several exemptions from the requirement to attend a "school". The first exemption, section 21(2)(a) of the Act, provides the legal basis for the ability of parents to send their children to independent schools. That section reads: "A child is excused from attendance at school if, (a) the child is receiving *satisfactory instruction* at home or *elsewhere*" (emphasis added). In practical terms, "elsewhere" means an independent school. If a child receives satisfactory instruction elsewhere, then a parent has fulfilled the obligation to send a child to school. (What level of instruction constitutes *satisfactory* instruction as required by the Act is a question which will be dealt with in Chapter 6.)

Section 16 of the *Education Act* is the only section which sets out the requirements which a private school must meet. Broken down by topic for ease of reference, the provisions of section 16 read as follows:

<u>The Notice of Intention to Operate</u>

16(1) No private school shall be operated in Ontario unless notice of intention to operate the private school has been submitted in accordance with this section.

(2) Every private school shall submit annually to the Ministry on or before the 1st day of September a notice of intention to operate a private school.

(3) A notice of intention to operate a private school shall be in such form and shall include such particulars as the Minister may require.

(4) Every person concerned in the management of a private school that is operated in contravention of subsection (1) is guilty of an offence and on conviction is liable to a fine of not more than $50 for every day such school is so operated.

<u>The September Return</u>

(5) The principal, headmaster, headmistress or person in charge of a private school shall make a return to the Ministry furnishing such statistical information regarding enrolment, staff, courses of study and other information as and when required by the Minister, and any such person who fails to make such return within sixty days of the request of the Minister is guilty of an offence and on conviction is liable to a fine of not more than $200.

<u>The General Power of the Ministry to Inspect Private Schools</u>

(6) The Minister may direct one or more supervisory officers to inspect a private school, in which case each such supervisory officer may enter the school at all reasonable hours and conduct an inspection of the school and any records or documents relating thereto, and every person who prevents or obstructs or

attempts to prevent or obstruct any such entry or inspection is guilty of an offence and on conviction is liable to a fine of not more than $500.

The Inspection of Ontario Diploma-Granting High Schools

(7) The Minister may, on the request of any person operating a private school, provide for inspection of the school in respect of the standard of instruction in the subjects leading to the Ontario secondary school diploma, the secondary school graduation diploma and to the secondary school honour graduation diploma, and may determine and charge a fee for such inspection.

Inspection of Teachers to Obtain Certification

(8) The Minister may, on the request of a person operating a private school or of a person in charge of a conservation authority school or field centre, provide for the inspection of a teacher in such school or centre who requires the recommendation of a supervisory officer for certification purposes.

Option to Participate in Province-Wide Tests

(8.1) The Minister may enter into agreements with a person operating,
(a) a private school;
(b) a school provided by a band, the council of a band or an education authority where the band, the council of the band or the education authority is authorized by the Crown in right of Canada to provide education for Indians; or
(c) a school provided by the Crown in right of Canada,

about administering tests to pupils enrolled in the school, marking the tests and reporting the results of the tests.

(8.2) Without limiting the generality of subsection (8.1), an agreement may provide for the charging of fees by the Minister to a person operating a school described in subsection (8.1).

Offences for Making False Statements

(9) Every person who knowingly makes a false statement in a notice of intention to operate a private school or an information return under this section is guilty of an offence and on conviction is liable to a fine of not more than $500.

With the exception of subsection 16(7), all the requirements of section 16 apply to both elementary and secondary independent schools. Subsection 16(7) applies only to independent secondary schools which offer graduating students an Ontario secondary school diploma. The practical effect and operation of each of the subsections of section 16 will be addressed in the remaining chapters of this book.

Finally, section 8(1) of the *Education Act* contains the only other provision relating to private schools. Ontario's education system traditionally has placed extensive powers in the hands of the Minister of Education and Training over almost all areas involved in the operation of schools. Section 8(1) para. 3.1 of the *Education Act* gives the Minister the following powers in respect of independent secondary schools which offer the Ontario diploma to their graduates:

8(1) The Minister may,

. . . . .

3.1 conduct reviews of classroom practices and the effectiveness of educational programs and require a board or *private school inspected under subsection 16(7)* to participate in the reviews and to provide information to the Minister for that purpose in such form as the Minister may prescribe; [Emphasis added.]

The Minister exercised this power in 1995 in an effort to require an independent school to participate in the grade 9 reading and writing test, but when the school commenced a legal action challenging the Minister's decision, the Minister recognized the ability of parents to exempt their children from writing the test.[32]

By way of summary, then, sections 8(1) para. 3.1, 16, 20 and 21(2), are the only sections of the *Education Act* affecting independent schools. Moreover, while a large number of regulations have been passed under the *Education Act* in respect of public and separate schools, the Province of Ontario has not passed any regulations specifically dealing with independent schools. From the perspective of those who wish to establish and operate independent schools, Ontario's legal framework possesses a refreshing simplicity.

---

[32] For a full discussion of the case, see "Early Years of Provincial Tests" in Chapter 6.

2

Establishing the Independent School: Corporate Issues

POSSIBLE LEGAL FORMS FOR AN INDEPENDENT SCHOOL

The *Education Act* does not require independent schools to use any particular legal form for their operation. The Act simply describes a private school as "an institution" and leaves the choice of the legal form or structure to those who establish the school. Several different legal structures are available: an independent school may operate as a sole proprietorship, a partnership, an unincorporated association, a business corporation (*i.e.*, a for-profit corporation) or a not-for-profit corporation. Each type of legal structure has its own benefits and disadvantages.

The Decision Whether to Incorporate

The founders of an independent school must first decide whether to incorporate a company to operate the school. The main advantages and disadvantages of incorporation compared to other legal forms are as follows:

1. *Personal liability* — If an independent school is not incorporated, liability for the obligations entered into by the school will rest personally with those who operate the school. For example, in the case of a person who runs a school as a sole proprietorship, the individual would be liable personally for any contractual obligations entered into in respect of the school. If the school is operated as a partnership, the liabilities would be shared personally by each of the partners; in the case of an unincorporated association, the liabilities would be spread among each member of the association. Those who operate an unincorporated independent school would also be personally liable for any damages caused to individuals from injuries incurred on school premises as a result of the negligence of school staff, subject to any protection provided by the school's insurance policies. Further, a variety of federal and provincial income tax and pension Acts require an employer to withhold from wages specified statutory deduc-

tions. An employer who fails to do so may become liable for the amounts which should have been withheld, together with a penalty.[1] Where a school is operated as a sole proprietorship, partnership or unincorporated association, such liability would fall personally on the owners of the school.

2. *Taxation of income* — Corporations without share capital may be exempt from taxation pursuant to s. 149(1) of the *Income Tax Act*, whereas the income of a partnership or sole proprietorship will be taxed in the hands of the partner or proprietor. Under some circumstances the income of an unincorporated association may be exempt from taxation.[2]

3. *Legal capacity* — A corporation possesses the legal capacity to enter into contracts in its own name. By contrast, an unincorporated association cannot sue or be sued in its own name. This sometimes gives rise to problems entering into a lease, contract or banking arrangement in the name of the unincorporated association; the other party to the contract may insist that all members of the association personally sign the contract.

4. *Government filings* — Unincorporated associations are easier to establish and less expensive to maintain because they are not usually subject to government approval and its attendant filing requirements. However, any organization which plans to operate as a charitable organization will be subject to regulation by the Public Guardian and Trustee and Revenue Canada.

5. *Permanence* — A corporation connotes more permanence to the organization; an unincorporated association suggests a more temporary enterprise.

6. *Holding real estate* — A corporation can hold real estate in its own name, whereas an unincorporated association must hold real estate in the name of trustees and not in its own name. When the members of the unincorporated association die or otherwise resign, there may be problems in re-registering the property. Revenue Canada has indicated that where a charity owns or is to acquire real estate in the course of carrying out its objectives, it should be incorporated unless title to the property is held by trustees for the benefit of the applicant.

Not-for-Profit Corporations and Business Corporations

Most Ontario independent schools are corporations. Incorporated companies take two forms — companies with shareholders and non-share companies. The former operate to generate a profit, whereas non-share companies generally run on a not-for-profit basis. Some schools operate as share corporations, especially those which offer secondary school education to foreign students or

---

[1] See for example, ss. 153 and 227 of the *Income Tax Act*, R.S.C. 1985, c. 1 (5th Supp.).
[2] See s. 149(1)(*l*) of the *Income Tax Act*.

Establishing the Independent School: Corporate Issues 15

more technical courses of study. These schools incorporate under the Ontario *Business Corporations Act*[3] by filing articles of incorporation with the Ministry of Consumer and Commercial Relations.

Non-share corporations are the legal vehicle of choice for Ontario independent schools. In Canada a non-share corporation can be incorporated either under federal legislation (the *Canada Corporations Act*[4]) or under provincial legislation (the Ontario *Corporations Act*[5]). Since independent schools in Ontario by and large incorporate under the provincial *Corporations Act*, the balance of this chapter will focus on the issues which must be considered when incorporating a school as a non-share corporation under the Ontario legislation.

THE PROCEDURE FOR INCORPORATING A NON-SHARE CORPORATION

Part III of the Ontario *Corporations Act* governs the incorporation of a general non-share capital corporation. Although Part III contains only 16 sections, other provisions of the Act apply by reference to non-share corporations. While the structure of the *Corporations Act* is somewhat archaic and difficult to navigate through, the Ministry of Consumer and Commercial Relations publishes a very helpful handbook which provides detailed guidance on how to incorporate a non-share corporation.[6]

An application for incorporation of an Ontario non-share corporation involves the following steps:

1. Obtaining a search report on the proposed name of the corporation.
2. Completing a prescribed application for incorporation.
3. Where the corporation will be a charitable organization, the application for incorporation must first be forwarded to the Charitable Property Division of the Office of the Public Guardian and Trustee.
4. Once the approval of the Public Guardian and Trustee is obtained, the application for incorporation is filed with the Ministry of Consumer and Commercial Relations.

---

[3] R.S.O. 1990, c. B.16.
[4] R.S.C. 1970, c. C-32.
[5] R.S.O. 1990, c. C.38.
[6] *Not-for-Profit Incorporators Handbook* (Toronto: Ministry of Consumer and Commercial Relations, Companies Branch, 1993) (the "Handbook"). The book may be ordered from Publications Ontario, 50 Grosvenor Street, Toronto. A useful legal text on the incorporation of non-share corporations is Donald J. Bourgeois, *The Law of Charitable and Non-Profit Organizations*, 2nd ed. (Toronto: Butterworths, 1995).

5. Within 60 days following the issuance of letters patent by the Ministry of Consumer and Commercial Relations, the company must file an initial notice.

Each of these steps will be considered in turn.

Corporate Name Search

The *Corporations Act* prohibits the incorporation of a new company with a name that is the same as, or similar to, the name of an existing corporation, association, partnership, individual or business, if the use of the name would be likely to deceive the public.[7] To avoid the possibility of similar names, the incorporators of a company must first determine if their proposed corporate name is available for use. This is done by obtaining an Ontario Biased Name Search Report, commonly called a NUANS Report, for the proposed corporate name. Several name search companies provide this service for a fee. They will search the registry of existing corporations and provide a list of any existing corporate names which may be the same as or similar to the name of the proposed corporation. The Ministry of Consumer and Commercial Relations ("MCCR") requires that the name search report be dated no more than 90 days before the submission of the application for incorporation.

If the name search report discloses that an existing corporation bears the same or similar name to the proposed corporation, then incorporators have one of two choices. They may either select a new name for their proposed corporation, or they may contact the existing corporation to obtain its consent to the use of the name. If the existing corporation consents, the consent must be filed at the time the application for incorporation is submitted.

The *Corporations Act* imposes some other limits on the choice of corporate names. For example, a corporate name cannot imply a connection with the Crown, the federal or provincial government or any member of the Royal Family, or be a name which is objectionable on any public grounds.[8] Where the corporation is to be a charitable organization, the Public Guardian and Trustee requires that the name reflect the charitable objects of the corporation. In the case of an independent school, the inclusion of the word "school" in its name will suffice. Where a school wishes to include the word "college" in its name, it must obtain the prior written consent of the Ministry of Colleges and Universities.[9]

In addition to the restrictions imposed by the *Corporations Act* on the choice of corporate names, other limitations may exist. Some religious schools may require the permission of their church or religious organization to use

---

[7] Section 13(1).
[8] R.R.O. 1990, Reg. 181, s. 3(1) under the *Corporations Act*.
[9] Regulation, s. 3(1).

certain words in their names. For example, no school may bear the title "catholic school" without the consent of the local Roman Catholic bishop.[10]

The MCCR will determine whether a proposed corporate name is acceptable. Even if the applicants have obtained the consent of a corporation with a similar name, the MCCR may impose conditions on, or deny, the use of the name.

Application for Incorporation
General Matters

The application for incorporation used by the MCCR is a short document, but requires care in its preparation. The name and the address of the head office of the corporation must be set out in the application. The address of the head office normally will be the address of the school. The application must name and be signed by at least three applicants for incorporation who are at least 18 years of age. On incorporation these applicants automatically become members of the corporation and its first directors.[11] While the directors of the corporation may be changed or increased following incorporation, the first directors should be chosen with a view that they will serve as directors of the school corporation for some period of time after its incorporation.

Corporate Objects

The application must set out the objects or purposes of the corporation. The objects should be drafted with care and with legal advice. A corporation set up under Part III of the *Corporations Act* cannot engage in activities which do not fall within, or are incidental to, its objects. The objects of an independent school typically will specify the nature of the instruction offered by the school — elementary, secondary or academic/technical — as well as whether the program of study follows any specific principles, either religious or pedagogic. Examples of objects used by several Ontario independent schools are reproduced in Appendix "C".

Where a not-for-profit corporation which operates an independent school plans to seek registration as a charitable organization, the objects of the corporation must be exclusively charitable. Often applications for the incorporation of a charitable organization are rejected because they contain both charitable and non-charitable objects. While the *Income Tax Act* does not define the term "charity", it has a well-established meaning in law: "Charity in its legal sense comprises four principal divisions: trusts for the relief of poverty; trusts for the advancement of education; trusts for the advancement of religion; and trusts for

---

[10] *The Code of Canon Law* (London: Collins Liturgical Publications, 1983), Canon 803(3).
[11] *Corporations Act*, ss. 119 and 121.

other purposes beneficial to the community, not falling under the preceding heads."[12] If any doubt exists whether the proposed objects of a corporation are of a charitable nature, then the incorporators should forward draft objects both to the Public Guardian and Trustee and to Revenue Canada for pre-approval before the application for incorporation is filed. It must be stressed that it is the approval from Revenue Canada, not from the MCCR, which is necessary in order for a corporation to be registered as a charitable organization.

Special Provisions

As a matter of practice the MCCR requires that all letters patent issued for charitable corporations include the following clauses as special provisions in the application for incorporation:

(a) the corporation shall be carried on without the purpose of gain for its members and any profits or other accretions to the corporation shall be used in promoting its objects;

(b) the directors shall serve as such without remuneration and no director shall directly or indirectly receive any profit from his or her position as such, provided that directors may be paid reasonable expenses incurred by them in the performance of their duties;

(c) the corporation shall be subject to the *Charities Accounting Act*[13] and the *Charitable Gifts Act*;[14]

(d) the borrowing power of the corporation pursuant to any by-law passed and confirmed in accordance with section 59 of the *Corporations Act* shall be limited to borrowing money for current operating expenses, provided that the borrowing power of the corporation shall not be so limited if it borrows on the security of real or personal property;

(e) on the dissolution of the corporation and after payment of all debts and liabilities, its remaining property shall be distributed or disposed of to charities which carry on their work solely in Ontario;[15] and

(f) if it is made to appear to the satisfaction of the Minister, on report of the Public Guardian and Trustee, that the corporation has failed to comply with any of the provisions of the *Charities Accounting Act* or the *Charitable Gifts Act*, the Minister may authorize an inquiry for the purpose of determining whether or not there is sufficient cause for the

---

[12] *Commissioners for Special Purposes of the Income Tax v. Pemsel*, [1891] A.C. 531 (H.L.) at p. 583.

[13] R.S.O. 1990, c. C.10.

[14] R.S.O. 1990, c. C.8.

[15] Maxwell Gotlieb, "Choosing Your Jurisdiction — Federal or Provincial and Operating Outside of Canada" (paper presented at *Charity and Not-for-Profit Law: The Emerging Specialty*, Canadian Bar Association — Ontario, Continuing Legal Education, May 15, 1997).

Lieutenant-Governor to make an order to cancel the letters patent of the corporation and declare it to be dissolved.

Pre-approval of the Public Guardian and Trustees Office in the Case of "Charitable Organizations"

Where the applicants plan to apply for registration of the corporation as a charitable organization under the *Income Tax Act* they must first obtain the approval of the Charitable Property Division of the Office of the Public Guardian and Trustee prior to submitting the application for incorporation. Duplicate copies of the draft application for incorporation should be submitted to the Charitable Property Division which will review the provisions of the proposed letters patent to ensure that they are exclusively charitable and to consider whether the corporation will be operated appropriately as a charity. If the application proves satisfactory, the incorporators must pay a fee whereupon the Public Guardian and Trustee will approve the draft application for incorporation.[16]

Filing the Application for Incorporation

Once the application for incorporation of the independent school has been prepared (and in the case of a charitable organization approved by the Charitable Property Division of the Public Guardian and Trustees Office), the applicants must submit the application to the MCCR together with a filing fee of $155 payable to the Minister of Finance. A copy of the NUANS name search report must accompany the application for incorporation.

No legal right exists to incorporate a non-share corporation. Technically, the incorporation of a non-share corporation in Ontario is made by application to the Lieutenant-Governor of Ontario (represented by the Minister of Consumer and Commercial Relations) who enjoys the discretion to grant, or refuse to grant, letters patent for non-share corporations. On approval of the application, letters patent will be issued and the corporation comes into existence on the date of their issuance.[17]

Corporations Information Return

Within 60 days of incorporation, the new corporation must file an Initial Notice with the Ministry of Consumer and Commercial Relations[18] providing information about the names and addresses of the directors and officers of the corporation, as well as the location of the corporation's head office.

---

[16] To determine the current fee, contact the Charitable Property Division, Public Trustee, 2nd Flr., 538 Yonge Street, Toronto, tel: (416) 326-1963. At the time of writing the fee was $120.
[17] *Corporations Act*, s. 12(1).
[18] *Corporations Information Act*, R.S.O. 1990, c. C.39.

CORPORATE GOVERNANCE — DRAFTING THE BY-LAWS

The issuance of letters patent for the new independent school marks only the first step in the legal organization of the school corporation. The letters patent provide the legal form, or skeleton, for the new school, including a statement of its objects, but they do not contain the rules for the corporate governance of the school. These rules are placed in the by-laws of the corporation. As their first act, the directors of the new school corporation must pass a general by-law describing the governance structure and procedures for the school corporation. Since applicants for incorporation may choose to place certain items relating to the governance structure and procedure either in the application for incorporation or in the by-laws, the general practice is to draft the by-laws at the same time as the articles of incorporation are prepared.

A fine balance must be struck in drafting the school's by-laws: they must clearly set out the governance structure for the new school, yet at the same time they should not delve into detailed matters of school policy. By-laws of new independent school corporations commonly deal with the following matters:

(a) classes of membership in the corporation;
(b) the number of directors, their election and replacement;
(c) the conduct of meetings of the board of directors;
(d) standing committees of the board of directors;
(e) the officers of the corporation and their duties; and
(f) annual and special meetings of the members.

Membership

Whereas in a business (for profit) corporation the shareholders own the corporation and must approve the major decisions made by the management of the corporation, in a non-share corporation the "member" stands in the place of the shareholder. When establishing an independent school, one of the fundamental governance issues is to determine the members, or classes of members, of the school corporation. The Ontario *Corporations Act* provides great flexibility on this issue. A non-share corporation may have more than one class of membership, each of which may possess different voting or other corporate rights. The identification of the classes of members may be made in the letters patent or in the by-laws of the corporation.[19] There is no limit on the number of members of the corporation unless the letters patent or by-laws specifically provide a limit.[20] Each member of each class of members of a corporation has

---

[19] *Corporations Act*, s. 120.
[20] Section 123.

one vote unless the letters patent or by-laws specifically provide that each member has more than one vote or no vote.[21]

Who should be members of the independent school corporation? There are as many answers to this question as there are types of independent schools. Ultimately, the answer to the question will reflect the fundamental characteristics of each school. Some independent school corporations open membership to any person whose children attend the school or, more broadly still, to any person who subscribes to the constitution or guiding principles of the school.[22] Schools which are operated by organizations, either religious or secular, may limit membership in the corporation to those associated with or approved by the organization.[23] Some of the older independent schools in the province have very broadly based membership, often including as voting members, past students, parents of past students and parents of present students. In some cases friends of the school — persons who have demonstrated a long-standing interest in the welfare of the school — are also included within the membership category.

Some corporations may wish to charge a membership fee in order to defray the costs of sending information and publications to members. While the board of directors may pass a by-law setting the fee, the by-law is subject to approval by the members of the corporation.[24]

The *Corporations Act* establishes two methods for admission to membership. The board of directors may pass resolutions admitting persons to membership in the school corporation. In addition, the letters patent or by-laws of the corporation may provide for the admission of members by virtue of their office — *e.g.*, all parents of students enrolled at the school.[25]

Directors

In the eyes of the law, directors are responsible for managing the business and affairs of the corporation. Directors must exercise their powers and discharge their duties with a view to the best interests of the corporation, and

---

[21] Section 125.
[22] For example, the model by-laws for the Ontario Alliance of Christian School Societies provide that membership in a school corporation (called a Christian Education Society) is open to any person 18 years of age or older who subscribes to the basis and purpose of the school of the promoting and advancing of Christian religion and Christian education. *Board Manual* (Ancaster: Ontario Alliance of Christian School Societies, 1990) at p. 17.
[23] In the by-law this can be achieved by the following language: "Membership in the corporation shall consist of the applicants for the incorporation of the corporation and such other individuals as are admitted as members by resolution of the Board of Directors."
[24] *Corporations Act*, s. 129(1)(b).
[25] Section 124.

they must exercise the care, diligence and skills that reasonably prudent persons would exercise in comparable circumstances.[26]

Who May Act as a Director

The applicants for incorporation are the first directors of the new school corporation until their replacement.[27] A director must be 18 or more years of age,[28] and must be a member of the corporation.[29] No undischarged bankrupt can be a director, and if a director becomes bankrupt, he thereupon ceases to be a director.[30]

The letters patent or by-laws may provide for persons becoming *ex officio* members of the board of directors.[31] For example, in the case of an independent school with strong links to a church or religious organization, the by-laws may stipulate that certain members of the church or religious organizations sit as *ex officio* members of the board. Similarly, in some schools the president of the parents' association is an *ex officio* member of the board.

Whether the principal of a school should be an *ex officio* member of the board is a more difficult question. On the one hand, the principal is an employee of the school and ultimately reports to and is subject to the direction of the board of directors. On the other hand, the sound operation of an independent school depends heavily on the activities of the principal, and a board of directors proceeds at its peril without maintaining strong communications with the principal. The Canadian Education Standards Institute, an accreditation body for many of the larger Canadian independent schools, recommends in its governance standard that employees of the school not be members of the school's governing body. Yet a governing structure appropriate for a school of some 500 to 900 students, requiring the maintenance of a firm distinction between the board of directors and the principal, may not be appropriate for a small elementary independent school where the principal has been one of the driving forces behind the creation of the school. In such a case, it may be unrealistic to exclude the principal from the board of directors. As a possible middle ground, the by-laws could provide that the principal not be a director of the school corporation, but that the board of directors should invite the principal to every meeting of the board.

---

[26] William I. Innes, "Liability of Directors and Officers of Charitable and Non-Profit Corporations" (1993), 13 E. & T.J. 151 at p. 153.
[27] *Corporations Act*, s. 284(1).
[28] Section 286(4).
[29] Section 286(1). A person may be a director of a corporation if he or she becomes a member within ten days after his or her election or appointment of director, but if a person fails to become a member within ten days he or she ceases to be a director (see s. 286(2)).
[30] Section 286(5).
[31] Section 127.

Remuneration of Directors

While the *Corporations Act* provides that a director may receive reasonable remuneration and expenses for his or her services to the corporation as a director, or for his or her services to the corporation in any other capacity, the letters patent or by-laws of the corporation may prohibit such payments.[32] If the school corporation is registered as a charitable organization, the present state of Ontario law prohibits a director of a charitable corporation from receiving remuneration for services rendered as an employee of the corporation without first obtaining court approval.[33] Although this prohibition has attracted criticism from many quarters as bad law, Ontario courts currently uphold the prohibition. For this reason, the principal of an independent school which is registered as a charitable organization could not act as a director of the school without court approval, or unless the special act incorporating the school so provides.[34]

Conflict of Interest

The *Corporations Act* requires every director of a school corporation who is in any way directly, or indirectly, interested in a proposed contract or a contract with the corporation to declare his interest at a meeting of the directors of the company.[35] A director must make this declaration at the first meeting of the board of directors at which the question of entering the contract is taken into consideration.[36] Once a director has made a declaration of interest in a proposed contract, he cannot vote in respect of the contract at a meeting of the board of directors.[37] It is unclear as a matter of law whether an interested director can be included in the determination of the quorum for the purposes of dealing with the proposed transaction and whether the director can be present in the room while the matter is being discussed. The prudent and generally accepted course would be for the director to leave the meeting of the board until the board has discussed the transaction and taken a vote.[38]

The *Corporations Act* provides that if a director makes a declaration of interest and refrains from voting in respect of the contract, then the director is not accountable to the corporation for any profit realized from the contract and the contract is not voidable by reason only of a director holding that office or

---

[32] Section 126(2).
[33] *Public Trustee v. Toronto Humane Society* (1987), 40 D.L.R. (4th) 111, 60 O.R. (2d) 236 (H.C.J.).
[34] See, for example, *Act to Incorporate St. Andrew's College*, S.O. 1911, c. 141, s. 6; *Act to Incorporate Appleby School*, S.O. 1911, c. 140, s. 7.
[35] *Corporations Act*, s. 71(1).
[36] Section 71(2).
[37] Section 71(4).
[38] William I. Innes, "Liability of Directors and Officers of Charitable and Non-Profit Corporations" (1993), 13 E. & T.J. 151 at p. 156.

of the fiduciary relationship established thereby.[39] Where a director fails to disclose his interest in a proposed contract in a meeting of a board of directors, the director will be shielded from any liability to account for the contract where two conditions are met: the contract is subsequently confirmed by a majority of the votes cast at a general members' meeting duly called for that purpose; and second, the director's interest in the contract is declared in the notice calling the meeting.[40]

If a director does not comply with these declaration of interest requirements in the *Corporations Act*, the director will become liable in respect of any profit realized from the contract, will be guilty of an offence and, on conviction, liable to a fine of not more than $200. As well, the contract can be set aside by the school corporation if it so wishes.[41]

As will be discussed below, the Public Guardian and Trustee takes the position that directors of charitable corporations are trustees and cannot benefit in any way from the assets of the corporation without court approval. In view of this position and its apparent acceptance by the courts, a director with a material pecuniary interest in a contract that is about to be entered into by a school corporation, which is a registered charity, should probably disclose his interest on becoming aware of it and resign from his director's office. Alternatively, the school corporation would have to seek a court order to sanction the transaction.[42]

The Number of Directors

An Ontario non-share corporation must have a minimum of three directors on its board of directors and the board of directors must consist of a fixed number of directors.[43] A corporation can always increase or decrease the number of its directors, but this would require the members to pass a special resolution to change the number.[44]

What is the appropriate size of the board of directors of an independent school? Although there is no correct answer to this question, "smaller is better" is a good rule of thumb. Since a board of directors oversees the affairs of the school, the board needs to be of a manageable size so that the directors can efficiently decide the questions facing the school. Boards which consist of 8 to 12 members usually provide the right combination of depth and efficiency; boards larger than 12 directors tend to become unwieldy and poor decision-makers.[45]

---

[39] *Corporations Act*, s. 71(4).
[40] Section 71(5).
[41] Section 71(6).
[42] Innes, *op. cit.*, footnote 38, at pp. 156-7.
[43] *Corporations Act*, s. 283(2).
[44] Section 285(1).
[45] For a useful analysis of the design for boards of non-profit organizations see: John

Term of Office for Directors

On incorporation, the persons named as first directors in the letters of application become the directors of the corporation until replaced by directors elected by the members at a general meeting.[46]

Before incorporating the independent school, a decision must be made about the term of office for directors because the *Corporations Act* provides that the election of directors shall take place yearly unless the letters patent provide otherwise.[47] The Act provides that directors are eligible for re-election.[48] As well, the Act permits the letters patent to provide for the election and retirement of directors in rotation, but in such a case no director can be elected for a term of more than five years and at least three directors shall retire from office in each year.[49] As a result, if the organizers of an independent school wish the directors' term of office to exceed one year, the letters patent must be drafted to contain such a special provision. The same will hold true when there is a desire to create a rotating board of directors.

Although directors may be re-elected after one-year terms (and the school thereby develops an experienced board of directors[50]), a school can provide for longer terms of service for directors in its letters patent. For example, some schools set a director's term of office at three years, thereby enabling a director to spend the first year of his term "learning the ropes", and then drawing on this experience in the second and third years of the term.

Directors' Meetings

The *Corporations Act* does not mandate a specific number of directors' meetings during the course of a year. There is no need to specify in the by-laws the frequency of directors' meetings; usually the by-laws indicate that the board of directors should hold regular meetings to be set in accordance with a resolution passed by the board.

The frequency of directors' meetings will vary to some degree with the age of a school. In the early years of a school, regular monthly meetings will prove necessary. As the school matures, directors' meetings may be moved to a bi-monthly or quarterly basis in accordance with the business cycle of the school. When unforeseen issues arise with which the board must deal quickly, a special meeting of the board of directors can be called. Whatever the frequency of the board meetings, it is a good practice for the board to establish, at

---

Carver, *Boards That Make a Difference* (San Francisco: Jossey-Bass Publishing, 1990).
[46] *Corporations Act*, ss. 284(1) and 287(1).
[47] Section 287(2).
[48] *Ibid.*
[49] Section 287(5).
[50] Section 287(2).

the beginning of each academic year, the dates of the regular board meetings for the forthcoming year.

The by-laws of the school corporation should contain provisions clearly dealing with where meetings are to be held, who can call board meetings, the amount of notice to be given for a meeting, the quorum for a meeting and the voting rules.

The *Corporations Act* provides that a majority of the board of directors constitutes a quorum unless the letters patent provide otherwise, but in no case shall a quorum of the board be less than two-fifths of the board of directors.[51] The Act provides that meetings of the board of directors shall be held at the head office of the corporation unless specific provision is made in the by-laws to hold the meetings elsewhere. The independent school's by-laws may provide for meetings of the board to be held at any place in or outside Ontario.[52] The Act does not contain any specific provision setting out notice requirements for meetings of directors. Although the Act does not provide for holding telephone meetings of directors of non-share corporations, given the ability of most other kinds of corporations to hold telephone meetings on proper notice, it is unlikely that a serious issue would arise if a school's by-law made provision for telephone board meetings.

Executive Committee of the Board of Directors

Where the board of directors consists of more than six directors, the directors may pass a by-law authorizing them to elect an executive committee consisting of not fewer than three directors.[53] The by-law may also authorize the board of directors to delegate to the executive committee any powers of the board of directors. The by-law may contain restrictions on which powers may be delegated to the executive committee, or the board of directors may impose restrictions on such delegated powers from time to time.[54] An executive committee may fix its quorum at not less than the majority of its members.[55]

The necessity for an executive committee of the board of directors will depend on both the size of the board of directors and the amount of work facing the board. An executive committee may prove useful where the need arises to deal with school matters on short notice and the size of the board makes the calling of a full board meeting time-consuming or cumbersome. An executive committee can also serve as an effective group to set the agenda for board meetings and to provide strategic leadership for a board.

---

[51] Section 288(1).
[52] Section 82(2).
[53] Section 70.
[54] Section 70(1). It is important to note that such a by-law will not be effective until it has been confirmed by at least two-thirds of the votes cast at a general meeting of the members called for that purpose.
[55] Section 70(3).

Chair of the Board of Directors

The board of directors may elect from among themselves a chair of the board where the school corporation has passed a special resolution to that effect. The special resolution may also define the duties of the chair and may assign to the chair any or all of the duties of the president or other officer of the corporation. The school corporation may have both a chair of the board and a president, but in that case, the special resolution must prescribe the duties of the chair and the president.[56]

Powers of the Board of Directors

The *Corporations Act* stipulates that the affairs of the corporation shall be managed by a board of directors.[57] To that end, the Act authorizes the directors to pass by-laws not contrary to the corporation's letters patent to regulate:

(a) the admission of persons as members, the qualification and conditions of membership, the fees and dues of members, the suspension and termination of memberships, and the transfer of members;
(b) the qualification and remuneration of the directors;
(c) the time for and the manner of election of directors;
(d) the time and place and the notice to be given for the holding of meetings of the members and of the board of directors, the quorum at meetings of members, the requirements as to proxies, and the procedure in all things at members meetings and at meetings of the board of directors;
(e) the appointment, remuneration, functions, duties and removals of officers and employees of the corporation; and
(f) the conduct in all other particulars of the affairs of the corporation.[58]

The *Corporations Act* does place some restrictions on this broad power of the board of directors to pass by-laws. First, it is open to the applicants who incorporate the companies to place restrictions in the letters patent on the power of directors to pass by-laws.[59] In addition, any by-law passed by the board of directors is only effective until the next annual meeting of the members of the corporation. At the next annual meeting, the members must confirm the by-law, otherwise the by-law ceases to have effect.[60]

The Act also provides that the directors of the corporation may pass by-laws providing for the division of its members into groups, the election of

---

[56] Section 290.
[57] Section 283(1).
[58] Section 129(1).
[59] *Ibid.*
[60] Section 129(2).

some or all of its directors by such groups on the basis of the number of members in each group, the election of delegates to reflect such groups and other similar matters.[61] Any by-law on such matters passed by the board of directors is not effective until it has been confirmed by at least two-thirds of the votes cast at a general meeting of the members duly called for considering the by-law.[62]

During the corporation's first year of existence its directors may pass a by-law by having all directors sign the by-law.[63] Thereafter, no business of the corporation can be transacted by the board of directors except at a meeting of the directors where a quorum of the board is present.[64]

Committees of the Board of Directors

The by-laws should identify any standing committees of the board of directors of the school. Since most of the detailed work performed by a board of directors generally falls to the board's standing committees, it is important that the by-laws clearly specify the number of committees, their duties and their membership.

What Standing Committees are Necessary?

As a general rule, the number of standing committees should be kept to a minimum. Three standing committees of the board usually are necessary for the operation of an independent school — finance and property, planning and governance.

The finance and property committee bears responsibility for the preparation of an annual budget and forecast for the school, oversees the keeping of financial records by the school staff, co-operates with the school auditors, develops procedures for the financial administration of the school, reviews the adequacy of the school's management and insurance programs, reviews the human resource policies for school employees, and supervises the management, maintenance and upkeep of the premises and buildings of the school. As this list of duties suggests, as a school grows in size, a need may emerge to divest some of these duties onto additional specialized standing committees, such as a separate property committee and human resources committee.

The planning committee primarily assesses the past, present and future position of the school. It identifies the internal and external factors and trends affecting the school, sets the priorities for the school and devises the plans and strategies to foster and promote the school's educational mission. A planning committee should also identify and propose methods by which the school can

---

[61] Section 130(1).
[62] Section 130(2).
[63] Section 298(1).
[64] Section 283(3).

examine, on an ongoing basis, all aspects of its operations to determine its strengths and weaknesses and to examine how well its programs fulfil its objectives.

The governance committee performs two main functions. A vibrant and effective board of directors requires the constant recruitment of qualified candidates. The primary role of the governance committee is to identify persons who, by reason of their expertise, training, position, resources or otherwise, would be qualified to serve on the board of directors of the school and on committees of the board of directors. The governance committee nominates persons to fill vacancies on the board of directors when they arise. For its second critical function, the governance committee should conduct annual evaluations of the chair of the board of directors, each member of the board of directors and the board as a whole. This process of self-assessment need not be highly formalized, but it is very important for a board to evaluate continuously whether it is effectively performing the responsibilities the school requires of it.

Beyond these core committees, there are several other committees which the board of an independent school may use depending on the stage of development and the needs of the school. An education committee may supervise a broad range of activities from student admissions, the hiring of faculty, the development of programs of study through to monitoring the academic standards of the school. Before establishing an education committee, a board must carefully consider its relationship with the principal of the school. The success of a school's program depends largely on the leadership provided by the principal. If a board, through an education committee, begins to involve itself in operational matters which are properly the responsibility of the principal, unnecessary tension may arise between the board and the principal. While there may be need for an education committee of the board in the case of a school which is starting from scratch — an education committee can support and assist a principal in building a school program in its formative years — once the school is on its feet, less justification exists for an education committee to involve itself in matters for which the principal bears responsibility. For schools which rest on the principle that parents must remain active educators of their children, an education committee may serve to supervise the school's program of study to ensure it continues to meet the objectives and purposes of the school. If a board does decide to establish an education committee, care should be taken to ensure that the committee's focus remains at the policy level, leaving the operation of the school's programs in the hands of the principal and the staff.

Some schools also maintain standing committees of the board which deal with development issues such as fundraising and alumni affairs, as well as communication, transportation and public relations.

The Structure of Standing Committees

The by-laws of an independent school may provide that the chair of any board standing committee be a member of the board of directors. The chair of the board of directors may be designated as an *ex officio* member of each standing committee. The treasurer of the school frequently is the chair of the finance committee.

Since the standing committees of a board of directors provide a natural method by which to involve and train new people in the affairs and activities of the board, the by-laws of the school should provide sufficient flexibility to allow the appointment of non-directors to standing committees of the board. Non-director members of standing committees who demonstrate dedication and skill in the performance of committee work often prove natural candidates for the board when vacancies arise.

The by-laws should be sufficiently flexible to allow for the expansion and contraction of the number of members of standing committees. A by-law could provide for a minimum number of members on a standing committee and then authorize the board of directors to appoint additional members to the standing committee if and when required. Similarly, the by-law should provide sufficient flexibility to standing committees to establish their own rules of procedure and to regulate their meetings as they think fit.

The by-laws of a school may provide that the board of directors can appoint from time to time such *ad hoc* committees as they consider necessary.

Officers

The *Corporations Act* requires the directors to elect a president from among themselves and to appoint a secretary.[65] Vice-presidents and other officers may be appointed by directors, but they are not mandatory.[66] Alternatively, the letters patent or by-laws of the corporation may provide that the members of the corporation elect or appoint the officers of the corporation at a general meeting called for that purpose. Absent such a provision, the *Corporations Act* provides that the power to elect and appoint officers rests with the board of directors.[67]

As mentioned above, the board of directors can also appoint a chair of the board and assign the chair some or all of the duties of the president.[68]

---

[65] Section 289(1), (2).
[66] Section 289(2).
[67] Section 289(3).
[68] Section 290.

Meetings of the Members of the School Corporation

Under the *Corporations Act*, a corporation must hold the first annual meeting of its members not later than 18 months after its incorporation. Thereafter, annual members' meetings must be held not more than 15 months after the holding of the last preceding annual meeting.[69] Where the directors fail to hold such meetings, the members may request the directors to call a general meeting of members[70] or apply to the court for an order directing the holding of a members' meeting.[71]

The by-laws of the corporation may provide that the meetings of the members be held at any place in Ontario.[72] If no such provision is inserted in the by-laws, then the *Corporations Act* requires that members' meetings be held at the head office of the school corporation.[73] If it is planned to hold members' meetings at any place outside Ontario, then specific provision for this must be inserted in the letters patent of the corporation.[74] As in the case of directors' meetings, the Act does not make any specific provision for the holding of telephone meetings of members.

At a members' meeting, each member of the school corporation has one vote unless the letters patent or by-laws specifically provide that a member has more than one vote or has no vote.[75] Since a member is entitled to vote at a meeting of members by means of a proxy, the by-laws of the school should deal with the responsibility of the secretary to distribute the proxies when requested and the means by which proxies may be exercised at a members' meeting.[76]

Section 93 of the *Corporations Act* sets out the procedure for calling and holding a members' meeting. Notice of the time and place for holding a members' meeting must be sent to each member by mail at least ten days before the date of the meeting. The school corporation may adopt by-laws which modify this procedure for the calling and holding of members' meetings, except that the by-laws cannot provide for fewer than ten days' notice and cannot provide that notice of the meeting may be given other than individually.[77]

No member in arrears of any membership dues is entitled to vote at a members' meeting. All questions proposed for the consideration of members at a meeting shall be determined by the majority of the votes cast, and the chair

---

[69] Section 293.
[70] Section 295.
[71] Section 332.
[72] Section 82(2).
[73] Section 82(1).
[74] Section 82(3).
[75] Section 125.
[76] Section 84(1).
[77] Section 93(2).

presiding at the meeting has a second or casting vote in case of an equality of votes. The chair may, with the consent of the meeting, adjourn the meeting from time to time and from place to place.

The president, or in his absence a vice-president who is a director, shall preside as chair at members' meetings. Where the board of directors has delegated to its chair the power to preside at members' meetings, then the chair of the board will chair such meetings.

Auditors

At the first general members' meeting, the members must appoint an auditor to hold office until the first annual meeting. If the members do not appoint an auditor, the directors must.[78] Thereafter, at each annual members' meeting, the members must appoint an auditor to hold office until the next members' meeting.[79] The auditor appointed may not be a director, officer or employee of the corporation.

Under the *Corporations Act* the appointment of an auditor is mandatory; the Act does not contain any provisions permitting the waiver of an audit.

By-Law Approval by Revenue Canada

Although the by-laws of the school corporation are not filed with the application for incorporation to the Ministry of Consumer and Commercial Relations, the by-laws must be filed with any application forwarded to Revenue Canada when seeking charitable status for the independent school.

ANNUAL CORPORATE FILINGS

Following incorporation, a school must file an annual return with the Ministry of Consumer and Commercial Relations. If the school fails to file a return for two consecutive years, the letters patent of the school may be cancelled. Penalties may be levied against a corporation in default of its reporting requirements, and a corporation in default is also incapable of commencing any action to enforce a contract in a court in Ontario.[80]

If there is a change in the directors, officers or head office of the school corporation, a notice of change form must be filed with the Ministry of Consumer and Commercial Relations within 15 days of the change.[81]

---

[78] Section 94(1).
[79] Section 94(2).
[80] *Corporations Information Act*, s. 18.
[81] Section 4.

PERSONAL LIABILITY OF MEMBERS AND DIRECTORS OF A NON-SHARE CORPORATION

One of the main legal advantages of using a non-share corporation to operate an independent school lies in minimizing the personal liability of members of the school corporation for the liabilities incurred by the school. The *Corporations Act* provides that a member of a non-share corporation shall not be held "answerable or responsible for any act, default, obligation or liability of the corporation or for any engagement, claim, payment, loss, injury, transaction, matter or thing relating to or connected with the corporation".[82]

A director of a non-share corporation must exercise the degree of skill which may reasonably be expected from a person of his knowledge and experience.[83] Although it is unusual for a court to impose personal liability on the directors of non-share corporations, many statutes make directors of the corporation potentially subject to some personal liability for the debts of the corporation. Since directors are charged with managing the affairs and business of the school corporation, the law requires directors to manage prudently the financial affairs of the school. If the directors permit the school to default on certain important financial obligations of the school, then the law will impose personal liability on the directors for such obligations. It is beyond the scope of this book to discuss in detail all the personal obligations which the law imposes on directors of corporations. Briefly, however, some of the more important personal liabilities which may arise for directors are:

(a) liability to employees for up to six months' wages and for vacation pay accrued for not more than 12 months under the *Employment Standards Act*, R.S.O. 1990, c. E.14;[84]
(b) liability for unremitted employee source deductions under the *Income Tax Act*;
(c) liability for the remittance of G.S.T.;
(d) liability for the failure to collect or remit retail sales tax;
(e) failure to remit tax under the *Employer Health Tax Act*;[85]
(f) making a false or misleading statement in the information provided to the MCCR;
(g) failure to keep the records of proceedings, documents, and registers, and books of account and accounting records at the head office of the

---

[82] *Corporations Act*, s. 122.
[83] Donald J. Bourgeois, *The Law of Charitable and Non-Profit Organizations*, 2nd ed. (Toronto: Butterworths, 1995) at pp. 134-5.
[84] *Corporations Act*, s. 81.
[85] R.S.O. 1990, c. E.11.

corporation or another authorized location so that the remedy may be open for inspection during normal business hours;[86] and

(h) failure to take reasonable care that the school corporation complies with the *Occupational Health and Safety Act*.[87]

In the event that a director of the school corporation is sued for any act done in the execution of his or her duties as a director, the school may indemnify the director out of its funds for all costs and expenses the director incurs in the lawsuit, except that a director is not entitled to be indemnified for any costs and expenses incurred or occasioned by his or her own wilful neglect or default. The decision by the school corporation to indemnify the director must be made at a meeting of members of the school corporation.[88] A school can purchase directors' and officers' liability insurance to protect against such risks. Directors' and officers' liability insurance policies normally provide for two separate agreements: one for the officers and directors, and one for the corporation. Such policies will cover losses arising from a "wrongful act" including negligence, breaches of duty, misstatements and omissions, but not for "knowingly wrongful acts", such as fraud or criminal acts. Other types of liability may also be excluded on the basis that extent of exposure is too uncertain for insurance companies to value.

With respect to the indemnification of directors of a non-share corporation which is a charitable organization, the Public Guardian and Trustee takes the position that the indemnification of directors is a form of remuneration and a charitable corporation is not permitted to indemnify its directors without first obtaining a court order. Whether the Public Guardian and Trustees' position is correct is open to debate,[89] but the Public Guardian and Trustee vigorously applies this policy in its dealings with charitable organizations. A recent amendment to the *Charities Accounting Act* now provides for a simplified procedure to obtain a court order for a charitable organization, including a court order authorizing the purchase of directors' and officers' liability insurance.

---

[86] *Corporations Act*, s. 304(4).
[87] R.S.O. 1990, c. O.1, s. 32.
[88] *Corporations Act*, s. 80.
[89] William I. Innes, "Liability of Directors and Officers and Non-Profit Corporations" (1993), 13 E. & T.J. 151 at p. 161. Bill 117 introduced in 1997 in the Ontario legislature would have amended the *Corporations Act* to clarify the situation. Bill 117 did not proceed past first reading.

THE INDEPENDENT SCHOOL AS A REGISTERED CHARITY

Application for Registration

Registering an independent school as a registered charity provides two benefits. First, a registered charity does not pay tax on its taxable income,[90] and also may qualify for special treatment regarding G.S.T. and provincial retail sales tax.[91] Second, a registered charity may issue tax receipts to those who make charitable donations to the registered charity and the donors are able to obtain some favourable tax treatment for their charitable donations.

Since the common law of Canada recognizes the pursuit of education as a charitable purpose, an independent school likely will be recognized by Revenue Canada as carrying on a charitable purpose. For an independent school to be accepted as a "registered charity" by Revenue Canada, it must qualify as a "charitable organization", which the *Income Tax Act* defines as:

> ... an organization, whether or not incorporated,
>
> (a) all the resources of which are devoted to charitable activities carried on by the organization itself,
> (b) no part of the income of which is payable to, or is otherwise available for, the personal benefit of any proprietor, member, shareholder, trustee or settlor thereof,
> (c) more than 50% of the directors, trustees, officers or like officials of which deal with each other and with each of the other directors, trustees, officers or officials at arms length ...[92]

An application for registration as a charitable organization is made by completing and filing a form (T-2050) with the Charities Division of Revenue Canada. Revenue Canada publishes a brochure entitled "Registering Your Charity For Income Tax Purposes (T4063)" which provides details about the requirements for applying for registration as a charity. Since all registered charities are required to maintain books and records at a Canadian address which is recorded with Revenue Canada, the application for registration must specify the address where books and records of the independent school will be kept. The following documentation must also accompany the application for registration as a charitable organization:

---

[90] *Income Tax Act*, s. 149(1)(*f*); Ontario *Corporations Tax Act*, R.S.O. 1990, c. C.40, s. 57(1).
[91] For a full discussion see Bourgeois, *op. cit.*, footnote 83, at pp. 189-97, or contact the local office of Revenue Canada or the Ontario Ministry of Revenue for further information.
[92] *Income Tax Act*, s. 149.1(1).

1. A copy of the letters patent and by-laws of the corporation.
2. A statement setting out the activities and programs to be carried on by the corporation to further each of the objectives or purposes set out in the letters patent. The statement of activities should be quite precise; a vague or incomplete description will result in a delay in processing the application. It is often helpful to include brochures or other materials about the school setting out its activities.
3. Financial information about the school. If the school has already completed a fiscal year of operation, the financial statements for the last completed year must be included. If the school is not yet in operation, a proposed budget or estimate of income and expenditures, as well as anticipated assets and liabilities of the first year of operation, should be included.
4. A full list of all the directors and officers of the school corporation.
5. An indication whether the school owns, or intends to own, real property. Revenue Canada takes the view that if an applicant for a registered charity intends to own land, it should be incorporated.

The application form contains other questions designed to identify into which category of "registered charity" the applicant school will fall. Under the *Income Tax Act*, there are three kinds of registered charities: a charitable organization, a public foundation or a private foundation. Foundations fund the charitable activities of other registered organizations, whereas a charitable organization initiates or carries out charitable activities. Independent schools usually will fall into the category of charitable organizations.

Additional Duties of Directors of a Registered Charity

The charitable objects of a registered charity impose additional duties on the directors of the corporation. The Public Guardian and Trustee takes the position that a charitable corporation holds its assets in trust for charitable purposes and that the corporation's directors consequently owe fiduciary duties to the corporation to ensure that it fulfils its obligation as a trustee. Whether this position is correct as a matter of law has generated some debate, but there can be no doubt that Ontario courts will hold directors of charitable corporations to a high standard of care approximating that imposed on a trustee.[93]

What this means in practical terms is that a director of a charitable corporation cannot profit from his position as a director. Courts have long recognized that the director of a charitable corporation stands in a fiduciary position and, as such, is not allowed to put himself in a position where his own interest and his duty to the corporation conflict. A fiduciary is not entitled to make a

---

[93] See Bourgeois, *op. cit.*, footnote 83, at pp. 135-8.

profit from the corporation whose assets he is charged to protect.[94] By way of illustrating this restriction, an Ontario court has held that directors of charitable corporations should not receive any payments as directors without the corporation first obtaining court approval. The court strongly suggested that a provision in the charitable corporation's by-laws permitting remuneration to be paid to directors would not be sufficient to lawfully authorize such payments without first obtaining court approval for the by-law.[95] Another Ontario case held that a lawyer who is a director of a charitable corporation cannot receive payment for professional services rendered to the corporation without first obtaining court approval of the payments.[96]

Given this clear legal prohibition against directors of charitable corporations profiting from their positions, an independent school which is a registered charity must not remunerate its directors, pay its directors salaries as employees, or pay its directors for services rendered other than as directors (*e.g.*, for legal services performed by them as lawyers) without first obtaining court approval.

These fiduciary duties of directors apply with equal force on the dissolution of a charitable corporation. Take the case of *Faith Haven Bible Training Centre (Re)*,[97] which involved an educational institution incorporated as a registered charity. When the school decided to cease operations, the board of directors voted to give the school's car to its principal and distribute the remaining assets of the school among those who had taught or contributed services to the school over the years. The Public Trustee objected to this disposition of the school's assets, and the court upheld the objection, finding that the distribution of the school's property to the principal and others was a breach of duty by the directors of the school. In the result, the court excused the breaches because on the facts of the case it was clear that the persons who received the payments had made significant contributions to the school over its years of operation and the court was prepared to award them fair and reasonable honoraria for their services. While the directors of the Faith Haven Bible Training Centre escaped personal liability for the unauthorized payments in that particular case, the court made it clear that where directors propose to deal with a corporation's assets in a manner contrary to the charitable objects of the corporation, the directors first must seek court approval for their planned actions.

---

[94] *Bray v. Ford*, [1896] A.C. 44 (H.L.) at p. 51; *French Protestant Hospital (Re)*, [1951] 1 Ch. 567 at pp. 570-71.
[95] *Public Trustee v. Toronto Humane Society* (1987), 40 D.L.R. (4th) 111, 60 O.R. (2d) 236 at pp. 246-8 (H.C.J.).
[96] *Harold G. Fox Education Fund v. Public Trustee* (1989), 69 O.R. (2d) 742 at p. 747, 34 E.T.R. 113 (H.C.J.).
[97] (1988), 29 E.T.R. 198 (Ont. Surr. Ct.) at p. 208.

MUNICIPAL APPROVALS FOR AN INDEPENDENT SCHOOL

Zoning

Local municipal zoning by-laws must be taken into account when selecting a site to construct or operate a school. Zoning by-laws usually classify the operation of an independent school as a non-residential use of property which, depending on the language of the zoning by-law for a particular municipality, may or may not be a permitted use in a residential area. Municipal by-laws often will exclude the operation of a school from permitted uses in a residential area and require that schools be operated in areas zoned for institutional use. Care must therefore be taken to ensure that the local zoning by-laws permit the use of a selected site for a school or that an exemption from the zoning by-law can be obtained.

If an independent school operates on property not zoned for that purpose, a municipality may seek an injunction to restrain the continuing use of the property for a school. In one case a church decided to use part of its building to operate an elementary school. Although the local zoning by-law permitted the use of the property as a church, including its use as a nursery and Sunday school, the zoning by-law required independent schools to operate on properties zoned for institutional purposes. When the municipality sought to restrain the operation of the school, its operators argued that the school was a permitted use because the mission of the church involved a teaching ministry, and therefore the school was simply an offshoot of the church. The court rejected this argument, holding that since the zoning by-law clearly distinguished between a church and a private school, the operation of an independent school could not fall under the definition of "church".[98] The court also held that the zoning by-law did not infringe the guarantee of freedom of religion under section 2(a) of the *Canadian Charter of Rights and Freedoms*, by distinguishing between a church and a school affiliated with the church. The court held that the municipal zoning by-law was blind to church affiliation, applying as a land use control instrument to all denominations.[99]

Building Code, Fire Marshall and Health Protection Compliance

An independent school must consult with municipal authorities to ensure that its premises comply with the Building Code, the Fire Code and the *Health Protection and Promotion Act*.[100] Under the *Health Protection and Promotion*

---

[98] *Milton (Town) v. Smith* (1986), 32 M.P.L.R. 107 (Ont. S.C.) at p. 118.
[99] *Supra*, at p. 122.
[100] R.S.O. 1990, c. H.7.

Establishing the Independent School: Corporate Issues 39

Act, the local medical officer of health must inspect premises for the purpose of preventing, eliminating and decreasing the effects of health hazards.[101] The inspection must include any premises such as a school cafeteria where food is offered for sale.[102] Regulations under that Act set out detailed requirements for the construction and operation of a food premise, such as a school cafeteria.[103]

The Ministry of Education and Training requires an independent school to file with its initial Notice of Intention to Operate letters from the municipal clerk, Fire Marshall, and public health office confirming that the site selected by the school is suitable for use as a school.

---

[101] Section 10(1).
[102] Section 10(2).
[103] See the detailed requirements of the regulation: Food Premises, R.R.O. 1990, Reg. 562 (as amended).

3

Dealing With the Ministry of Education and Training

THE NOTICE OF INTENTION TO OPERATE

The Legal Obligation to File

No independent school can operate in Ontario unless it files a Notice of Intention to Operate a Private School with the Ministry of Education and Training[1] (the "Ministry"). A Notice of Intention to Operate a Private School must be in the form prescribed by the Ministry and include such details as the Minister may require.[2] If a Notice of Intention to Operate is not filed with the Ministry, section 16(4) the *Education Act* provides that "every person concerned in the management of a private school . . . is guilty of an offence and on conviction is liable to a fine of not more than $50 for every day such school is so operated". Since the Act does not define those who are involved in the management of an independent school, this penalty section potentially could impose liability on a broad range of people — the incorporators of the independent school, the directors and officers of the school, and those involved in the administration of the school, for example, the principals and vice-principals.

Content of the Notice

The present form of the Notice of Intention to Operate a Private School used by the Ministry serves as an information return, application for inspection and contract to adopt the Ontario Student Transcript Common Course Coding, all rolled into one. Since the principal of an independent school must sign the notice and certify that the information contained in the notice is true and correct, and since the notice may create a contractual obligation between the independent school with the Ministry, care must be taken when completing the form.

---

[1] *Education Act*, R.S.O. 1990, c. E.2, s. 16(1).
[2] Section 16(3).

Much of the information requested on the Notice of Intention to Operate consists of basic information about the school such as its name, location, language of instruction, affiliation and corporate status. The notice also requests statistical information about student enrolment, the size of the teaching staff, level of instruction (elementary, secondary, or elementary and secondary) and the curriculum. A copy of the Ministry's current Notice of Intention to Operate a Private School can be found in Appendix "E".

Most of the form is self-explanatory, but two sections merit specific mention. First, the Notice of Intention to Operate requires the school principal to confirm that the use of the premises has been approved by the local municipal clerk or building commission, the Fire Marshall and the medical officer of health. Letters should be obtained from each of these agencies confirming that the site has been approved for use as an independent school. A school should obtain these approvals in advance and file the three required letters with its initial Notice of Intention to Operate. Once a new independent school has received Ministry approval, it is not required to resubmit these letters of approval with each annual filing of its Notice of Intention to Operate. If, however, an existing school decides to relocate to a new site, it would have to submit new letters of approval for the new site. Second, as will be discussed in Chapter 6 "Programs of Study", elementary independent schools are not required to follow the curriculum used in public and separate schools, and only inspected secondary independent schools are required to conform to the courses of study offered in secondary public and separate schools. This freedom of an independent school to choose whether or not to follow the public and separate school curriculum is reflected in that part of the Notice of Intention to Operate which requires a school to indicate whether it will follow the Ontario curriculum and offer Ontario Academic Courses.

As presently designed, the lower portion of the Notice of Intention to Operate consists of an application for inspection of a private school at the secondary level pursuant to section 16(7) of the *Education Act*. The form only requires some basic information on estimated student enrolment in the secondary grades, the opening and closing dates of school semesters, and the number of candidates for an Ontario secondary school diploma at the end of the semester. The application for inspection does not deal with the requirements for the program of study at an inspected private secondary school.

From a legal point of view, the application for inspection at the secondary level contained in the Notice of Intention to Operate, when signed by the school principal, creates a contract between the independent school and the Ministry of Education and Training in three respects. First, the school effectively agrees to follow the Ministry's prescribed program of study leading up to the Ontario secondary school diploma, thereby relinquishing its ability to set its own courses of study.

Second, the school agrees that no part of an inspection report will be used in any advertising or promotional material concerning the school. A school may identify itself on its promotional material as an inspected private secondary school, but the school cannot use or incorporate any comments or remarks contained in an annual inspection report in its promotional material. It is also important to note that the Notice of Intention to Operate specifically states that the inclusion of a school on the list of private schools maintained at the Ministry does not imply that the school has been accepted, approved or recognized as providing satisfactory instruction. By the terms of the Notice of Intention to Operate, a private school may not advertise that it offers satisfactory instruction simply on the basis that it has filed a Notice of Intention to Operate.

Finally, the application for inspection also gives rise to a contract under which the independent school agrees to adopt the Ontario Student Transcript Common Course Coding which identifies each course offered at the secondary level leading to an Ontario secondary school diploma. The list of common course codes also contains the codes used to report completion of the grade 9 program.[3]

Filing

The initial Notice of Intention to Operate must be submitted to the Ministry on or before the first day of September of the year in which the school intends to commence operation.[4] The completed Notice of Intention to Operate must be forwarded to the Ministry of Education and Training, Operations and Fields Services Branch. The *Education Act* makes it an offence for any person to knowingly make false statements in a Notice of Intention to Operate and imposes a fine of up to $500.[5]

Before an initial inspection occurs, a new independent school must send the Ministry all relevant documentation, including the letters of approval from the municipal clerk, Fire Marshall and medical officer of health, together with its Notice of Intention to Operate and school year calendar.

The Ministry inspects all new independent schools in their first year of operation, and these inspections are called NOI (or Notice of Intention to Operate) inspections. The Ministry seeks to conduct NOI inspections no later than October 30th of the school's first year of operation and a Ministry inspector will arrive unannounced at the new school to conduct the inspection.[6] At the present time the Ministry does not charge a fee for a NOI inspection.

---

[3] The list of common course codes can be found on the Ministry of Education and Training website: www.edu.gov.on.ca.
[4] *Education Act*, s. 16(2).
[5] Section 16(9).
[6] Although the Ministry previously scheduled initial NOI inspections for new private

In conducting an initial NOI inspection, the Ministry inspector first seeks to ensure that the new school meets the definition of "private school" in the *Education Act*. The definition[7] requires that a private school provide instruction for five or more pupils who are of or over compulsory school age. A child is of compulsory school age if he or she attains the age of six years on or before the first school day in September, and remains of compulsory school age until 16 years.[8] A private school therefore must have five or more pupils who are over the age of six as of September 1st in the school year. A school may enrol pupils in junior kindergarten and kindergarten classes.[9] Any children attending a school's kindergarten or junior kindergarten program are not counted as part of the five or more pupils required to constitute a private school. An independent school cannot enrol children who have not attained the age of four by December 31st, as such an operation would be subject to the provisions of the *Day Nurseries Act*.[10] A new school must also demonstrate that it provides instruction between the hours of 9:00 a.m. and 4:00 p.m. on any school day.

The inspector will ascertain the type of instruction and curriculum used by the school, primarily to confirm that the school does have an organized program of study as well as assessment and evaluation strategies. Finally, the inspector will review the new school's record-keeping to ensure that the school uses some method to record the attendance of students and track their academic progress.

Following the NOI inspection, the Ministry will send the new independent school a letter which will either approve or not approve the school as a private school. Where the Ministry approves a new private school, the letter will provide the school with its Ministry Identification Number ("MIDENT") and will include the school in the Ministry's directory of private schools which is issued each year.[11]

If the school does not meet the requirements of the NOI inspection, the Ministry will not approve it as a private school. In many circumstances a new school will fail to comply with NOI requirements because it does not enrol the

---

schools, the Ministry occasionally found the new school would tailor its operations for the day of inspection, thereby not providing an accurate picture of the school's operation.

[7] Section 1(1) "'private school' means an institution at which instruction is provided at any time between the hours of 9 a.m. and 4 p.m. on any school day for five or more pupils who are of or over compulsory school age in any of the subjects of the elementary or secondary school courses of study and that is not a school as defined in this section."

[8] Section 21(1)(a).

[9] The Ministry considers a child eligible for junior kindergarten if the child attains the age of four by December 31st; a child is eligible for kindergarten if he or she attains the age of five by December 31st of the school year.

[10] R.S.O. 1990, c. D.2.

[11] The Directory of Private Schools is posted on the Ministry's website.

required minimum of five students of compulsory school age. When a school does not receive Ministry approval, the Ministry will so inform the local school boards, both public and Roman Catholic.

Annual Filing

The Act requires every private school to submit to the Ministry, on or before the first day of September in each year, a Notice of Intention to Operate a Private School.[12] Failure to make an annual filing is an offence, exposing every person concerned in the management of a school to a daily fine of not more than $50 for every day the school is operated without making the annual filing.[13] If a school does not make its annual filing, the Ministry will consider the school to have ceased operation and will remove it from the Ministry's published directory of elementary and secondary private schools.

SEPTEMBER STATISTICAL FILING

The *Education Act* requires a principal, headmaster, headmistress or person in charge of a private school to make a return to the Ministry furnishing "such statistical information regarding enrolment, staff, courses of study or other information as and when required by the Minister".[14] Failure to make such a return within 60 days of the request is an offence, subject on conviction to a fine of not more than $200.[15]

The Ministry commonly refers to this statistical information return as the "September Report". A September Report form is sent to each independent school in October and the Ministry requires the school to collect and submit the requested data shortly thereafter.[16] The specific date varies from year to year. (A copy of the current September Report form can be found in Appendix "F".)

INSPECTIONS OF INDEPENDENT SCHOOLS BY THE MINISTRY OF EDUCATION AND TRAINING

Section 16 of the *Education Act* provides for two types of private school inspections. First, section 16(6) of the Act authorizes Ministry supervisory offi-

---

[12] *Education Act*, s. 16(2).
[13] Section 16(4).
[14] Section 16(5).
[15] *Ibid.*
[16] *Private School Manual: Information for Inspected Private Schools* (Ministry of Education and Training, August, 1997) at p. 6.

cers to inspect *any* private school during reasonable hours, and to conduct an inspection of the school and any records or documents relating to the school. Under this provision, all private elementary and secondary schools may be inspected by Ministry supervisory officers. As a matter of practice, the Ministry will conduct initial NOI inspections for all new elementary and non-credit granting secondary private schools, but will not inspect those schools in subsequent years of operation unless exceptional circumstances arise.

Section 16(7) of the Act deals with the second kind of inspection, that of a private secondary school which offers subjects leading to an Ontario secondary school diploma. Such inspections are designed to review the standard of instruction offered in the subjects leading to an Ontario diploma. Although all independent schools are subject to inspection, it is common practice to use the term "inspected independent schools" when referring to private secondary schools which offer programs of study leading to an Ontario diploma.

While one benefit of the short, and somewhat terse, provisions in the *Education Act* dealing with independent schools is the resulting flexibility and latitude granted to schools in their operations, an accompanying drawback is the uncertainty surrounding the proper scope of Ministry inspections. Under the Act, the Ministry possesses the authority to inspect private schools, but as a matter of administrative law, any inspection must accord with the statutory purpose of the inspection. How does the *Education Act* describe the purpose of Ministry inspections of private schools? Here the vagueness of the *Education Act* takes over, section 16(6) of the Act authorizes supervisory officers to enter a private school to "conduct an inspection of the school and any records or documents relating thereto". On its face, this is a very broad power. At the same time, the *Education Act*, in its compulsory attendance provision, provides that students attending an independent school must receive "satisfactory instruction".[17] In view of this, any inspection of an independent school by a Ministry supervisory officer must be confined to matters relating to whether the school provides its students with "satisfactory instruction".

Over the years, Ministry inspections of independent schools for the most part have focused on aspects of the school's operation pertaining to satisfactory instruction. Yet at times, tension arises between Ministry inspectors and independent schools when the inspectors make demands which the school considers unreasonable or unrelated to the issue of satisfactory instruction. At the end of the day, a spirit of common sense must be brought to the process by both the Ministry inspecting officer and the school staff, with each recognizing the legitimate roles, responsibilities and principles of the other.[18]

---

[17] Section 21(2)(a).

[18] A solution to this problem may be in sight. With the reduction in the past few years of the number of provincial civil servants, and the consequent strains this has placed on the resources of the Ministry to conduct independent school inspections, inde-

INSPECTED INDEPENDENT SECONDARY SCHOOLS

The Private School Manual

Beyond the very simple guidance provided by the language of the inspection provisions contained in section 16(6) and (7) of the *Education Act*, the only other source of information about the procedures used during independent school inspections lies in the *Private School Manual* published by the Ministry of Education and Training. Before reviewing some of the procedures outlined in the manual, it must be emphasized that the Ministry's *Private School Manual* does not have any legal force or effect. Neither the *Education Act* nor any statutorily authorized policy of the Minister specify how Ministry officials should conduct an inspection. The *Private School Manual* is simply a statement by Ministry staff of the approach they will take when inspecting independent secondary schools which grant credits and Ontario secondary school diplomas. (Excerpts from the *Private School Manual* are reproduced in Appendix "G".)

Much of the manual seeks to provide independent secondary schools with information to enable them to prepare for Ministry inspections. The *Private School Manual* identifies eight purposes for inspection visits:

1. To discuss the organization of the school as outlined in the Notice of Intention to Operate a Private School form, the September Report, OS:IS and related policy memoranda.

2. To ensure that the courses of study adhere to the intent of the guidelines.

3. To discuss the courses of study, school course calendars and timetables which the principal may be requested to submit.

4. To inspect, as requested, teachers who apply for a Certificate of Qualification.

5. To observe teachers in order to assess the quality of program for the granting of credits and diplomas.

6. To inspect Ontario Student Record folders and Ontario Student Transcripts.

7. To discuss the assessments and recommendations with the principal.

8. To ascertain the congruency between the curriculum guideline, the course of study and student work.[19]

In the past, the Ministry inspected credit-granting independent secondary schools every year. Recent reductions in the staffing of the Ministry seem to

---

pendent school associations are exploring ways to move independent school inspections out of the Ministry and into the hands of an independent inspection or accreditation body. A move in this direction would mark a first step towards the creation of a self-regulating environment for Ontario independent schools, perhaps along the lines of Ontario public hospitals which undergo periodic accreditation by a professional inspection organization.

[19] *Private School Manual, op. cit.*, footnote 16, at p. 46.

have resulted in less frequent inspections of schools, with some schools reporting breaks of two or three years between Ministry inspections.

Preparing for an Inspection

A Ministry supervisory officer will contact a secondary school principal by letter to arrange a date for the inspection, and will advise the principal of the procedures which will be followed for that year's inspection. Although pre-inspection practices vary among Ministry inspectors, many supervisory officers will request the principal to submit in advance of the inspection details of the courses offered by the school, teacher timetables, the master school timetable, the names of teachers requesting inspection to obtain a Certificate of Qualification, courses of study for all courses and the school's course calendar.[20] The Ministry requires this information to confirm that the school's courses meet the instruction time requirements set out in OS:IS[21] for credit courses.

In recent years, the Ministry has sought to secure from the school copies of its courses of study well in advance of the actual inspection. (There are always exceptions to this practice. Sometimes the date of inspection will be advanced and the Ministry inspector will pick up the courses of study at the school during the course of the inspection and review them afterwards.) If a Ministry inspector concludes that the courses of study submitted by a school in advance of the inspection contain serious problems, the inspector may advise a school that an inspection will not take place until the school revises and improves its courses of study and resubmits them for review by the Ministry.

The Ministry inspector's review and critique of a school's course of study is based on the course guidelines issued by the Ministry for each secondary school credit course. Some inspectors will return the reviewed course outlines to the school in advance of the inspection and discuss their comments and recommendations with the principal at that time.

A school only has to submit one course of study for each course offered. For example, if a school offers three classes of grade 10 English, the school need submit only one course of study for the grade 10 English course. If a school does not submit a course of study to the Ministry, or provide the Ministry with a copy of the course of study when requested during an inspection, in all likelihood the Ministry will not allow the school to offer the course for credit.

Although the extent of the preparation required for an inspection will vary from school to school, as a general matter, a school should pay close attention to three areas. First, the school's student records should be well-

---

[20] *Ibid.*, at p. 47.
[21] OS:IS is the abbreviated title of "Ontario Schools: Intermediate and Senior Divisions, Program and Diploma Requirements, 1989" which contains the requirements for secondary school programs leading to an Ontario diploma.

organized and up to date. If the independent school uses the Ministry's Ontario Student Records, they should comply with the requirements of the *Ontario Student Record (OSR): Guideline 1989.* Second, all courses of study should be in order. Third, if any teacher wishes to be inspected for certification, all the prerequisite documentation should be completed and sent to the Ministry by October 30th of the school year.

The Inspection

An inspection usually will begin by the inspector meeting with the principal. A principal should provide the inspector with a proposed timetable of the classes to be observed. Past experience suggests that Ministry supervisory officers generally wish to observe several OAC and senior grade classes. If the previous inspection report recommended changes to specific courses, an inspector likely will wish to observe those classes as well. The inspector may ask the principal if there are specific classes which the principal would like the inspector to observe during the day. An inspector usually tries to attend part or all of a class during each period in order to observe classroom performance and pedagogical methods.

Depending on the inspector involved, much of the time spent on an inspection may focus on a review of paper work to ascertain whether the school demonstrates a planned and organized program of study. According to the *Private School Manual*, teachers must make available a copy of their course of study, a complete, detailed record of daily lessons, a set of marked student notes, assignments, projects, tests and examinations reflective of the work in the entire course to date and a record of student evaluation which follows the weight for each component assigned in the course of study.[22] A supervisory officer may also review a school's written safety policies and practices for in-school programs, field trips and extended travel programs.[23] The *Private School Manual* identifies those issues to which the Ministry pays particular attention during an inspection:

- OSR maintenance: documentation of equivalent credits, Grade 9 documentation, procedures for access to OSRs, storage of OSRs, documentation for waiving prerequisites;
- OSTs: documentation of Grade 9 program, course names and codes for courses grades 10-12/OAC;
- Report Cards: course codes for Grade 9, attendance report, credit value for course grades 10-12/OAC;

---

[22] *Private School Manual: Information for Inspected Private Schools* (Ministry of Education and Training, August, 1997) at p. 47.
[23] *Ibid.*, at p. 48.

- School Course Calendar: required components, course names and codes, prerequisites;
- Courses of Study: adherence to the curriculum guidelines, details of teaching/learning activities in each unit;
- Examinations: correspondence with examination handbooks;
- Instructions: evidence of higher level thinking skills activities, detail in lesson plans, evaluation records which reflect the weighting listed in the course of study;
- General: materials required for the inspection (lesson plans, evaluation records, student work).[24]

As this list suggests, the Ministry designs its inspections to ascertain that the school has an organized, planned and documented program of study and maintains the appropriate student records and transcripts.

Ministry inspections usually take one day to conduct and generally only one Ministry inspector will perform the inspection. At the end of the day's inspection, the Ministry inspector will discuss with the principal the inspector's observations and recommendations. Most inspectors will engage in a thorough discussion with the principal of their recommendations, as well as the method and timing in which the school can reasonably implement the recommendations.

Inspection Costs

At the present time, the Minister charges a fee for the inspection of a secondary school. The fee is based on the number of students enrolled in the school.

Where a school is not located on a highway or improved road, it is the policy of the Ministry to request that the school pay the travel expenses for the inspection. A travel advance payable to the supervisory officer must be received by the supervisory officer at least two weeks prior to the scheduled visit. If the cheque is not received, the trip will be cancelled. Following the inspection, an itemized expense account, receipts and any surplus money will be returned to the school operator.[25]

Inspection Reports

As soon as possible following the inspection, the supervisory officer will issue an inspection report to the school. The private school inspection report is sent to the school principal, with a copy also sent to the Provincial Co-ordinator of Private Schools in the Ministry of Education and Train-

---

[24] *Ibid.*, at pp. 54-5.
[25] *Ibid.*, at p. 48.

ing.[26] (A copy of the Private School Inspection Report currently used by the Ministry is reproduced in Appendix "H".) A private school inspection report outlines the total number of students enrolled in each secondary grade on the day of inspection, the number of Ontario secondary school diplomas and certificates requested by the principal and the secondary school courses for which approval has been granted.[27] The report also specifies whether the principal is authorized to grant Ontario diploma credits and for what period of time. Where the Ministry approves the granting by the school of a credit for a course, the approval signifies that the Ministry has approved the instructional standards for the course.[28]

Where the inspection uncovers significant problems in a secondary school's program of instruction, an inspector's report may specify that limits are placed on the ability of the school's principal to grant credits. The report may require the school to obtain authorization from the supervisory office of the Ministry in order to grant credits in specified subjects. In more serious cases, the report may provide that the Ministry's supervisory officer must authorize the granting of all credits, effectively suspending the principal's power to grant credits and vesting the power in the supervisory office of the Ministry. In order for the school's principal to resume his authority to grant credits, the school will be required to implement the recommendations specified by the inspector in the inspection report.

A report will attach a list of recommendations. The Ministry expects a school to act on recommendations made by the inspector. When the inspection report is sent to the school, the Ministry generally requests the school to develop a plan for the implementation of the recommendations and advise the Ministry of the plan within four to six weeks. In cases where the Ministry's inspection has revealed serious problems with a secondary school program, the Ministry may require the independent school to present a remedial plan within a shorter period of time.

Sometimes disagreements may arise between a school and the Ministry as to the legitimate scope of recommendations which an inspector may make. In resolving such disagreements, the Ministry must respect the fact that an independent school is an autonomous educational institute with a specific educational mandate, while the school must recognize that it relinquishes a certain degree of autonomy when it wishes to grant credits towards an Ontario diploma.

---

[26] *Ibid.*, at p. 54.
[27] *Ibid.*, at p. 53.
[28] *Ibid.*, at p. 48.

Powers of the Ministry in the Event of an Unsatisfactory Inspection Report

In the event that an inspector's report concludes that an independent school's program of study is deficient or unsatisfactory in some respect, what steps can the Ministry take against the school? The *Education Act* does not contain any specific provision authorizing the Minister of Education and Training to take action against an independent school in the event of an unsatisfactory inspection report. The absence of a specific section in the Act does not end the inquiry. The Supreme Court of Canada has recognized that a province possesses a legitimate interest in ensuring the education of children.[29] A court would likely find that several sections of the *Education Act* authorize the Minister, by implication, to act in the event an independent school receives an unsatisfactory inspection report.

In the case of inspected high schools, the Act requires that the independent secondary school request inspection by the Minister in respect of instruction leading to the Ontario secondary school diploma.[30] Since the *Education Act* grants the Minister the authority to prescribe the conditions under which high school diplomas are granted,[31] by implication, the Minister would possess the power to refuse to grant Ontario diplomas to students graduating from an independent secondary school which fails to meet the appropriate standard of instruction in its secondary school program. The Minister may also possess the implied power to refuse to permit a secondary school from granting credits to its students in the event of an unsatisfactory inspection report.

Notwithstanding these potentially severe powers of the Minister, general principles of administrative law impose two significant restraints on the Minister's power to act in response to an unsatisfactory inspection report. First, any course of action taken by the Ministry following an unsatisfactory inspection report must accord with principles of procedural fairness. That is to say, the Ministry must give the school notice of the specific areas in which its program of instruction is unsatisfactory, provide the school with an opportunity to comment on and discuss the inspection report with the Ministry, and also provide the school with the opportunity to rectify those portions of the program which are unsatisfactory. Only in the most exceptional case would the Ministry be justified in taking immediate action against a school: for example, where an inspection report revealed that conditions in a school posed an immediate danger to the health and safety of its students.

In addition to the obligation of procedural fairness, principles of administrative law also impose on the Ministry an obligation to take remedial and

---

[29] See, for example, *R. v. Jones* (1986), 31 D.L.R. (4th) 569, [1986] 2 S.C.R. 284.
[30] *Education Act*, s. 16(7).
[31] Section 8(1), para. 1.

enforcement steps which are proportionate to the deficiencies found in a school's program of study. In the vernacular, the Minister of Education and Training, as a matter of law, is not entitled to "use an elephant gun to kill a mouse". In legal terms, any decisions made by the Minister, or his employees, must be made in good faith,[32] must be consistent with the principles contained in the *Education Act*, must not infringe rights protected by Canadian constitutional law and cannot be taken for an improper purpose. Any decision by the Minister or his delegates also must not take extraneous factors or irrelevant considerations into account, but must consider all relevant factors.[33] Moreover, the Minister cannot make a decision which is so unreasonable that no reasonable authority would come to it.[34]

In other words, any response by the Ministry to deficiencies revealed in an independent school's inspection report must be tailored to, and relate to, the deficiencies revealed by the inspection, and those deficiencies must reasonably relate to the issue of "satisfactory instruction". The Ministry cannot focus on deficiencies in one area of a school's program to improperly sanction the school in respect of other areas of its program which are satisfactory. For example, if an inspection report revealed that a school's grade 10 computer studies program was so unsatisfactory that the standard of instruction did not permit the granting of a credit in computer studies, it would be improper for the Ministry, and an abuse of the Minister's decision-making powers, to prevent the school from granting credits in other grade 10 subjects where the level of instruction proves satisfactory.

In the case of elementary schools and secondary schools which do not offer an Ontario diploma, the results of an inspection must be measured against the statutory standard of providing "satisfactory instruction" to the children in attendance in those schools. The principles of procedural fairness and proportionality discussed above in the context of inspected secondary schools would apply equally to any action proposed to be taken by the Minister in response to an unsatisfactory inspection report for elementary schools or secondary schools which do not offer an Ontario diploma.

In the extreme circumstance where an inspection report revealed such fundamental deficiencies in a school's program of study that children were not receiving "satisfactory instruction", it might be open to the Ministry to request the appropriate district school board attendance counsellor or the Provincial School Attendance Counsellor, to conclude that the children should not be excused from attendance at the local public or separate school and to direct that they attend such a school.[35] Under such circumstances, a formal inquiry would

---

[32] David J. Mullan, *Administrative Law*, 3rd ed. (Toronto: Carswell, 1996) at §477.
[33] *Ibid.*, at § 482.
[34] *Ibid.*, at § 487.
[35] *Education Act*, s. 24(2).

have to be held under the *Education Act* to determine whether the children were receiving satisfactory instruction at the school.

CAN AN INDEPENDENT SCHOOL OPERATE HOME CAMPUSES?

Recent years have witnessed an increase in the number of parents who choose to school their children at home. The school attendance provisions of the *Education Act* permit parents to excuse their children from attending a school if they are receiving "satisfactory instruction at home or elsewhere". The elasticity of the concept of "satisfactory instruction" sometimes gives rise to conflicts between home-schooling parents and district school boards because the *Education Act* requires school attendance counsellors of district school boards to enforce the Act's compulsory school attendance provisions.[36] Principals of every public elementary and secondary school must report to the appropriate school attendance counsellor the names, ages and residences of all pupils of compulsory school age who do not attend school,[37] including the names of children who are schooled at home. In the event a board's school attendance counsellor forms the opinion that a child is not receiving satisfactory instruction at home and the parents disagree with his assessment, the *Education Act* authorizes the Provincial School Attendance Counsellor to convene an inquiry hearing to determine whether the child is properly excused from school.[38] Some district school boards have seized on the school attendance provisions of the *Education Act* to develop detailed requirements for home-schooling parents, notwithstanding that the *Education Act* does not give any authority to the boards to develop or enforce such home-schooling policies. School boards have taken the position that it is the responsibility of each school board to define what constitutes a satisfactory instruction[39] with the result that district school boards display varying degrees of sympathy and support to parents who home school.

In an effort to avoid potential conflict with their district school board, some parents have explored the possibility of joining with other parents to form a loose co-operative arrangement which would qualify as an independent school for the purposes of the *Education Act*, while their children continue to receive their instruction at home. One of the advantages of establishing an independent school arrangement is that parents thereby minimize their dealings

---

[36] Section 25(5).
[37] Section 28(1)(a).
[38] Section 24(2).
[39] See the reference to the testimony of the superintendent of school operations for the Halton Board of Education in *R. (L.M.) v. B. (R.C.)*, [1997] O.J. No. 4578 (QL) at para. 89.

with the district school board because the supervision of independent schools falls into the hands of inspectors appointed by the Ministry of Education and Training.[40] Some involved in the home-schooling movement have argued that school boards generally presume that home-schooled children are not receiving satisfactory instruction and therefore require periodic testing by the board, whereas the presumption is reversed for a child who attends an independent school. There is a certain amount of truth to this perception given the way the laws are presently applied throughout the province.

Can parents who school their children at home enter into a co-operative arrangement with other parents to establish an independent school where the classrooms are located in the parents' homes? The question can be answered with a qualified "yes", but a clear distinction first must be made between home schooling and independent schools. Home schooling is not defined in the Act, but the Act permits parents to excuse their children from attendance at a public school as long as they receive "satisfactory instruction at home".[41] A parent who schools a child at home need not notify the Ministry that they are conducting home schooling, keep enrolment information, nor be subject to inspection by the Ministry. By contrast, section 16 of the Act applies to an independent school which must maintain and report enrolment information to the Ministry and permit inspection by the Ministry. A child may not be in an independent school and a home school at the same time, although a child's instructional day could involve both types of schooling at different times.

The definition of "private school" in the *Education Act* is very broad –"private school" means an institution at which instruction is provided and contains two key elements: a private school must be an "institution", and the "institution" must provide instruction. The word "institution" has a broad meaning capable of covering several kinds of educational settings. For example, the *Education Act* provides that a private school may provide instruction at "*any time* between the hours of 9:00 a.m. and 4:00 p.m. on *any school day* for five or more pupils". Accordingly, the definition of "private school" does not contain a minimum number of daily hours during which instruction must be provided at the institution, and the use of the phrase "any school day" allows an argument to be made that instruction need not be given at the institution on every school day.

As a second key element, the definition of "private school" requires that the "institution" provide instruction to the students. The Ministry has taken the position that an independent school may operate on various campuses and the Act does not require that students of an independent school must be physically located at a certain building or location. In the 1985 case of *R. v. Prentice*,[42]

---

[40] *Education Act*, s. 16(6).
[41] Section 21(2)(a).
[42] [1985] O.J. No. 771 (QL) (Ont. Prov. Ct.).

witnesses from the Ministry took the position that an arrangement under which children were educated at a "home campus" of a private school satisfied the definition of private school in the *Education Act*. (The judge in the case did not comment on whether such an interpretation of the Act by the Ministry witnesses was a proper one.)

Although the Ministry interprets section 16 of the Act as permitting multi-campus private schools, which would include homes, it regards an "institution" as an entity which must be organized and which accepts responsibility for the instruction of its students. In the Ministry's view, a network of parents teaching at home while supported by a central organization which acts as a distribution centre for curriculum documents and resource materials would not constitute an "institution", and therefore not qualify as an independent school. On the other hand, an arrangement under which a central organization controlled the content of the program or course of study at each home campus, monitored the quality of instruction and evaluation of student achievement and recorded the attendance of pupils, would qualify as an independent school.

If home-schooling parents do form an independent school, it will be subject to the reporting and inspection requirements contained in section 16 of the *Education Act* and each home campus of the private school would be subject to inspection by the Ministry. While an independent school may comprise several home campuses, the current attendance provisions of the *Education Act* do not authorize an independent school to assess whether home-schooled children are receiving "satisfactory instruction at home". Such a responsibility rests with a district board school attendance counsellor or the Provincial School Attendance Counsellor.[43]

---

[43] *Education Act*, ss. 24 and 25.

4

The Contract of Instruction

THE CONTRACTUAL RELATIONSHIP BETWEEN PARENT AND SCHOOL

One of the hallmarks of the independent school is the nature of the legal relationship between the school and students' parents. Whereas in the public and separate school systems the obligations of the school to the parents are governed by the *Education Act*,[1] in independent schools, the relationship between the parents and the school is governed by the law of contract. At the heart of the relationship lies the contract of instruction under which the parents of each student contract for the school to provide a specified kind of instruction in return for the payment of tuition by the parents.[2] A contract of instruction, like any contract, must clearly set out the expectations and obligations of the parties: what the parents expect the school to provide to their children, what the school expects the parents to pay and the rules to which it expects a student to adhere. Accordingly, an independent school must take care to ensure that its contract of instruction is clear, comprehensive and enforceable.

A school's contract of instruction must contain all the elements necessary to form a binding contract:

(i) the parties to the contract must have the capacity to enter into the contract;
(ii) the contract must contain a clear exchange of promises by the parties;
(iii) the contract must be accompanied by some financial or economic consideration to support the promises.

If a contract does not contain these elements, it may not be enforceable.

---

[1] R.S.O. 1990, c. E.2.
[2] *Wisch v. Sanford School, Inc.*, 420 F. Supp. 1310 (1976) at p. 1315.

THE LEGAL CAPACITY OF THE PARTIES

Both parties to a contract must possess the legal capacity to enter into the contract. Since most independent schools are corporations (either non-share or business), they thereby enjoy the power of any corporation to enter into contracts. If an independent school is not a corporation, then it will be a partnership, an unincorporated association or a sole proprietorship. While the law of contract recognizes that any of these three forms of business organizations may enter into contracts, a school operating under one of these legal forms should disclose its legal status on the contract of instruction so that parents are aware that they are not dealing with a corporate entity.

The other party to the contract of instruction is the parent, and in some cases, the student. Until a child reaches the age of majority, which in Ontario is 18 years of age,[3] the child lacks the legal capacity to enter into a contract, and the parents must enter into the contract of instruction with the school for the benefit of their child. Once the student reaches the age of 18 years, he may contract on his own behalf and the parents no longer possess the legal ability to enter into a contract for their child without his consent. As a practical matter, most 18 year olds do not have the financial resources to pay for school tuition and it is usually expected that the parents will pay the student's tuition. In the case of the 18-year-old student, a school should require both the student and the parents to sign the contract of instruction.

Where a student is not residing with both his parents, the school must take care to ensure that the contract of instruction is entered into by an adult who enjoys the legal authority to arrange for the education of the child. In the case of a child whose parents are separated or divorced, the school should require that the parent, or parents, who enjoy legal custody of the child sign the contract of instruction. Where a child's parents are dead, or for other reasons the child does not reside with either parent, the school must ensure that the student's legal guardian signs the contract of instruction.

THE DOCUMENTS CONSTITUTING THE CONTRACT OF INSTRUCTION

Several documents typically constitute the contract of instruction: the school's brochure or catalogue, the application for admission, the letter of acceptance and any handbook distributed to students on acceptance or at the start of the school year.[4]

---

[3] *Age of Majority and Accountability Act*, R.S.O. 1990, c. A.7, ss. 1 and 3.
[4] *Corpus Juris Secondum*, Vol. 78A (St. Paul, Minn.: West Publishing Co., 1995) ss. 815 and 816; *Kentucky Military Institute v. Bramblet*, 164 S.W. 808 (Ky. Ct. App., 1914) at p. 809; *Miami Military Institute v. Leff*, 220 N.Y.S. 799 (1926) at p. 807.

School Brochure or Catalogue

An independent school's brochure to prospective students typically should include a description of the general educational principles underlying the school, the program of study, the school's facilities, extracurricular activities and the cost of tuition. The brochure should clearly set out the amount of tuition, any additional fees or charges, as well as any capital contribution or loan requirements.

Since parents rely on the representations about the program of study made by the school in its brochure in deciding whether to enrol their children in the school, care must be taken to ensure the accuracy of all information contained in the brochure. If, for example, a brochure creates the impression that the school offers a music program at all levels, when in fact the program is limited to senior grades, the parents of a junior grade student who entered into a contract of instruction with the school on the basis that a music program would be available for their child could later ask to be relieved of their obligations under the contract of instruction on the basis that the school had made a material misrepresentation in its brochure.

A school also uses its brochure or catalogue to convey to parents of prospective students information about the school's educational philosophy and program with the expectation that any parents who decide to send their children to the school will accept the information and agree to abide by any obligations it imposes. For example, the school's brochure might refer to a student code of conduct or a requirement to participate in religious exercises. In order for statements in a brochure or catalogue to be binding on a parent or student, the school should ensure that the statements are made known to, or called to the attention of, a prospective pupil or the person contracting for his instruction. This can be accomplished in two ways. First, the format and presentation of the brochure can highlight or draw particular attention to material information such as educational philosophy, tuition and codes of conduct. In addition, a school can include on its application for admission form an acknowledgment to be signed by the parents that they have read and understood the information contained in the school's brochure or catalogue and agree to be bound by any statements contained in it.

Even if parents neglect to read the terms and conditions contained in a school's catalogue, courts likely will regard the act of registering the student as acceptance of the contract's obligations by the parents. For example, in the case of *Sutcliffe v. Acadia University (Governors)*,[5] the court concluded that the calendar formed part of the contract in the sense that it was part of the offer forwarded by the university to the student with the registration kit and accepted

---

[5] (1978), 85 D.L.R. (3d) 115 (N.S. Co. Ct.), affd 95 D.L.R. (3d) 95 (N.S.C.A.).

by the student by his act of registering and paying the initial instalment called for by the plaintiff. The court continued:

> It is immaterial whether the [student] read the calendar or not. Such a term as the paragraph dealing with the refunds is not so exotic as to take the [student] by surprise or as to be outside the ordinary course of commerce, and there is no evidence of any representations or other activity on the part of the [university] that would in any way mislead the [student] concerning this term.[6]

In the *Sutcliffe* case, the university's calendar provided that "fees for the academic year are assessed at time of registration in September, with one-half of the total payable in full prior to completion of the student's official registration, and the remaining half is payable on or before January 6, 1975".[7] The court found that on registration, the student became liable for the full year's academic and student organization fees because the word "assessed" in its context meant fixed and imposed at the time of registration. Although the student was given the privilege of paying the amount in half-yearly instalments, the student became liable for the full amount on registration.[8]

Application for Enrolment

The second document making up the contract of instruction is the application for enrolment completed and submitted by the pupil's parents. An application form should be designed to meet five objectives:

1. The form should require parents to provide the school with all information about the student and the parents necessary for the school's records such as: name, address, emergency contact numbers, health insurance information, dietary restrictions, known medical problems of the student, etc.
2. An application form should disclose all information about a student which the school requires to decide whether to admit the student. Typically an application form will require the parents to submit copies of the student's transcripts from schools previously attended and perhaps letters of recommendation from the principal or teachers of former schools or other community members who know the student.
3. The language used on the form must truly reflect that the parents are applying to the school for consideration of their child for a place in the school. The form should clearly state that the school retains the final discretion to accept or reject any application.
4. The application form should contain an acknowledgment by the parents that they have read and understood the information provided to them by

---

[6] *Supra*, 85 D.L.R., at p. 116.
[7] *Supra*, at p. 117.
[8] *Supra*, 95 D.L.R., at pp. 101-2.

the school through its catalogue or other material, and that the parents and the student agree to abide by any requirements imposed by those materials. For example, where a school has a student code of conduct or behaviour, it would be prudent for the school to provide the parents of prospective students with information about the code before they apply to the school and specifically include in the application form an agreement by the parents that their children will abide by the terms of the code of conduct.
5. The application form should contain a clear promise, or agreement by the parents, to pay the specified school tuition and any other fees or charges at the times required by the school's payment plan.

Letter of Acceptance

The letter of acceptance sent by the school to parents whose children are accepted for enrolment forms the third document of the contract of instruction. When the school sends out a letter of acceptance, a binding agreement between the school and the parents is created. The letter of acceptance acknowledges that the school accepts the parents' offer to enrol their children in the school. If a school intends its letter of acceptance only to create a conditional contract which will not become binding until certain conditions are fulfilled, the letter of acceptance should clearly set out such conditions and the date by which they must be fulfilled. A school, for example, may send out a letter of acceptance which stipulates that the parents must pay a first instalment of the tuition by a certain date, failing which the letter of acceptance is withdrawn. In legal terms, a conditional letter of acceptance creates a contract between the school and the parent which is subject to the fulfilment of a subsequent condition and if the parents do not satisfy the condition, a contract is not created.

Student Handbook

A fourth document which may form part of a contract of instruction is the school's student handbook. Some schools publish separate student handbooks which contain the rules and regulations of the school relating to academic advancement, as well as a student code of conduct. Often, this information finds its way into a daytimer or planner provided to each student at the beginning of the school year. In either event, a school should ensure that the contents of a handbook or code of conduct are called to the attention of the student and his parents. If a student engages in some conduct which the school wishes to discipline by suspension or expulsion, procedural fairness requires that the parents and the student were aware that the school considers the conduct to be a discipline matter.

A school can ensure that parents are made aware of the contents of the student handbook in a variety of ways: the school can include the handbook in the general information package distributed about the school before the parents apply; the handbook can be sent to the parents at the time they apply to the school; or, if the handbook is given to the students at the beginning of the school year, the school can require the students to return the handbook signed by them and their parents with an acknowledgment that they have read and understood the school's rules and regulations.

RETURNING STUDENTS

From a legal perspective, the process of re-enrolling a student in a school is simpler and requires less documentation than a new admission because there already exists an understanding and acceptance between the school and the parents of the fundamental terms and conditions governing the education of the school's pupils. The enrolment documentation for a returning student requires no more than a brochure from the school setting out the program of study for the forthcoming year, a re-enrolment form signed by the parents and in the case of secondary schools, a course selection form completed by the student. The school's brochure describing the program for the forthcoming year should include, or be accompanied by, a statement of the tuition and fees for the forthcoming year and details of the payment plan. The documentation should require the parent to request the re-enrolment of their child in the school together with a promise to pay the tuition and fees for the forthcoming year. As in the case of an application for a new student, the re-enrolment form should use language which clearly indicates that the school retains the discretion to accept or reject any application for re-enrolment.

If a school proposes to make material changes in its program of study in the forthcoming academic year, those changes should be clearly communicated to the parents of existing pupils so that they can take the information into account in deciding whether or not to re-enrol their children in the school. If a school does not clearly communicate proposed changes, a court may find that it was an implied term of the re-enrolment contract of instruction that the school's program of study would be offered on the same terms and conditions as in the past year.

In *High Park Montessori School v. Vidgen*,[9] the High Park Montessori School had operated for many years on the basis that two certified Association Montessori Internationale ("AMI") teachers were in each primary classroom. The re-enrolment package sent out in February of the school year was completed by the Vidgens and returned together with post-dated cheques for the payment of tuition for the forthcoming year. During the summer, the parents discovered that the school planned to reduce the number of certified AMI teachers in the primary classrooms to one teacher with an assistant. The

---

[9] (1989), 14 A.C.W.S. (3d) 349 (Ont. Prov. Ct.).

Vidgens put a stop payment order on the post-dated cheques and the school sued the Vidgens for the tuition. The court concluded that the contract of instruction formed by the return of the re-enrolment package contained an implied term that the number of qualified AMI teachers would be the same as in the previous school year. The reduction by the High Park Montessori School of the number of qualified AMI teachers in the primary classroom constituted a fundamental breach of the contract which meant the Vidgens were entitled to the return of their deposit and the school was prevented from seeking payment of the tuition.

REFUNDS OF TUITION

A contract of instruction between a school and parents to give a complete course of instruction, or to furnish instruction and board for a specified period of time, is an entire contract so that the school is entitled either to payment of the whole sum agreed on or to nothing. There can be no part performance or partial recovery of a contract of instruction absent any agreement or stipulation to the contrary.[10] As a result, in order to avoid disputes between the school and parents which may arise out of ambiguities contained in the contract of instruction, a school's contract of instruction should spell out clearly both the time period over which tuition payments are to be made and the school's tuition refund policy. Many schools utilize a refund policy which permits the refund of tuition on a sliding scale depending on the time of year at which the student withdraws from the program of study. Whatever refund policy a school may adopt, the policy should be clear and disclosed to parents before they submit their application for admission or renewal of admission.

HUMAN RIGHTS CONSIDERATIONS FOR ADMISSIONS

The Ontario *Human Rights Code* applies to independent schools, whether they operate as a corporation, charitable or otherwise, or as an unincorporated association, partnership or sole proprietorship.[11] The *Human Rights Code* provides that "every person has a right to equal treatment with respect to *services* . . . and *facilities*, without discrimination because of race, ancestry, place of origin, colour, ethnic origin, citizenship, creed, sex, sexual orientation, age,

---

[10] *Corpus Juris Secondum*, Vol. 78A, *op. cit.*, footnote 4, Schools and School Districts, s. 815.
[11] *Sehdev (Litigation Guardian of) v. Bayview Glen Junior Schools Ltd.* (1988), 9 C.H.R.R. D/4881 (Ont. Bd. Inq.) at para. 37740; see also the definition of "person" in s. 29(1) of the *Interpretation Act*, R.S.O. 1990, c. I.11 and s. 46 of the *Human Rights Code*, R.S.O. 1990, c. H.19.

marital status, family status or handicap".[12] The Code prohibits any person from infringing this right[13] either by directly and intentionally discriminating against a person, or by constructively discriminating against a person. Constructive discrimination arises where a "requirement, qualification or factor" exists that is not discrimination on a prohibited ground, but that results in the exclusion, restriction or preference of a group of persons who are identified by a prohibited ground of discrimination. If, for example, a dress code appears to be neutral on its face, but in its application would exclude certain persons on the grounds of a prohibited ground of discrimination, such as creed, then the otherwise neutral rule would become a source of constructive discrimination. A finding of constructive discrimination can be avoided where the person can show that the requirement, qualification, or factor, is reasonable and *bona fide* in the circumstances.[14]

A finding of constructive discrimination was made in the case of *Sehdev (Litigation Guardian of) v. Bayview Glen Junior Schools Ltd.*[15] The school refused admission to two Sikh children because the school considered their wearing turbans to be inconsistent with the school's strict uniform policy. The Bayview Glen school operated on the principle that God is the supreme being and creator of the universe, and the school actively promoted precepts and concepts common to all major organized faiths in order to inculcate an awareness of the sameness that exists among persons. As a reflection of this policy, the school's dress code required that all students dress outwardly the same: no additions or deletions were allowed from that policy since the school considered that they would detract from the outward promotion of sameness.

When the mother of the Sehdev children applied for admission, she was told that there were no exceptions allowed to the school's strict uniform policy and that any outwardly appearing articles of religion were precluded. The school told Ms. Sehdev that just as they could not accept her children if they wore turbans, the school would not accept for admission an Orthodox Jew wearing a yarmulka.[16]

A Board of Inquiry struck to consider the Sehdevs' complaint under the *Human Rights Code* found that the Bayview Glen School constructively, or indirectly, discriminated against the Sehdevs because the effect of the school's uniform policy was to deny entry to the Sehdev children because the practice of their creed required them to wear turbans. The Board of Inquiry also found that the Bayview Glen School had not demonstrated that strict adherence to the

---

[12] Section 1 (emphasis added).
[13] Section 9.
[14] Section 11(1).
[15] *Supra*, footnote 11.
[16] *Supra*, footnote 11, at para. 37727.

uniform policy was a reasonable and *bona fide* requirement in the circumstances. The Board stated:

> The [school has] not, in my opinion, established that the uniform policy "requirement" is "reasonable and *bona fide* in the circumstances," and the onus is upon them to do so. The essence of the situation is a balancing of interests. The school's preference for a strict uniform policy is not a relevant reason for compromising the complainant's religion. Moreover, the [school is] obliged to reasonably accommodate the complainant . . . and the [school] could easily do so by modifying ever so slightly the uniform policy, but the [school] refused to do so.
>
> I emphasize that, in my opinion, the objectives of a uniform policy will not really be compromised by making the slight exception required for practicing Sikh students.
>
> . . . . .
>
> In the instant situation . . . the objectives of a uniform policy will not be compromised by making a slight exception for practicing Sikh students and Orthodox Jew students. That is, the school can accommodate practicing Sikh and practicing Orthodox Jew students without undue hardship. It is not reasonable in the circumstances to impose the uniform policy requirement upon practicing Sikhs or Orthodox Jews.[17]

Standing alone, the provisions of the *Human Rights Code* against direct and indirect discrimination would prohibit independent schools from restricting admissions on the basis of religion or sex. Section 18 of the *Human Rights Code*, however, creates an exception to the right to equal treatment in the case of religious and educational institutions. Section 18 reads:

> 18. The rights under Part I to equal treatment with respect to services and facilities, with or without accommodation, are not infringed where membership or participation in a religious, philanthropic, educational, fraternal or social institution or organization that is primarily engaged in serving the interests of persons identified by a prohibited ground of discrimination is restricted to persons who are similarly identified.

As a result, an independent school which primarily serves, for example, the interests of members of a religious faith or denomination, may restrict the admission to or participation in the school to persons of that religious faith or denomination.

In the *Bayview Glen Junior School* case, the Board of Inquiry determined that the school did not fit within the exception of section 18 and made the following comments about the scope and operation of section 18 of the *Human Rights Code*:[18]

---

[17] *Supra*, footnote 11, at paras. 37770-71 and 37776.
[18] *Supra*, footnote 11, at paras. 37782-90.

1. The exception contained in section 18 is consistent with an underlying value of respect for the diversity of religion and culture in Ontario. True respect for a person's religion implies the right to have one's children in an independent school where all the other children are adherents to the same religion.
2. Nevertheless, the exception contained in section 18 should be narrowly construed, and does not give a blanket exemption to independent schools to do as they wish in the area of admissions.
3. For a school to obtain the benefit of section 18, it must demonstrate that it is "primarily engaged in serving the interests of persons identified by a prohibited ground of discrimination". If an Anglican school positively stated that all students must be Anglicans, the school would fall within the exception of section 18.
4. If a school intends to seek an exemption under section 18, it must publicly adopt and state its policy of exclusion.
5. If a school fits within the exception in section 18, it is thereby protected against breaches of the Code involving both direct and indirect discrimination.
6. Section 18, however, does not exempt a school for every act of discrimination that is a violation of the protected right under Part I of the *Human Rights Code*. For example, an Anglican school that only takes Anglican students could not rely upon section 18 to excuse discrimination against a black Anglican applicant for admission.

Religious independent schools in Ontario exhibit a variety of practices in their admissions policies. Some schools require that parents of any student become members of the school corporation and restrict membership in the corporation to adherents of a specific faith or denomination. Other religious schools do not place restrictions on who may apply, but require the parents of any student to sign an agreement that they will observe and respect the principles and practice of the faith or denomination on which the school bases its program of study. At the end of the day it is up to each independent school and religious community to decide on the approach appropriate for its school. Whatever the approach, the school should clearly explain to the parents of prospective students the religious or philosophical principles and requirements underlying its program of study so that the parents can determine whether the school offers a program which conforms with their desires for their children.

5

Financial and Operational Issues

ABSENCE OF GOVERNMENT FUNDING

Unlike many other provinces, Ontario does not provide any funding to independent schools.[1]

In the early 1990s, a group of Christian and Jewish parents commenced court applications challenging as unconstitutional the absence of any provincial funding for religious independent schools in Ontario. Both groups of parents argued that the absence of government funding imposed a burden on the practice of their religions because the precepts of their religions required them to secure an education for their children consistent with their faiths. This burden, they contended, infringed their freedom of religion guaranteed by section 2(a) of the *Canadian Charter of Rights and Freedoms*. The parents also asserted that the absence of government funding resulted in discriminatory treatment contrary to their equality guarantees contained in section 15(1) of the Charter. The groups took slightly different approaches in their equality arguments. The Jewish parents argued that since Roman Catholic schools received government funding in Ontario, it was discriminatory not to fund the schools of other religions. The Christian parents contended that since parents who sought a secular education for their children received one at government expense through the public schools, it was discriminatory to require parents who wish to secure a religious environment for their children's education to bear personally all the costs of such an education.

In its 1996 decision, *Adler v. Ontario*,[2] the Supreme Court of Canada rejected these claims. The majority of the court held that section 93 of the *Constitution Act, 1867*, constitutes a comprehensive code with respect to denominational school rights and, in the case of Ontario, limits the funding of

---

[1] For example, in Quebec, independent schools receive 85% of the per pupil grant made to the public system; in Manitoba, 63% of the per pupil grant; Alberta, 50-60% of the per pupil grant; and in British Columbia 10-50% of the per pupil grant.
[2] (1996), 140 D.L.R. (4th) 385, [1996] 3 S.C.R. 609 at p. 642, para. 35.

denominational schools to Roman Catholic schools. The court held that there was nothing in the Canadian *Constitution* which prohibited a provincial government from funding independent schools, but there was nothing in the *Constitution* which required them to fund such schools. As stated by Justice Iacobucci:

> One thing should, however, be made clear. The province remains free to exercise its plenary power with regard to education in whatever way it sees fit, subject to the restrictions relating to separate schools imposed by s. 93(1). Section 93 grants to the province of Ontario the power to legislate with regard to public schools and separate schools. However, nothing in these reasons should be taken to mean that the province's legislative power is limited to these two school systems. In other words, the province could, if it so chose, pass legislation extending funding to denominational schools other than Roman Catholic schools without infringing the rights guaranteed to Roman Catholic separate schools under s. 93(1) . . . However, an ability to pass such legislation does not amount to an obligation to do so.[3]

Some members of the court also held that the failure of the government to fund religious independent schools did not constitute interference with freedom of religion, holding that the cost of sending their children to independent religious schools was a "natural cost" of the parents' religion and therefore did not constitute an infringement of their freedom of religion protected by section 2(a) of the Charter.[4]

Following the release of the Supreme Court of Canada's decision in the *Adler* case, there was some speculation as to whether the Ontario government would consider providing some operating grants to independent schools. The Minister of Education publicly stated that he would take the matter under consideration, but the years 1997 and 1998 were consumed by the major restructuring of the public and separate school systems undertaken by the Ontario government. Some have suggested that the centralization of the financing of public and separate schools put in place by the *Education Quality Improvement Act, 1997*,[5] would facilitate the province's ability to extend some funding to independent schools in the event it chose to do so. Yet to date, the Ontario government has taken no steps in that direction, nor is there any indication that the funding of independent schools ranks high on the government's legislative agenda.

---

[3] *Supra*, at pp. 648-9, para. 48.
[4] *Supra, per* Sopinka J., at p. 703, para. 176.
[5] S.O. 1997, c. 31.

SOURCES OF REVENUE

In the absence of any government funding, independent schools must look to other sources of revenue to finance their operations. The first and largest component of any school's revenue consists of the tuition charged to parents who send their children to the school. No law regulates what tuition may be charged, and the level of any school's tuition will be a function of the school's necessary expenditures.

Fund-raising drives within the school population form the second source of revenue for a school. The range of fund-raising activities is limited only by the imagination of the members of the school community. For some schools, fund-raising drives represent a significant portion of the school's income.

The third source of income lies in donations made to the school by members of the school community, alumni or friends of the school. Where the school is a registered charity, a school may issue tax receipts to such donors who may then receive some favourable tax treatment for their donation.

Increasingly, charitable organizations, including independent schools, are turning to various forms of lottery schemes to raise money. As prevalent as the schemes may be, it must be remembered that in Canada gambling is contrary to the *Criminal Code*, except in certain circumstances. Charitable organizations may raise funds from a lottery scheme for a charitable purpose or object, but they must first obtain a licence to conduct the lottery.[6] In Ontario, the government has authorized the director under the *Gaming Control Act, 1992*[7] and municipalities, to issue licences for lottery schemes for charitable purposes. Accordingly, any independent school which plans to raise funds by holding a lottery (*e.g.*, a tuition raffle, casino night, etc.) must first obtain a licence from the appropriate authority.[8]

TAXATION OF REVENUE

An independent school, large or small, should seek the advice of a chartered accountant on any issue relating to its payment of tax and its operation as a registered charity. The following sections seek to provide an overview of the law in these areas, but specific advice should be sought for particular problems which arise.

The *Income Tax Act* provides two exemptions from taxation of taxable income which may be available to independent schools. First, a school which is

---

[6] *Criminal Code*, R.S.C. 1985, c. C-46, s. 207(1).
[7] S.O. 1992, c. 24.
[8] For further information, contact the Ontario Gaming Control Commission, 1099 Bay Street, 2nd Flr., Toronto, Ontario, tel: (416) 326-8700.

a registered charity is not required to pay income tax on its taxable income.[9] Second, if the school is not a registered charity, it still might qualify for an exemption from the payment of income tax if it qualifies under the non-profit organization exemption contained in section 149(1)(l) of the *Income Tax Act* which provides that no tax is payable on the taxable income of a:

> . . . club, society or association that, in the opinion of the Minister, was not a charity within the meaning assigned by subsection 149.1(1) and that was organized and operated exclusively for social welfare, civic improvement, pleasure or recreation or for any other purpose except profit, no part of the income of which was payable to, was otherwise available for the personal benefit of, any proprietor, member or shareholder thereof unless the proprietor, member or shareholder was a club, society or association the primary purpose and function of which was the promotion of amateur athletics in Canada.[10]

In the case of a not-for-profit corporation, income is not to include taxable capital gains.[11]

TUITION AS A CHARITABLE DONATION

"Gifts" and the McBurney Case

Under Canadian tax laws, individuals are entitled to a federal non-refundable tax credit on charitable donations.[12] For any payment to attract such a credit it must qualify as a "charitable gift" which is defined in the *Income Tax Act* as a "gift" to a "registered charity". A registered charity is authorized to issue official donation receipts for income tax purposes showing the amount of the cash donations.[13]

Can some or all of the tuition paid by a parent to an independent school qualify as a "charitable gift" for which the school can issue an official receipt and for which the parent may claim a tax credit? The short answer to this question is that Revenue Canada only permits official receipts to be issued for that portion of tuition fees which relate to religious education.[14]

Over the years, efforts have been made by taxpayers to have qualified as gifts the amounts they paid to schools which their children attended.[15] The

---

[9] *Income Tax Act*, R.S.C. 1985, c. 1 (5th Supp.), s. 149(1)(f). See also the Ontario *Corporations Tax Act*, R.S.O. 1990, c. C.40, s. 57(1).
[10] See also Interpretation Bulletin IT-83R3, at para. 1.
[11] *Income Tax Act*, s. 149(2).
[12] Section 118.1(3).
[13] *Income Tax Regulation*, C.R.C. 1978, c. 945, s. 3501(1).
[14] Information Circular 75-23, at paras. 4-6.
[15] *R. v. Zandstra*, [1974] C.T.C. 503, 74 D.T.C. 6416 (F.C.T.D.); *Getkate v. Minister of National Revenue*, [1980] C.T.C. 2830, 80 D.T.C. 1695 (T.R.B.).

leading court case in this area is the decision in *R. v. McBurney*.[16] Mr. McBurney enrolled his children in Christian independent schools in the Ottawa area because he considered that his children would not receive a Christian education in the area's public schools. Each of the schools was a non-profit corporation registered as a charity with Revenue Canada. Each school offered both secular and religious courses and all courses were taught "as vehicles for the expression and inculcation of religious faith".[17] As described by the trial judge, religious teaching in the schools "was and is blended with [the teaching of secular subjects] such that, if the secular and religious teachings were . . . chemical elements, they would be combined in solution of varying proportions from hour to hour throughout the school year".[18]

Mr. McBurney contended that the schools his children attended did not charge parents tuition, instead they issued guidelines setting out the amount each family should consider giving to the school to cover operating costs and the guidelines were scaled to the income of the family.[19] From time to time the school also appealed to the larger church community for donations. The evidence revealed that the schools had never refused admission to, nor asked a child to leave a school, simply because the parents were not contributing their fair share to the school's operating costs.

Mr. McBurney deducted the payments he made to the schools as gifts to registered charities. The Minister of Revenue disallowed the deductions and Mr. McBurney appealed to the courts. The progress of his appeal through the courts is worth reviewing in some detail because the issues raised by Mr. McBurney are ones which often confront the administrations of many independent schools.

Mr. McBurney won at trial, persuading the court that his payments were not tuition payments. The trial court gave the following definition of tuition:

> What is a tuition fee? It is the monetary consideration (money or, possibly money's worth of goods or services) payable to a pedagogue or school authority for enrolling a pupil or student in an instructional, training or educational lecture or course of lectures. ("Lecture" signifies a more or less controlled learning situation including seminars, discussions, demonstrations or student experience.) Failure to pay or make good the tuition in such contractual circumstances legitimately and morally entitles the pedagogue or school authority to bar the pupil from attending the lecture or course or, if it be too late for that, entitles the pedagogue or school authority to demand and sue for the promised money (or money's worth).[20]

---

[16] [1984] C.T.C. 466, 84 D.T.C. 6494 (F.C.T.D.), revd [1985] 2 C.T.C. 214, 85 D.T.C. 5433 (F.C.A.).
[17] *Supra*, 84 D.T.C., at p. 6498.
[18] *Supra*, at p. 6499.
[19] *Supra*, at p. 6502.
[20] *Supra*.

The trial judge likened Mr. McBurney's payments to the school to contributions made by parishioners to their church:

> There were no tuition fees charged by any of the three charitable corporations. The plaintiff's payments were made as much without consideration as are contributions to a parish church. It is clear that the plaintiff and other like-minded contributors banded together in a community (or congregation) in order to support each other's ideals of Christian Education, to develop or maintain each school and to meet, as a community, the common expenses entailed in their project. In that regard they were and are indistinguishable from the congregation of a parish, about the deductibility of whose gifts there is no doubt.[21]

The Federal Court of Appeal overturned the trial decision, holding that the Minister of Revenue had properly disallowed Mr. McBurney's deduction of the payments as gifts. The Federal Court of Appeal adopted the following definition of "gift" for tax purposes:

> ". . . to constitute a 'gift', it must appear that the property transferred was transferred voluntarily and not as the result of a contractual obligation to transfer it and that no advantage of a material character was received by the transferor by way of return."[22]

The court then proceeded to find that Mr. McBurney did not make voluntary payments to the schools, rather he made the payments under a moral and legal duty to secure an education for his children and, in return, the school educated his children:

> There can be little doubt that here, too, the respondent saw it as his Christian duty to ensure his children receive the kind of education these schools provided. The payments were made in pursuance of that duty and according to a clear understanding with the charities that while his children were attending these schools he would contribute within his means toward the costs of operating them. I cannot accept the argument that because the respondent may have been under no legal obligation to contribute, the payments are to be regarded as "gifts". The securing of the kind of education he desired for his children and the making of the payments went hand-in-hand.[23]

As a result of the decision in the *McBurney* case, any payment made by a taxpayer to an independent school "in response to a material advantage received in turn" does not qualify as a "gift" for income tax purposes.

Revenue Canada Information Circular 75-23

While payments to secure a secular education may not qualify as gifts, the law has recognized the right of a taxpayer to deduct donations to a religious

---

[21] *Supra*, at p. 6504.
[22] *Supra*, 85 D.T.C., at pp. 5435-6.
[23] *Supra*, at p. 5436.

school society for religious training and education.[24] Revenue Canada has adopted an administrative practice reflecting this legal principle which permits taxpayers to claim as charitable gifts that portion of the tuition paid to an independent school in respect of the religious education component of its program of study.[25] This administrative practice is set out in Revenue Canada's Information Circular 75-23, "Tuition Fees and Charity Donations Paid to Privately Supported Secular and Religious Schools", which is reproduced in Appendix "I".

After reciting the general rule that tuition payments are not considered charitable donations, Information Circular 75-23 then recognizes an exception in the case of schools which operate in a dual capacity of providing both "secular (academic) and religious education":

> 4. The provisions of the *Income Tax Act* do not permit a deduction, as a charitable donation, of an [a]mount paid to a school for academic tuition, whether the amount was paid for set fees or was a voluntary contribution. A gift, to be allowable within the concept of paragraph 110(1)(a) of the Act, must be a voluntary transference of property without consideration. The consideration here is the academic training received by the children attending the school. *On the other hand religious training is not viewed as consideration for purposes of the definition of a gift.*
>
> 5. School fees are normally based on the costs of operation. However, there are some schools in Canada, usually connected with a church, which do not levy set fees and operate solely through contributions of parents or guardians and other members of the church. These schools, which are subject to the inspection of provincial educational authorities, operate in a dual capacity providing both secular and religious education.
>
> 6. Under certain circumstances receipts for charitable donations may be issued for a portion of an amount paid to attend schools, other than post-secondary institutions or designated educational institutions, which operate in this dual capacity. There are two methods of calculating the donation portion of amounts paid, depending on how the school maintains its accounting records. [Emphasis added.]

Information Circular 75-23 then proceeds to set out two formulae for calculating the portion of tuition payments characterized as a charitable donation for religious training — one formula for schools which segregate the costs of operating the secular portion of the school and the costs of providing religious education, and a second formula for those schools which do not segregate their accounting records.

---

[24] *Koetsier v. M.N.R.* (1974), 74 D.T.C. 1001 (T.R.B.); Information Circular 75-23, at para. 3.
[25] *R. v. Woolner* (unreported, December 6, 1997, T.C.C.), under appeal to F.C.A.

Schools Which Segregate Operating Costs

Where an independent school segregates the costs of secular and religious education, the school may calculate the donation portion of a tuition payment in accordance with the following guidelines:

1. Determine the net cost of operating the secular portion of the school: the total operating costs of that portion of the school (excluding capital expenditures and depreciation) less miscellaneous income, grants received and donations received from persons with no children in attendance, unless such grants or donations were designated for a capital purpose.
2. Divide, or pro rate, this net cost over the number of pupils enrolled during the school year to determine a cost per pupil for the secular training.
3. Deduct this cost per pupil from the amount of tuition paid by the parent for the pupil and then official donation receipts can be issued for the difference.[26]

By way of illustration:

Net Operating Costs of Secular Portion	$500,000
Number of Pupils	110
Cost Per Pupil – Secular Portion	$4,545
Tuition Paid by Student's Parent	$5,200
less Cost Per Pupil	($4,545)
Amount of Charitable Donation	$655

If a taxpayer has more than one child in attendance at the school, the amount to be deducted from his total tuition payment to determine the donation portion is the "cost per pupil" for academic training multiplied by the number of his children enrolled during the school year.[27] This approach applies even where the school sets tuition on a "per family" basis.[28] By way of illustration, if a taxpayer sends three children to the same independent school, and the school charges tuition on a sliding scale (charging less for the second and third child in attendance), the calculation would be:

Cost Per Pupil – Secular Portion	$4,545
Number of Children of Taxpayer at School	3
Total Cost Per Pupil for Taxpayer	$13,635

---

[26] Information Circular 75-23, at paras. 7 and 8.
[27] *Ibid.*, at para. 7.
[28] *R. v. Zandstra*, [1974] C.T.C. 503, 74 D.T.C. 6416 (F.C.T.D.).

Tuition for First Child	$5,200
Tuition for Second Child	$5,000
Tuition for Third Child	$4,750
Total Tuition Paid by Taxpayer	$14,950
less Total Cost Per Pupil	$13,635
Amount of Charitable Donation	$1,315

Schools Which Do Not Segregate Operating Costs

Revenue Canada grants less favourable tax treatment to independent schools which do not segregate the costs of operating the secular portion of the school from those providing religious training. For such schools, a donation receipt can be issued only for that part of the payment which is in excess of the net operating costs per pupil of the whole school for a school year. In this case, the net operating costs of the whole school will be the total operating costs of the school including both secular and religious education (excluding capital expenditures and depreciation) less miscellaneous income, grants and donations from persons with no children in attendance, unless such grants or donations were designated for capital purposes, divided by the number of students enrolled in the school. By way of illustration:

Net Operating Costs of Secular and Religious Portion	$550,000
Number of Pupils	110
Cost Per Pupil – Total Costs	$5,000
Tuition Paid By Student's Parent	$5,200
less Cost Per Pupil	$5,000
Amount of Charitable Donation	$200

If the taxpayer has more than one child in attendance in the school, the amount to be deducted from his total payment to determine the donation portion is the cost per pupil for the whole school multiplied by the number of his children enrolled during a school year.[29]

OTHER CHARITABLE DONATIONS

Some schools request that parents make contributions to the school's capital fund, either by way of loan or donation. Since Revenue Canada regards tuition as based upon the operational costs of a school,[30] contributions to a

---

[29] Information Circular 75-23, at paras. 7 and 9.
[30] *Ibid.*, at para. 5.

school's capital fund could be treated as gifts provided such contributions are voluntary and do not give rise to a material benefit or advantage.[31] Although this can be an area of some dispute with Revenue Canada, generally contributions to a school's capital fund will be treated as gifts for which a charitable receipt may be issued.[32]

Independent schools engage in a variety of fund-raising activities, and questions frequently arise as to whether donations made in specific fund-raising campaigns qualify as gifts for the purposes of issuing a tax receipt to the payor. Revenue Canada has issued Information Circular 80-10R, "Registered Charities and Operating a Registered Charity", which provides guidelines on the treatment of certain payments. Revenue Canada defines a gift as:

> ... a voluntary transfer of property without consideration. There must be a donor who freely disposes of the property and there must be a donee who receives the property given. No right, privilege, material benefit or advantage may be conferred on the donor or on a person designated by the donor as a consequence of the gift.[33]

Revenue Canada takes the position that the following types of payments made to a registered charity do not normally qualify as donations, are not deductible for income tax purposes, and are not payments in respect of which official receipts can be issued:

(a) payment for members that convey an advantage of material character to the member (the right to vote at meetings and to receive financial statements and reports on the activities of the charity is not considered to be a material advantage);

(b) amounts received by loose collection (*i.e.*, where a particular donor cannot be identified as having made a particular donation);

(c) donations of services where the donor requests that, instead of payment for his services, he be supplied with a donation receipt to the value of services rendered (Revenue Canada considers that it is acceptable for a person who has been paid for services rendered to then make a donation for which a receipt can be issued);

---

[31] Information Circular 80-10R, at para. 29.

[32] The simple fact is that most donors to a charity get some benefit or advantage from making a contribution. The real issue is whether the benefit is direct enough to disqualify the gift. Over the years various donations to churches and synagogues have been sources of contention with Revenue Canada, but usually have been resolved in favour of the taxpayer. For a full discussion on this point, see Arthur B.C. Drache, Q.C., *Canadian Taxation of Charities and Donations* (Toronto: Carswell, 1993) at pp. 5-13 to 5-22.

[33] Information Circular 80-10R, at para. 29.

(d) donations of old clothes, furniture, home baking, hobby crafts, etc. (an exception may be made for articles of unusually high value);[34]
(e) amounts paid for admission to concerts, dinners and similar fund-raising functions, except for any amounts paid that were in excess of the fair market value of any consideration (such as the dinner) received by the donor;[35] and
(f) any portion of the purchase of a lottery ticket, despite the fact that the lottery proceeds accrue to one or more charities.[36]

No receipt can be issued where goods are bought at a charity-sponsored auction, whether or not the purchaser paid more or less than the actual value of the goods. The purchase of an item at an auction involves a contract of sale, not a gift.[37]

Where a school which is a registered charity secures an undertaking by a donor to pay a donation over a period of years, the school is not entitled to issue to the donor an official receipt for the entire amount in the year in which the pledge is made. An official receipt may be made only after the amount pledged has actually been received by the school, and the donor may claim a deduction only in each of the years in which the amounts pledged are actually paid to the school.[38]

RECEIPTS FOR CHARITABLE DONATIONS

The required contents of the official receipt issued to a donor are set out in detail in the *Income Tax Regulations*.[39] An official receipt must include the following information:

(a) the name and address in Canada of the organization as recorded with the Minister of Revenue;
(b) the registration number assigned by the Minister to the organization;
(c) the serial number of the receipt;

---

[34] For such articles, see Revenue Canada Information Pamphlet "Gifts in Kind" and Interpretation Bulletin IT-297R.
[35] See Revenue Canada Interpretation Bulletin IT-110R, at para. 5, and Donald J. Bourgeois, *The Law of Charitable and Non-Profit Organizations*, 2nd ed. (Toronto: Butterworths, 1995) at p. 183; *Aspinall v. Minister of National Revenue* (1970), 70 D.T.C. 1669 (T.A.B.).
[36] Information Circular 80-10R, at para. 30.
[37] See, for example, *Tite v. Minister of National Revenue*, [1986] 2 C.T.C. 2343, 86 D.T.C. 1788 (T.C.C.).
[38] Information Circular 80-10R, at para. 31.
[39] Section 3500.

(d) the place where the receipt was issued;
(e) the date on which the cash donation was received;
(f) the date on which the receipt was issued where it differs from the date on which the donation was received;
(g) the name and address of the donor;
(h) the amount of the cash donation or the fair market value at the time of the donation for the gift of any property; and
(i) the signature of a responsible individual who has been authorized by the organization to acknowledge donations.

The regulation permits a facsimile signature subject to certain conditions.[40] A receipt for donations received after the calendar year end may be issued for the previous year only if the donation was mailed in that year and the cheque or other instrument was dated in that year. Otherwise, the receipt applies to the current year.[41]

If a receipt does not comply with these conditions, the donation claimed by the donor may be disallowed. In addition, a charity that issues receipts which do not comply with the regulation may furnish Revenue Canada with grounds to revoke its registration as a charity.[42]

TUITION AS AN EMPLOYEE "FRINGE BENEFIT"

Where a school provides tuition free of charge, or at a reduced amount, to a child of an employee of the school, the fair market value of the tuition must be included in the employee's income.[43]

EXPENDITURES

Not-for-Profit Corporation

Where an independent school is a not-for-profit corporation, but is not a registered charity, few rules govern the expenditures made by the school. As a matter of corporate law, the school must engage in activities which are in furtherance of, or incidental to, its objects as stated in the school's letters patent. Accordingly, any expenditures by the school must be in furtherance of, or incidental to, the objects of the school.

---

[40] Section 3501.
[41] Information Circular 80-10R, at para. 33.
[42] See Information Circular 80-10R and s. 168(1)(d) of the *Income Tax Act*.
[43] *Income Tax Act*, s. 6(1)(a); Interpretation Bulletin IT-47OR, at para. 20.

Expenditures must be properly recorded by the school and an annual financial statement prepared. The school's auditors must review annually the school's financial statements and express an opinion on whether or not the financial statements fairly represent the financial position of the corporation.[44]

Registered Charity

Where an independent school is also a registered charity, it must comply with the disbursement quota for charitable organizations contained in the *Income Tax Act*. In order to ensure that most of a charity's funds are used for charitable purposes, and to discourage inappropriate accumulation of capital, the *Income Tax Act* requires a registered charity to expend its annual disbursement quota. For most charities this means spending on authorized expenditures a minimum of 80% of the income for which it issued donation receipts in the immediately preceding taxation year.[45] Expenditures which qualify for the disbursement quota include: the payment of salaries to individuals who perform duties directly related to the charitable activities; the acquisition of equipment or property that is used in conjunction with charitable activities; as well as amounts given under a program to provide scholarships or assistance to persons in need and expenditures to other Canadian persons in need. Amounts paid for purely administrative expenses such as fund-raising costs, legal or accounting fees, or the like, are not expenditures included in the disbursement quota.[46]

Given the constant need of most independent schools for additional funds, most schools likely will not encounter any difficulty in expending their disbursement quota on charitable activities.[47] Nonetheless a school must monitor carefully its compliance with its disbursement quota because failure to spend the required amount on charitable activities constitutes one ground for the deregistration of the charity.[48] Where a school wants to accumulate property for a particular charitable purpose such as raising funds for a new school building, the school can seek permission from Revenue Canada for temporary relief from the disbursement quota requirements.[49]

The Ontario *Charities Accounting Act* and *Charitable Gifts Act* implicitly place some restrictions on the spending of charitable organizations. The *Charities Accounting Act* prohibits a charitable organization from owning lands as an investment. A charitable organization may hold land if it is used or occupied

---

[44] *Corporations Act*, R.S.O. 1990, c. C.38, s. 96.
[45] *Income Tax Act*, s. 149.1(1), (2)(b); Information Circular 80-10R, at paras. 34-6.
[46] Information Circular 80-10R, at para. 36.
[47] For a more detailed discussion of disbursement quotas, see Information Circular 80-10R, Part IV, and Donald J. Bourgeois, *The Law of Charitable and Non-Profit Organizations*, 2nd ed. (Toronto: Butterworths, 1995) at pp. 180-82.
[48] *Income Tax Act*, s. 149.1(4)(b).
[49] Section 149.1(8); Information Circular 80-10R, at para. 39.

for charitable purposes, but if the land is no longer required for charitable purposes, the Act requires the charitable organization to dispose of it within three years.[50]

The *Charitable Gifts Act* seeks to ensure that charitable organizations are not carrying on business. It discourages charitable organizations from placing funds at risk in capital markets and prohibits charitable organizations from owning more than 10% of the shares of a business. If a charitable organization receives a gift or bequest of an interest in a business that is greater than 10% of the shares of a business, the *Charitable Gifts Act* empowers and directs the corporation to dispose of the surplus within seven years of the receipt of the gift or bequest.[51]

INTEREST RATES ON OVERDUE STUDENT ACCOUNTS

If a school charges interest on overdue student accounts, it must comply with the provisions of the *Interest Act*.[52] If the school and the parents have agreed that interest will be paid on overdue accounts, but no rate is specified, then the *Interest Act* only permits the school to charge interest at a rate of 5% per annum.[53] Consequently, a school's contract of instruction with parents should specify the rate of interest payable on overdue accounts. In addition, if the contract of instruction states the rate of interest as a daily, weekly or monthly rate, it must also contain an express statement of the yearly rate of interest to which the other rate is equivalent, otherwise the *Interest Act* does not permit the school to charge interest at a rate greater than 5% a year.[54]

BOOKS AND RECORDS

The Ontario *Corporations Act* requires a corporation to keep proper books of account and accounting records for the corporation's financial and other transactions, including records of all moneys received and disbursed, sales and purchases, the assets and liabilities of the corporation, and all other transactions affecting the financial position of the corporation.[55] The corporation must also keep a copy of the letters patent, by-laws and special resolutions of the corporation, a register of members for the previous ten years, a register of all directors and a minute book of all proceedings of the members, directors

---

[50] R.S.O. 1990, c. C.10, s. 8(2).
[51] R.S.O. 1990, c. C.8, s. 2.
[52] R.S.C. 1985, c. I-15.
[53] Section 3.
[54] Section 4.
[55] *Corporations Act*, s. 302.

and of any executive committee.[56] These records are to be kept at the head office of the school corporation.[57]

The *Income Tax Act* requires that every person who carries on business must keep records and books of account containing the information necessary to enable Revenue Canada to determine taxes payable under the Act.[58]

A registered charity must keep at its designated address: records and books of account which contain information in such form as will enable the Minister of Revenue to determine whether there are any grounds for the revocation of its registration; a duplicate of each receipt containing prescribed information for any donation received by it; and other information in such form as will enable the Minister to verify the donations for which deduction or tax credit is available under the *Income Tax Act*.[59]

FILINGS

Not-for-Profit Corporation

A school which is a not-for-profit corporation will be required to make the following filings with government agencies on an annual basis:

(a) an annual information return filed with the Ontario Ministry of Consumer and Commercial Relations pursuant to section 3.1 of the *Corporations Information Act*[60] identifying the head office, directors and officers of the corporation; and

(b) an annual income tax return within six months of the corporate year end.[61]

Registered Charity

Where the independent school corporation is a registered charity, it must make the following annual filings:

(a) an information return under the *Corporations Information Act*;

(b) a registered charity return with Revenue Canada within six months of the end of the organization's fiscal year;[62] and

---

[56] Sections 299 and 300.
[57] Section 304.
[58] *Income Tax Act*, s. 230(1).
[59] Section 230(2).
[60] R.S.O. 1990, c. C.39.
[61] *Income Tax Act*, s. 150(1).
[62] Section 149.1(14).

(c) an annual filing of its financial statements with the Public Guardian and Trustee pursuant to the *Charities Accounting Act*.[63]

The registered charity return includes a calculation of the revenue and expenditures of the organization, financial statements (although they need not be audited), a list of liabilities and assets, a list of the officers and their addresses and information describing its activities. Failure to file the annual registered charity return may result in Revenue Canada revoking the school's registration as a registered charity.[64]

MUNICIPAL TAXES

Municipal taxes are levied against assessed property. Under the *Assessment Act*[65] all real property in Ontario is liable to assessment and municipal taxation, subject to specified exemptions. Two exemptions contained in section 3 of the *Assessment Act* provide the basis for most independent schools to claim exemption from assessment for municipal taxation:

> 3. All real property in Ontario is liable to assessment and taxation, subject to the following exemptions from taxation:
>
> . . . . .
>
> 4. Land owned, used and occupied solely by a university, college, community college or school as defined in the *Education Act* or land leased and occupied by any of them if the land would be exempt from taxation if it was occupied by the owner.
> 5. Land owned, used and occupied solely by a non-profit philanthropic, religious or educational seminary of learning or land leased and occupied by any of them if the land would be exempt from taxation if it was occupied by the owner. This paragraph does not apply to land with an area of more than 50 acres.

Occasionally disputes arise between independent schools and municipal assessment authorities as to what part of the buildings and grounds of property are used in connection with and for the purposes of the independent school. In *St. Andrew's College v. York (County) Assessment Commissioner*,[66] St. Andrew's College operated a boarding and day school for boys from grades 7 to OAC. The Township of King decided to assess as taxable property those portions of the boys' residences which contained the living quarters for the school's housemasters and headmaster, as well as the detached buildings on the

---

[63] *Charities Accounting Act*, s. 2.
[64] *Income Tax Act*, s. 168(1).
[65] R.S.O. 1990, c. A.31.
[66] (1971), 19 D.L.R. (3d) 503, [1971] 3 O.R. 91 (H.C.J.).

school campus which served as residences for the school's nurses, maintenance and kitchen staff. The school successfully challenged the assessment in court, arguing that the residences were used in connection with the school since it was necessary to ensure that staff resided on the property to provide constant supervision over the young boys boarding at the school.

Notwithstanding that some of the staff paid a small sum to occupy the premises, the court found that the staff did not "occupy" the premises for the purposes of the *Assessment Act*, but that the school maintained control over the premises:

> It must, therefore, be clear that where a person as a term of his employment is required to occupy certain premises for the purposes of the institution by which he is employed and by reason of the necessity of using him in the way he is used does not constitute him a tenant of the property or an occupant of it. It is said that while he may physically live in it the occupation is that of the institution which employs him of which he in effect is the servant and the school the master.[67]

The court continued:

> . . . none of the persons described by [the headmaster] occupying the premises in question are occupying them as tenants of the college even though they may in some cases be paying a small amount for them . . . [T]he occupation of these persons . . . is in law not their occupation but the occupation of their employer, *i.e.*, the incorporated college.
>
> It would appear to be that in caring for boys as young as 12 years of age there must be an immense amount of personal supervision and it has to be available when it is needed. That is why the nurses and matrons are necessary in the college organization and they are particularly useful in connection with the younger boys. Where boys are being fed at an early hour in the morning it is also essential I think to have the cook live in just as it is essential to be able to supply heat at all times and the person responsible for the state of the furnace may be called on at any hour of the day or night. The consequence of leaving particularly young children exposed to the exigencies of a Canadian winter is not one which seems reasonable under the circumstances and in my opinion, in respect to all these various persons, the occupation is a necessary one and only exists because they are doing certain work for the college which requires their immediate presence.[68]

What of property that is used for purposes connected with the school only during part of the year? The exemptions contained in section 3(4) and (5) of the *Assessment Act* are limited to lands "owned, used and occupied solely" by educational institutions. In *National Ballet School v. Assessment Commissioner, Region 9*,[69] a benefactor of the National Ballet School donated some

---

[67] *Supra*, at p. 96.
[68] *Supra*, at p. 99.
[69] (1979), 100 D.L.R. (3d) 559, 25 O.R. (2d) 50 (H.C.J.).

residential property to the school. The property was located two miles from the National Ballet School's facilities. The National Ballet School used the residence to hold meetings of the board of directors and various committees and to host fund-raising events. Although the school maintained a full-time employee on the property for security and maintenance, the property was only used for about 50% of the year. Nevertheless, the court held that the buildings and grounds clearly were used for the purpose of the seminary of learning and the fact that the residence was not used each day during the year did not disentitle it from exemption from assessment. The court stated:

> Where does one draw the line? I think the only thing to do is go back to the statute. So long as the property is *bona fide* used for the purposes of the seminary, it does not matter that the whole is not used for the purpose or is not used constantly. There may well come a point where the use is so little and of such short duration that the exemption can no longer be claimed. But in my view that would not be because the property was not used for the purposes but because it was not used *bona fide*. Here the use clearly meets that latter test.
>
> . . . . .
>
> These premises are needed in part and legitimately used in part. If the premises are not used at all for the purposes of the seminary . . . or are used for only one day in the year . . . it can hardly be said to be "actually used" by the school. Similarly, if they were used solely for the purpose of obtaining tax exemption, they could hardly be said to be "*bona fide* used in connection with" the school. If they are used as they are used here "*bona fide* in connection with" the school, they are exempt while actually so used and occupied.[70]

The exemption of educational institutions from municipal taxes will affect a school's decision whether to buy or lease property. As the owner of property used for educational purposes, the school can secure the municipal tax exemption. Where a school leases property, the exemption will only be available "if the land would be exempt from taxation if it was occupied by the owner". Where the owner or landlord would not qualify for an exemption from assessment, the landlord invariably will include applicable municipal taxes in the rent charged to the independent school.

INSURANCE

Every independent school requires some insurance coverage. A school's board of directors should develop and implement a risk management strategy which identifies what assets the school possesses, what it would take to put it back together in the event of an accident, and what risks associated with the school's operation should be insured against. It is beyond the scope of this

---

[70] *Supra*, at pp. 54-5.

book to engage in a detailed discussion of insurance risks which arise during the operation of a school and appropriate levels of coverage. A board of directors should discuss such issues in detail with an insurance broker. Briefly, however, the following list identifies the basic kinds of insurance policies which an independent school should consider when developing its risk management strategy:[71]

1. Property Insurance: In addition to covering all basic risks, a school should decide whether it requires coverage for special risks as well as whether its policy covers the properties of others, such as staff, students or rental equipment.
2. Primary Liability Insurance: A school should ensure that its primary and umbrella liability policies cover all school activities, including sports, as well as naming as additional insured all employees, volunteers and alumni who may be engaged in running or supervising school activities.
3. Boiler and Machinery Coverage: A school should determine whether it requires this coverage for its building operations, either as owner or occupant.
4. Fidelity Insurance: This policy would cover any employee or volunteer who handles, or is responsible for, money in the operation of a school.
5. School Automobile and Bus Insurance.
6. Business Interruption Insurance: If there is a destruction of the school building, business interruption insurance can provide coverage to permit the generation of revenue necessary to cover expenses for the continued operation of the school.
7. Directors and Officers Liability Insurance: This insurance will indemnify the school's directors and officers if they are accused of negligence in their decision-making while sitting on the board of directors.
8. Electronic Data Processing Insurance: In light of the increased role played by information technology in school courses of study and administration, it is increasingly important to consider obtaining insurance coverage not only for the replacement values of computer equipment and software, but to cover losses in the event of a major collapse in a school's computer system.

---

[71] Based on notes from a presentation at the Annual Meeting of the Canadian Educational Standards Institute by Mr. Paul Smith, Vice-President of Hargraft Wood Fleming, Toronto.

CO-OPERATION AGREEMENTS WITH SCHOOL BOARDS

In some areas of the province, independent schools have entered into co-operative agreements with school boards for the use of school buildings and school buses. Some school boards have resisted making such agreements, taking the position that the *Education Act* only authorizes a board to enter into co-operative agreements with other school boards.[72] This is too narrow a view of the Act. Section 171 of the *Education Act* clearly gives boards of education the power to "permit the school buildings and premises and school buses owned by the Board to be used for any educational or other lawful purpose".[73] This power appears broad enough to authorize school boards to enter into cost-sharing agreements with independent schools regarding the use of school board buildings and the busing of students.

---

[72] *Education Act*, s. 171.1(2).
[73] Section 171(1), para. 24.

6

Programs of Study

OVERVIEW

By their nature, independent schools offer a diverse range of programs of study and pedagogical approaches which differ in focus, content, method and standards from their public school counterparts. The present structure of the *Education Act* facilitates this diversity of independent school programs at the elementary school level, but places some restrictions at the secondary level. Briefly stated, the *Education Act* contains the following legal requirements for the programs of study in independent schools:

1. There is no requirement that elementary schools follow a Ministry specified program of study, but any program of study in an independent elementary school must meet the general statutory standard of providing "satisfactory instruction".
2. If an independent secondary school does *not* offer its graduates the Ontario secondary school diploma, the secondary school graduation diploma or the secondary school honour graduation diploma, then the Act does not prescribe a specific program of study for the secondary school, save that the program of study in the secondary school must ensure "satisfactory instruction".
3. If the independent secondary school offers its graduates the Ontario secondary school diploma, the secondary school graduation diploma or the secondary school honour graduation diploma, then the secondary school must be inspected by the Ministry of Education and Training "in respect of the standard of instruction in the subjects leading to" the diplomas[1] and follow the Ministry's secondary school program of study.

Not all of Ontario's independent secondary schools offer the Ontario secondary school diploma nor request inspection by the Ministry. According to the

---

[1] *Education Act*, R.S.O. 1990, c. E.2, s. 16(7).

roster of private secondary schools published by the Ministry in June, 1997, 238 independent schools offered instruction at the secondary level, of which 150, or 63%, requested inspection by the Ministry.[2]

ELEMENTARY SCHOOLS

The *Education Act* excuses a child from attendance at a public or separate school if the child is receiving "satisfactory instruction at home or elsewhere". This is the only standard established in the *Education Act* regarding the required level of instruction in an independent elementary school. The *Education Act* does not contain any provision specifying the program of instruction in an independent elementary school, or mandating that independent elementary schools offer the same program as public schools.

The *Education Act* authorizes the inspection of a private elementary school by a Ministry supervisor who may enter the school at all reasonable hours and conduct an inspection of the school and any records or documents relating to the school.[3] In light of the language contained in the Act about such inspections, there would be two legitimate purposes to an inspection of an independent elementary school by a Ministry supervisory officer:

(i) to ensure that the students in the school are receiving "satisfactory instruction"; and
(ii) to ensure that the school maintains any records or documents relating to its operations which the *Education Act* requires it to maintain.

Until the 1997-98 school year, public and separate elementary schools were required to organize their courses of study in accordance with the principles contained in five Ministry of Education and Training policy documents: (1) *A Common Curriculum, Policies and Outcomes, Grades 1-9* (the Common Curriculum);[4] (2) *The Common Curriculum: Provincial Standards, Mathematics Grades 1-9*; (3) *The Common Curriculum: Provincial Standards, Language, Grades 1-9;* (4) *Transition Years, Grades 7, 8 and 9, 1992*; and (5) Policy Memorandum No. 115 (1994). These last two policy statements introduced the process of de-crediting grade 9 courses.

None of the requirements contained in these policy manuals and curriculum documents applied to an independent elementary school program from kindergarten through to grade 8. Those policies which dealt with the grade 9

---

[2] "Private Elementary and Secondary Schools in Ontario" (Ministry of Education and Training, June 1997) website: www.edu.gov.on.ca/eng/general/list private.html.
[3] *Education Act*, s. 16(6).
[4] (Ministry of Education and Training, 1995).

program may have applied to the grade 9 program in independent secondary schools which offered their graduating students an Ontario diploma because the Common Curriculum provided that it "must be used in all publicly-funded schools and in other schools whose program leads to an Ontario diploma".[5] Policy Memorandum No. 115 (1994) also appeared to regard the successful completion of the grade 9 program as part of the credits required for an Ontario diploma.[6] As a result, independent elementary schools were not required to follow the Ministry's program of study from grades 1 to 8, and the only legal standard which their programs had to meet was the standard of "satisfactory instruction".

Beginning in June, 1997, the Ministry of Education and Training began to revise portions of the Ontario elementary school curriculum, replacing those sections of the Common Curriculum dealing with language and mathematics by new programs of study called the *Ontario Curriculum, Grades 1-8*.[7] A new science curriculum was released in March, 1998. As further portions of the Ontario Curriculum are released, the Common Curriculum will be phased out entirely. The new *Ontario Curriculum, Grades 1-8*, does *not* apply to independent elementary schools. Independent elementary schools are free to follow some or all of the *Ontario Curriculum, Grades 1-8*, or ignore it completely in developing their own programs of study.

INDEPENDENT SECONDARY SCHOOLS WHICH DO NOT GRANT ONTARIO DIPLOMAS

For most of the last decade, the governing policy document for Ontario's public and separate secondary schools has been *Ontario Schools, Intermediate and Senior Divisions, Program and Diploma Requirements, 1989* (more commonly referred to as OS:IS) which establishes and describes those courses for which students may earn credits which count towards obtaining an Ontario diploma. Where an independent secondary school does not offer its graduates an Ontario graduation diploma OS:IS does not apply and the *Education Act* does not impose any requirements on the school's program of study, save the general requirement that the program must provide "satisfactory instruction".

---

[5] *Ibid.*, at p. 14.
[6] (Ministry of Education and Training, 1994) amending s. 4.9 of OS:IS.
[7] (Ministry of Education and Training, 1997).

INSPECTED INDEPENDENT SECONDARY SCHOOLS

Independent secondary schools offering Ontario secondary school diplomas to their graduates are required to comply with OS:IS in their programs of study.[8] Students attending such schools must obtain the same number and kind of credits as their public and separate school counterparts, and the independent secondary schools must follow the curriculum guidelines and common course codes issued by the Ministry of Education and Training.

What is the purpose of an independent secondary school if it has to comply with the Ministry's secondary school program of study? Notwithstanding the requirements of OS:IS, independent secondary schools enjoy considerable flexibility in the actual implementation of a secondary school program. For example, the flip-flops of the past decade by the Ministry of Education and Training over the streaming of secondary school courses — starting with a streamed program in the 1980s, which was then destreamed by the provincial government in the early 1990s, and has been restreamed at the end of the 1990s — had little effect on independent secondary schools. Independent secondary schools are free to offer instruction at the level compatible with their overall program of study and educational objectives. Nor do independent secondary schools have to diffuse their resources to offer the broad range of credit courses authorized under OS:IS. Many independent secondary schools focus their resources on offering instruction in a core liberal arts and sciences curriculum. Finally, independent secondary schools are free to select their own textbooks and are not required to purchase only those textbooks approved by the Ministry in *Circular 14*.

For most independent secondary schools, these three areas of flexibility enable them to offer a secondary school program which is distinctive from that in public schools. That having been said, it does seem incongruous that independent schools, which are the product of parents choosing to opt out of the public and separate school system for a variety of reasons, must conform to a secondary school curriculum set by the Ministry of Education and Training simply to offer their graduates a diploma with which Ontario universities feel comfortable. If independent secondary schools are to satisfy parental choice in education, a greater degree of independence in the secondary school program would seem desirable.

There are several possible solutions to this problem, one of which already exists while the others would require future policy changes. The immediate solution can be found in the International Baccalareate program, a secondary school program of study offered and administered by the International Baccalareate organization.[9] Used by only a few independent schools in Ontario, the

---

[8] OS:IS, s. 6.8, at p. 32.
[9] Information about the International Baccalareate program can be obtained from In-

International Bacculareate involves a rigorous senior secondary school program leading to the granting of an International Bacculareate which is recognized by universities throughout the world. Three significant constraints exist, however, in the International Bacculareate program. First, a significant per pupil fee must be paid each year to the International Bacculareate for the program. Second, schools must send their teachers for extensive specialized training with its attendant costs. Third, while the International Bacculareate program of study is rigorous, its requirements may not offer sufficient flexibility to be compatible with the educational missions of some independent schools.

Another possible method of extricating independent secondary schools from the demands of Ministry-set programs of study would lie in the creation of an alternative graduation diploma. This solution effectively would require the establishment of a provincial independent school accreditation agency which would create the broad requirements and standards for offering an independent school graduation diploma. Establishing an independent secondary school diploma would require that Ontario's independent secondary schools demonstrate a higher degree of collective organization and political will than they presently display. The fierce independence which necessarily characterizes most of Ontario's independent secondary schools at the same time often prevents greater actions by them towards a common end. Given the major shifts in Ontario's public secondary school programs which seem to occur with each provincial election and the attendant costs of such changes, the time may well be ripe for Ontario's independent schools to establish a provincial accreditation agency which would ensure a greater degree of stability for the independent secondary school program.

Commencing with the start of the school year in September, 1999, Ontario's public secondary schools will move to a four-year program leading to an Ontario diploma. Just as the requirements of OS:IS have applied to independent secondary schools offering an Ontario graduating diploma, the requirements of the new four-year high school program will also apply to Ontario's independent secondary schools. As of the date of writing this book, the structure and content of the proposed four-year high school program remains uncertain. The Ministry of Education and Training has announced that students will be required to complete 30 credits over four years, of which 18 will be compulsory credits, and the remaining 12 optional credits designed to enable students to pursue individual interests and meet university or work requirements. The program will reflect an increased emphasis on mathematics, language and science. The government also plans to require high school students to complete 40 hours of community involvement prior to graduation and implement a

---

ternational Bacculareate North America, 200 Madison Ave., Suite 2007, New York, N.Y. 10016, tel. (212) 696-4464.

teacher advisory system.[10] The Ministry also plans to reintroduce a form of graduated streaming which will see students choosing in grade 10 to move in courses designed to prepare them for university, college or work.

It remains to be seen whether the new high school program will provide independent secondary schools with greater flexibility than OS:IS in their courses of study.

WHAT DOES "SATISFACTORY INSTRUCTION" MEAN?

The *Education Act* requires independent schools to provide "satisfactory instruction" to their pupils,[11] but the Act does not define what constitutes "satisfactory instruction". Neither has the Ministry of Education and Training published any policy statements defining "satisfactory instruction", nor does the Ministry's *Private School Manual* expressly define the term. Nonetheless, the content of the requirement of "satisfactory instruction" can be gleaned from the few court cases which have examined the term, as well as from the overall approach set out in the Ministry's *Private School Manual*.

Court Cases

Two reported court decisions have considered the meaning of the term "satisfactory instruction" as used in the *Education Act*. Both involved parents who home schooled their children and were charged under the *Education Act* for refusing to cause their children to attend school. In both cases the local school boards and the Provincial School Attendance Counsellor took the position that the children were not receiving satisfactory instruction at home. Notwithstanding the home-schooling context of the cases, the decisions do provide some guidance on the meaning of the term "satisfactory instruction".

In the first case, *Lambton County Board of Education v. Beauchamp*,[12] the parent educated her child at home using correspondence materials from a Christian academy in the United States. As the result of a disagreement between the mother and the local school board over the quality of instruction her child was receiving, the mother was charged with refusing to cause her child to attend school.[13] The court acquitted the mother of the charges, and in the course of its decision made two comments on the meaning of the term "satisfactory instruction". First, while the *Education Act* did not spell out exactly what form of alternative education is acceptable, the court thought that the Ontario legislature intended to assure that "the alternative program be of a

---

[10] Ministry of Education and Training, News Release (January 9, 1998).
[11] *Education Act*, s. 21(2)(a).
[12] (1979), 10 R.F.L. (2d) 354 (Ont. Prov. Ct.).
[13] *Education Act*, s. 30(1).

quality comparable to that of the public school system".[14] Second, the court recognized the existence of a tension between the competing interests of parents and the state in the education of the child, and the necessity for any interpretation of the requirement of "satisfactory instruction" to balance these interests:

> I have no doubt that the legislature of Ontario, in enacting the *Education Act*, intended a purpose with which the majority of the population agrees, and that is to maintain at least a minimum degree or standard of education for its citizens; and to that end the state is accorded the right to interfere with the rights of parents to educate their children as they wish.
>
> Obviously, there will always be persons who for religious, cultural or other sectarian purposes reject all or part of the public educational system, and pressing against them will be the intent of the state to protect their children from what may be the ignorance, excess, or folly of their parents which may in turn deprive their children of the right to full and free development and may result in them becoming a burden and a charge upon society as a whole.
>
> It is very important that there be a fine balance between these contending rights and interests.[15]

While it may be understandable that a court would regard the public school system as the benchmark of "satisfactory instruction", it is disquieting to see a court imply that a choice by a parent to remove a child from the public school system may be described as one of "ignorance, excess or folly". Such an approach suggests that the state knows what is best for the child; not the parents. Despite this language, the court proceeded to place a high burden on any local school board, or the Provincial Attendance Counsellor, which sought to invoke the compulsory attendance provisions contained in the *Education Act*. The court stated that a board bears a substantial burden of proof in a case where a parent is charged and must conclusively prove its case against the parent through the introduction of substantial, detailed and, if necessary, expert testimony.[16] Since the reports filed in the *Lambton County* case by the investigators regarding the instruction the mother was providing to her child indicated that the child's educational progress was adequate, and that it was premature to determine whether the home study plan was working, the court concluded that the local school board had failed to establish beyond a reasonable doubt that the parent was guilty of the offence charged.[17]

The second case, *R. v. Prentice*,[18] also involved parents who educated their children at home. The children were registered as students at a private

---

[14] *Supra*, footnote 12, at p. 356.
[15] *Supra*, at p. 361.
[16] *Supra*, at p. 362.
[17] *Supra*.
[18] [1985] O.J. No. 771 (QL) (Ont. Prov. Ct.).

school, and the parents' home was classified as a "home campus" of the private school. The parents were charged with failing to cause their children to attend school because they were not providing satisfactory instruction. Whereas the court in the *Lambton County* case placed the onus on the school authorities to prove that a child schooled at home was not receiving satisfactory instruction, the court in *Prentice* took a different approach, making the following observations:

1. The clear intent of Part II of the *Education Act* on a broad reading of its provisions is to ensure that every child shall receive competent teaching wherever and under whatever auspices it occurs and whoever is the teacher.[19]
2. Section 30 of the *Education Act* creates a public welfare offence imposing strict liability on the parents, subject to a defence available to the parents, showing that they had taken due diligence. What this means is that proof by the educational authorities of a child's failure to attend school *prima facie* imports the offence under section 30, leaving it open to the parent to avoid liability by proving, either during the prosecution's case or by defence evidence, that he or she took all reasonable care.[20]

Given the results published in recent years about the mediocre performance of Ontario's public school students on national and international tests, one might question the court's presumption that if a child does not attend a public school then he or she is not receiving a satisfactory instruction. The court also displayed a disregard for the primacy of parental responsibility in ensuring the education of children.

Although in *Prentice* the court did not define the term "satisfactory instruction", the judge's comments on the evidence suggest that the court regarded the following elements as critical or necessary parts of "satisfactory instruction":

(a) the careful planning of a program of study and careful correlation between means and ends;[21]
(b) adequate record-keeping procedures which demonstrate that the educational program is organized, scheduled and can be evaluated;
(c) the periodic evaluation of a program of study to determine whether a child demonstrates an increase in learning; and
(d) a demonstration that the instructional program displays some purpose and direction, in the sense that there is a specific daily time schedule

---

[19] *Supra*, at para. 5.
[20] *Supra*, at para. 27.
[21] *Supra*, at paras. 21 and 22.

for a child to be engaged in the teaching and learning process, and that a curriculum is followed.[22]

The core of satisfactory instruction, in the court's view, is that a program of study possess some structure and organization. It is interesting to note that the evidence filed by the Board of Education at the trial in the *Prentice* case did not take issue so much with the content of the home-schooling program, as with its lack of organization and lack of planning.

Private School Manual

The Ministry's *Private School Manual* does not contain any definition of "satisfactory instruction" for an independent school. By examining what aspects of a school's operation the Ministry assesses during an inspection, one can infer what the Ministry regards as satisfactory instruction. First and foremost, the Ministry places great emphasis on the presence of a planned and organized program of instruction in the school. In this regard, the Ministry appears to regard the presence of defined courses of study and a written course of study for each course as key components to satisfactory instruction. The Ministry places great emphasis on the formalities of a course of study, looking for courses of study which provide information on the rationale, objectives, topics and sequence, time line, teaching strategies, resources, and assessment and evaluation techniques for each unit of study. At the classroom level, the Ministry considers the preparation and maintenance of daily records of lessons for each unit of study as another indicator of satisfactory instruction. A school which maintains on file up-to-date courses of study for each course offered by the school should encounter little difficulty in persuading a Ministry inspector that it meets the standard of a planned and organized program of study.

A second component of the Ministry's view of satisfactory instruction relates to the keeping of proper student records. While the specific student records which must be kept by different independent schools will be considered in Chapter 8, as a general matter, the Ministry will evaluate a school's records to see whether they contain the following features: accurate, secure and up-to-date student records and transcripts; the issuance of report cards; proper attendance reporting; the presence of a master timetable for all courses; a list of teachers with their teaching schedules; and a list of the students attending the school.[23]

A final element of satisfactory instruction in the eyes of the Ministry is the quality of the actual classroom instruction provided in independent schools. The Ministry's *Private School Manual* indicates that the Ministry will assess

---

[22] *Supra*, at para. 23.
[23] *Private School Manual*, at p. 31.

the school's teacher learning strategies, examination format and marking schemes, other evaluation strategies, homework and assignments, teacher lesson plans and the teacher's mark book. It has been the experience of many independent schools that the extent to which the Ministry assesses the school's in-classroom instruction will vary significantly from inspector to inspector. Some inspections are characterized by a complete absence of observation of in-classroom instruction, with the inspector focusing exclusively on the records and teaching plans maintained by the school.

TEXTBOOKS

Learning materials and textbooks approved by the Ministry of Education and Training for the use in Ontario's public and separate schools are listed in a document entitled *Circular 14*. Public and separate schools must select textbooks from the list in *Circular 14* in all subject areas for which approved learning materials are listed in the document.[24] In practice, public and separate school teachers may only use the specific textbooks and learning materials listed in *Circular 14*.

Some confusion exists as to whether the requirements of *Circular 14* also apply to independent schools. This should not be so, for the *Education Act* clearly does not require Ontario's independent elementary or secondary schools to select their textbooks from *Circular 14*. As the *Education Act* is currently written, the Minister of Education and Training does not possess any statutory power to specify or prescribe the textbooks and learning materials used in independent schools. Although section 8(1) of the *Education Act* confers upon the Minister extensive powers to select and approve textbooks, library books, reference books and other learning materials, as well as to publish lists of such books for use in elementary and secondary schools, all of these powers relate only to "schools", a term which does not include independent schools.[25] Section 11 of the *Education Act* authorizes the Minister to make regulations regarding textbooks, but only regulations which require "boards" to purchase books for the use of pupils.[26] Section 11 also authorizes the Minister to make regulations listing the textbooks that are selected and approved "for use in schools".[27] Again, since boards govern only public and separate schools, and the term "schools" does not include independent schools, the Minister does not possess the statutory power to make regulations regarding books to be used in independent schools.

---

[24] *Circular 14* (1995) at p. x, s. 3(a).
[25] *Education Act*, s. 8(1), paras. 4, 5, 6 and 7.
[26] Section 11(1), para. 8.
[27] Section 11(1), para. 24.

The Minister has exercised his regulation-making power with respect to the use of textbooks in public and separate schools. Regulation 298[28] made under the *Education Act* provides that the principal of a school, in consultation with the teachers, shall select textbooks from the list of textbooks approved by the Minister.[29] Since this requirement relates only to principals in "schools" (*i.e.*, public and separate schools), it does not apply to independent schools.

As to independent secondary schools which offer an Ontario diploma, the Minister does possess the statutory power to require such independent schools to participate in reviews of classroom practices and the effectiveness of educational programs and to provide information to the Minister for that purpose.[30] This power, however, does not confer upon the Minister any authority to prescribe the textbooks which must be used by independent secondary schools which offer an Ontario diploma. Nor does the Notice of Intention to Operate a Private School require an independent school to agree with the Ministry to select only textbooks from *Circular 14*.[31]

It is important for the principals and boards of directors of independent schools to understand properly the existing powers of the Minister with respect to the use of textbooks in independent schools. While independent secondary schools which offer an Ontario diploma certainly must submit to inspection in respect of "the standard of instruction in the subjects leading to the Ontario secondary school diploma",[32] as the *Education Act* now stands, this required inspection does not confer upon the Minister the power to prescribe the textbooks which must be used by those secondary schools.

It is open to an independent school to use textbooks from *Circular 14*, and many schools may find it convenient to use those textbooks since they are tailored to provincial courses of study. Yet Ontario's independent schools enjoy a broad freedom to choose the textbooks and reference materials which they find most compatible with their courses of study.

PROVINCE-WIDE TESTS

Early Years of Provincial Tests

In 1993, as part of the introduction of the Common Curriculum, the Ministry of Education and Training requested all schools, public and private, to administer a standardized grade 9 reading and writing test. The test was not

---

[28] Operation of Schools — General, R.R.O. 1990, Reg. 298 (as amended).
[29] Section 7(1).
[30] *Education Act*, s. 8(1), para. 3.1.
[31] If it did, the Ministry's request probably would be invalid since it lacks any statutory basis.
[32] *Education Act*, s. 16(7).

designed to determine whether a student passed or failed grade 9 English, but sought to determine on a province-wide basis the English proficiency of grade 9 students. Some independent schools objected to administering the grade 9 reading and writing test, in part because of the poor quality of the test and also because for some schools such standardized tests run counter to their pedagogical principles. Although the Ministry did not insist that independent schools administer the standardized tests in 1993-94, by the 1994-95 school year, the Ministry was taking the position that all independent schools were required to administer the grade 9 test. In support of its position, the Ministry relied upon section 8(1) of the *Education Act* which authorizes the Minister to conduct reviews of classroom practices and the effectiveness of educational programs in independent secondary schools inspected for Ontario diploma purposes.[33]

Despite the Ministry's position, one private school, The Toronto Waldorf School, continued to refuse to administer the test. As a result, the Ministry advised the school that if the test was not administered by the end of the 1994-95 school year, the school's grade 9 students would not be granted their grade 9 credit equivalence nor would the school be able to issue diplomas to its graduating students. Consequently, in June, 1995, the school went to court to challenge the Ministry's decision, arguing that the Ministry's grade 9 policy and curriculum documents did not make the test part of the grade 9 curriculum, and that the Ministry's policy on the test permitted parents to request, and principals to grant, exemptions from writing the test "if it is in the best interest of a student, from an educational or personal well-being perspective".[34] The court never had to rule on the private school's arguments because the Ministry altered its position and permitted the school's students to obtain exemptions from writing the standardized test.

The Education Quality and Accountability Office Act

Shortly after the *Toronto Waldorf School* case was settled, a provincial election brought a change of government. One of the first steps of the new provincial government in the education realm was to pass the *Education Quality and Accountability Office Act, 1996*[35] which set up an office by that name to evaluate the quality and effectiveness of elementary and secondary school education in Ontario. The Ministry of Education and Training plans to require students in elementary and secondary schools to write a series of provincial examinations at various stages of their academic careers designed by the Education Quality and Accountability Office (the "EQAO") to test their skills in several subject areas, primarily English language and mathematics. A province-

---

[33] Section 8(1), para. 3.1.
[34] *Toronto Waldorf School v. Minister of Education* (unreported, Ont. Div. Ct., Court File No. 328/95).
[35] S.O. 1996, c. 11 (the "EQAOA").

wide grade 3 English test was administered during the 1996-97 school year and the Ministry's plans call for further tests to be written at the grades 6, 9 and 11 levels.

Participation by independent schools in provincial tests administered by the EQAO is voluntary.[36] The *Education Quality and Accountability Office Act, 1996*, does not require students who attend independent schools to participate in provincial tests administered by the EQAO.[37] It is open to an independent school to enter into an agreement with the EQAO under which its students would write a test on a voluntary basis, and the EQAO may charge a fee to the school for administering any test.[38] Currently the office charges independent schools a fee of $45 per student to participate in a test. This fee covers the costs of all assessment materials, teacher training, marking and reporting.[39]

SPECIAL EDUCATION

The *Education Act* requires district school boards to make available, free of charge, special education programs and services to all exceptional children, and to establish within each board a Special Education Identification Placement and Review Committee.[40] These requirements do not apply to independent schools.

Under the Ontario *Health Insurance Act*[41] a group of health services termed "school health support services" are made available as OHIP-paid services. School health support services are provided to needy students at their school during school hours, and the services include physiotherapy, nursing services, nutrition and speech therapy. Although the purpose of the program is to assist disabled children to obtain an education which their disability might otherwise make difficult,[42] OHIP only pays for the services if they are provided in a public or separate school. Disabled children who attend an independent school may obtain the services, but their parents must pay for them.[43] In the

---

[36] In the 1996-97 school year about 20 independent schools participated in the grade 3 provincial test.

[37] The Education Quality and Accountability Office only possesses the power to require boards of education to administer provincial tests to their students: EQAOA, s. 4(1).

[38] EQAOA, s. 5(1)(a) and (2).

[39] Information about provincial standardized tests can be obtained by contacting the EQAO at 1-888-327-7377, or by visiting its web page (www.eqao.com).

[40] *Education Act*, s. 8(3) and Identification and Placement of Exceptional Pupils, O. Reg. 181/98.

[41] R.S.O. 1990, c. H.6. See also R.R.O. 1990, Reg. 552, ss. 13 and 14.

[42] *Adler v. Ontario* (1996), 140 D.L.R. (4th) 385, [1996] 3 S.C.R. 609 at p. 723, para. 227, *per* McLachlin J.

[43] Section 14 of Reg. 552 under the *Health Insurance Act* limits the services to stu-

Adler case the Supreme Court of Canada ruled that this differential treatment of disabled children in independent religious schools was not discriminatory and therefore did not infringe the guarantee of equality in s. 15(1) of the *Canadian Charter of Rights and Freedoms*.[44]

SCHOOL HEALTH PROGRAMS AND SERVICES

Under the *Health Protection and Promotion Act*[45] every local board of health is required to provided stipulated health programs and services to the pupils attending schools within the area served by the local board of health. This provision applies to an independent school since the Act defines "school" as including a "private school".[46] The health programs and services stipulated by the regulations under the Act include speech, hearing, vision and dental screening, assessment and recording of immunization status, "counseling services on health related problems", "mandatory health programs and services" as specified in the guidelines "and certain dental services".[47]

Recognizing that some of the health services specified under the regulation may not accord with the religious or conscientious beliefs of parents whose children attend a school, the Act provides that the stipulated health programs and services do not apply to pupils attending a school "unless the person or organization that operates the school has agreed to the provisions of the particular health program or service for the pupils attending the school".[48] Accordingly, sex or reproductive education programs offered by local boards of health cannot be provided in an independent school unless the school expressly agrees to the provision of the particular health program or service.

SCHOOL YEAR AND HOLIDAYS

Under the *Education Act*, the Ministry of Education and Training may make regulations prescribing the school year, school holidays, school terms and instructional days.[49] Amendments to the *Education Act* by Bill 160 limit examination days to ten in any school year and professional activity days to four in

---

dents in "schools" as that term is defined in the *Education Act*, thereby excluding students in independent schools.

[44] *Supra*, footnote 42, *per* Iacobucci J., at pp. 649-51, paras. 51-4 and *per* Sopinka and Major JJ., at p. 709, paras. 190-91.
[45] R.S.O. 1990, c. H.7, s. 6(1).
[46] Section 1(1).
[47] School Health Services and Programs, R.R.O. 1990, Reg. 570.
[48] *Health Protection and Promotion Act*, s. 6(2).
[49] *Education Act*, s. 11(7).

any school year.[50] None of these provisions apply to independent schools.[51] Accordingly, an independent school is free to set its school year, terms, holidays, instructional days, number of examination days and number of professional activity days.

For the same reason, independent schools are not subject to the minimum average class size requirements and average weekly minutes of instruction which were enacted by Bill 160.[52]

COURSE HOURS

Independent inspected secondary schools which offer credit courses leading to an Ontario diploma are required to comply with the minimum hour requirements for each credit course.[53] Currently a secondary school credit is granted in recognition of the successful completion of a course that has been scheduled for a minimum of 110 hours.[54] Fractional credits may be granted for short courses based on 30 hour modules.[55] These requirements may change with the implementation of the four-year secondary school program in the 1999-2000 academic year.

RELIGIOUS EDUCATION CREDITS

For many years, the Ministry of Education and Training took the position that an independent secondary school could not grant credits for religious education courses notwithstanding that credit courses in religious education in grades 9 and 10 of Roman Catholic separate schools were permitted.[56] When this discriminatory policy was challenged in court by several independent religious schools,[57] the Ministry amended its policy to permit any independent religious school to grant credits toward an Ontario diploma for grade 9 and 10 religion courses.[58] Although there are no Ministry approved credit courses for religious education in grades 11 and 12, many schools, both independent and

---

[50] Section 11(7.1).
[51] Section 11(7) and (7.1) of the *Education Act* apply only to schools under boards.
[52] *Education Act*, ss. 170.1 and 170.2.
[53] OS:IS, s. 4.4.
[54] *Ibid.*
[55] *Ibid.*, s. 4.5.
[56] *Ibid.*, s. 6.10.
[57] *Ontario Alliance of Christian Schools Societies v. Minister of Education* (unreported, Ont. Div. Ct., Application No. 580/92).
[58] Ministry of Education, Policy/Program Memorandum No. 118 (April 28, 1993). Such courses must be approved by the Ministry as non-guideline courses under OS:IS.

Roman Catholic separate, provide such courses through their grade 11 World Religion and grade 12 Society, Challenge and Change courses.

7

Principals and Teachers

THE ROLE OF PRINCIPALS AND TEACHERS

Principals and teachers play the vital role of contributing to the integral human formation of their students. Each school is a community and the members of the school community — principal, teachers, parents and students — must have a shared life and actions. The principal and teachers must act as members of the school community striving towards the common goal of the school society.

Several recent decisions of Canadian courts have recognized the central role played by principals and teachers in the education of students and the corresponding duties placed on them by their vocation as educators. In *Ross v. New Brunswick School District No. 15*,[1] the Supreme Court of Canada described a public school as: "a communication centre for a whole range of values and aspirations of a society. In large part, it defines the values that transcend society through the educational medium." Within each school:

> Teachers are inextricably linked to the integrity of the school system. Teachers occupy positions of trust and confidence, and exert considerable influence over their students as a result of their positions. The conduct of a teacher bears directly upon the community's perception of the ability of the teacher to fulfil such a position of trust and influence, and upon the community's confidence in the public school system as a whole.
>
> . . . . .
>
> By their conduct, teachers as "medium" must be perceived to uphold the values, beliefs and knowledge sought to be transmitted by the school system. The conduct of a teacher is evaluated on the basis of his or her position, rather than whether the conduct occurs within the classroom or beyond. Teachers are seen by the community to be the medium for the educational message and because of the community position they occupy, they are not able to "choose which hat they will wear on what occasion" . . . teachers do not necessarily check their teaching

---

[1] (1996), 133 D.L.R. (4th) 1 at p. 20, [1996] 1 S.C.R. 825.

hats at the school-yard gate and may be perceived to be wearing their teaching hats even off duty.

. . . . .

It is on the basis of the position of trust and influence that we hold the teacher to high standards both on and off duty, and it is an erosion of these standards that may lead to a loss in the community of confidence in the public school system.[2]

Teachers serve as models for their students to emulate, in large part because teachers derive their authority to teach from a student's parents. In *R. v. Audet*,[3] the Supreme Court of Canada stated:

In my view, no evidence is required to prove that teachers play a role in our society that places them in a direct position of trust and authority towards their students. Parents delegate their parental authority to teachers and entrust them with the responsibility of instilling in their children a large part of the store of learning they will acquire during their development.

Or as put by an Ontario court judge:

In so far as persons in the profession of . . . teachers, it is quite apparent that they hold a special role in the life of young people. In our society the role of the teacher is second in importance only to the parent. I dare say that the parent views the teacher as being in his or her place while the child is away from the control of the parent. The parent entrusts the teacher with the parent's responsibilities, preparing the youths to compete and to contribute and to develop their individual talents in this very difficult world, both in our own community, in our national community and in the international community, an extremely difficult time for young people and their parents. The role, therefore, of the teacher, in my opinion, has to be seen in the context of what challenges face teachers and young people in our community in the context to which I have just referred.[4]

For decades the *Education Act* has contained a provision which articulates the role and duties of a teacher in a public school. Section 264(1) of the Act provides that it is the duty of a teacher:

(a) to teach diligently and faithfully the classes or subjects assigned to the teacher by the principal;
(b) to encourage the pupils in the pursuit of learning;
(c) to inculcate by precept and example respect for religion and the principles of Judaeo-Christian morality and the highest regard for truth, justice, loyalty, love of country, humanity, benevolence, sobriety, industry, frugality, purity, temperance and all other virtues;

---

[2] *Supra*, at pp. 20-21.
[3] (1996), 135 D.L.R. (4th) 20 at p. 40, [1996] 2 S.C.R. 171.
[4] *R. v. Forde* (1992), 17 W.C.B. (2d) 89 (Ont. Ct. (Gen. Div.)) quoted in *R. v. Audet*, *supra*, at pp. 41-2.

Although the Supreme Court of Canada recently described section 264(1) as using language of "another era",[5] an assessment which undoubtedly would draw a mixed reaction from members of the populace at large, the court did recognize that the language of the section continues to set the ideal to which teachers must strive:

> The requirements it sets for teachers reflect the ideal and not the minimal standard. They are so idealistically high that even the most conscientious, earnest and diligent teacher could not meet all of them at all times. Angels might comply but not mere mortals. It follows that every breach of the section cannot be considered to infringe upon the values that are essential to the make-up of a good teacher. However, the section does indicate that teachers are very properly expected to maintain a higher standard of conduct than other employees because they occupy such an extremely important position in society.
>
> . . . . .
>
> Section 264(1)(c) requires teachers to inculcate by precept and example the highest regard for truth, justice, loyalty, love of country, humanity and benevolence. These are values that all parents wish their children to learn. In their position of trust, teachers must teach by example as well as by lesson, and that example is set just as much by their conduct outside the classroom as by their performance within it. Thus misconduct which occurs outside regular teaching hours can be the basis for discipline proceedings.[6]

While these cases considered the role of teachers in public schools, the principles apply with equal force to teachers in independent schools.

APPLICATION OF THE EDUCATION ACT TO INDEPENDENT SCHOOL TEACHERS AND PRINCIPALS

Terms and Conditions of Employment

The *Education Act* contains detailed provisions regarding the terms and conditions of employment of teachers and principals. As a matter of law, these provisions do not apply to independent school teachers, but only to teachers employed by a public or separate district school board or authority.[7] If an independent school's teachers are unionized, the general provisions of the *Labour Relations Act, 1995*[8] will apply.

---

[5] *Toronto (City) Board of Education v. O.S.S.T.F., District 15* (1997), 144 D.L.R. (4th) 385 at p. 401, [1997] 1 S.C.R. 487.
[6] *Supra, per* Cory J., at pp. 401-2.
[7] *Education Act*, R.S.O. 1990, c. E.2, Parts X and X.I.
[8] S.O. 1995, c. 1 (as amended).

Duties of Principals and Teachers

The Act also contains provisions setting out the duties of teachers and principals, including section 264 just discussed. Until the passage in December, 1997, of Bill 160, the *Education Quality Improvement Act, 1997*,[9] one could say with certainty that these provisions of the *Education Act* did not apply to teachers and principals in independent schools. Until the passage of Bill 160 the definition of "teacher" in the *Education Act* meant a person who held a valid certificate of qualification as a teacher in "an elementary or secondary school in Ontario", which would exclude teachers in independent schools.[10] Similarly, the Act defined "principal" as a teacher appointed by "a board to perform in respect of a school" the duties of a principal, again the reference to board and school excluding principals in independent schools.

On its face, Bill 160 slightly clouded the issue because it changed the definition of "teacher" to mean "a member of the Ontario College of Teachers".[11] The *Ontario College of Teachers Act, 1996*[12] provides that "every person who holds a certificate of qualification and registration is a member of the College". As a result, independent school teachers who hold certificates of qualification and registration become members of the Ontario College of Teachers and, therefore, a "teacher" within the meaning of the *Education Act.*

Does this change in the definition of "teacher" now mean that certified independent school teachers are subject to the duties imposed by section 264(1) of the *Education Act?* In a strictly legal sense, probably not, for the description of the duties of a teacher contained in section 264 of the *Education Act* is laced with references to "school", "board", "supervisory officers" and "principal", all of which refer only to the public and separate school system. Although the drafters of Bill 160 could have been clearer in the language which they chose, it appears that teachers in independent schools are not subject, as a matter of statute, to the duties and obligations imposed by the *Education Act,* but must look to their contract of employment to ascertain the scope of their duties and responsibilities.

In the case of principals, Bill 160 did not spawn any confusion because it did not change the definition of principal as a "teacher appointed by a board to perform in respect of a school the duties of a principal", a definition clearly restricting the term "principal" to those in the public and separate school systems.

That having been said, while section 264 of the *Education Act* does not apply as a matter of statutory interpretation to independent school teachers and principals, the section, dealing as it does with the duties of a teacher, illustrates

---

[9] S.O. 1997, c. 31.
[10] *Education Act*, s. 1(1).
[11] *Education Quality Improvement Act*, s. 1(1).
[12] S.O. 1996, c. 12, s. 14(1).

standards of professional conduct which one would expect to guide teachers in any independent school. For example, section 264 states that it is the duty of a teacher to teach diligently and faithfully the classes assigned to the teacher by the principal, to encourage the pupils in the pursuit of learning, to assist in developing co-operation and co-ordination of effort among the members of the staff of the school, and to maintain proper order and discipline in the classroom and while on duty in the school.[13] Each of these responsibilities would be considered implied terms of any contract of employment entered into by a teacher with an independent school simply because they reflect the fundamental duties of a teacher in any educational context. Similarly, the Act's enumeration of the duties of a principal — including the maintenance of proper order and discipline in the school, the development of co-operation and co-ordination of effort among members of the staff, maintenance of proper student records and the preparation of a timetable for the year — are so fundamental to the duties of a principal in any school that they would be considered implied terms of any contract of employment for a principal in an independent school.[14]

Nonetheless, at the end of the day the relationships between an independent school and its principal and teachers are not governed by the *Education Act*, but by the contracts of employment entered into between the school and its principal and teachers, as well as any policies of the school or its board of directors governing the duties and obligations of the school's principal and teachers.

PRINCIPALS

Duties

A principal, in a fundamental sense, performs two roles in a school: he is both the principal administrator and the principal educator of the school. Whether a school's organizational structure is vertical (under which the teachers report to the principal and the principal reports to the board) or horizontal (under which the principal is the first among equals who act in a collegial fashion) the two fundamental roles of a principal remain.

A principal acts as the chief administrator of the school and in the broadest sense is responsible for seeing that the school operates in a way which fulfils the mission of the school as set by the board of directors. As part of his administrative duties, a principal generally hires, promotes and dismisses faculty members and administrative staff, recommends to the board any changes in staff remuneration and benefits, initiates the school's budget process and

---

[13] *Education Act*, s. 264(1)(a), (b), (d) and (e).
[14] Section 265(a), (b) and (c).

oversees the expenditures of school funds, recommends capital repairs, improvements and the acquisition of new equipment, directs the school's academic program and makes recommendations to the board regarding major changes in the school's program of study. Most important of all, the principal is responsible for the academic, moral, and where applicable, religious tone of the school.

Given the broad range of responsibilities borne by a principal, it is imperative that the board of directors set clear lines of responsibility and authority for a principal in his contract of employment. A principal's contract should clearly demarcate those areas in which the principal has final authority from those in which he makes recommendations to the board for its approval. A school's success in large part depends upon establishing clear lines of authority for its principal, and the board's ability to evaluate a principal's performance depends upon a clear statement of the principal's responsibilities.

Some schools employ organizational models far removed from the traditional hierarchical structure of a school. Yet even in schools which operate on the basis of consensus decision-making among the faculty and the principal, there will be, of necessity, some areas where only one person speaks for the school. These areas should be reflected in the school's policy statements.

Membership on the Board of Directors

While there is no legal proscription against a principal sitting on the board of directors of a non-share corporation,[15] Ontario law prohibits any member of the board of directors of a registered charity from receiving remuneration from the school corporation without court approval. A principal therefore cannot sit on the board of directors of an independent school which is a registered charity unless the school obtains court approval or a special act incorporating the school so provides.

Nevertheless, the proper operation of a school requires that the principal not only report to the school's board of directors, but have constant access to the board's thinking about the school. A principal therefore should be invited to all meetings of the board of directors, and its committees, save for those meetings or committees which evaluate the principal's performance.

Evaluation

Every independent school should have in place a policy and process for the evaluation of its principal. The complexity and formality of the evaluation process will vary from school to school, according to the circumstances of each, but a school's board of directors should take time each year to evaluate

---

[15] See Chapter 2, under heading "Additional Duties of Directors of a Registered Charity".

the principal's performance and discuss the evaluation with the principal. No matter how small the school, it is always useful for the board of directors to set a series of goals or objectives for the principal, and then to review the principal's performance against those objectives at the end of each school year.

QUALIFICATIONS OF TEACHERS

Certificate of Qualification and Registration

While the *Education Act* requires that all teachers in elementary and secondary public and separate schools be members of the Ontario College of Teachers,[16] the Act does not impose the same requirements on teachers in independent schools. As a result, a teacher in an independent school is not required to hold a certificate of qualification and registration (or, the predecessor Ontario teacher's certificate or letter of standing).

Nevertheless most teachers in Ontario's independent schools do hold Ontario teacher certificates or certificates of qualification and registration. This number often varies with the stage of development of the school. Newly founded schools frequently include some non-certified teachers as part of their staff since these schools invariably face budgetary constraints in their start-up years and rely to some degree on the assistance of volunteer teachers. As a school becomes well established and increases in size, it usually moves towards increasing the number of certified teachers on staff so that by the time a school reaches its mature stage, its teachers invariably hold the same, or better, qualifications than their public system counterparts.

Inspection of Teachers for Certification

The *Education Act* recognizes the fact that some independent schools employ non-certified teachers. Section 16(8) of the Act enables independent schools to request that the Ministry inspect teachers in their schools for the purpose of receiving recommendation for certification. At the secondary school level, these inspections usually take place at the same time the Ministry performs its inspection of the school's secondary school program under section 16(7) of the Act, provided that the teacher has satisfied all the prerequisites for an inspection.

If a teacher holds a certificate of qualification from outside Ontario, the teacher may apply to the Ontario College of Teachers for a letter of eligibility.[17] This letter indicates that the person's academic and professional education

---

[16] *Education Act*, s. 262.
[17] Teachers Qualifications, O. Reg. 184/97, ss. 12 and 13. See also discussion in the *Private School Manual* (August, 1997) at pp. 36-9.

qualifies him or her to seek employment as a teacher in Ontario. Once the letter of eligibility is signed by a supervisory officer attesting to the offer of a teaching position and submitted to the Ontario College of Teachers, an interim certificate of qualification is then issued.[18] Following at least ten months of successful teaching, a teacher may request an inspection by a supervisory officer pursuant to section 16(8) of the Act for the purpose of receiving a certificate of qualification.[19]

The Ministry requires that a request for an inspection for the purpose of obtaining a certificate of qualification include a copy of the interim certificate of qualification. Upon receipt of an inspection request, the supervisory officer will contact the teacher to make the necessary arrangements.

The Ministry requires teachers seeking to obtain a certificate of qualification to gather the following materials and make them available for review during a supervisory officer's visit: courses of study, unit plans and the day book for the school year; a folder showing a variety of student work in all courses for which the teacher is responsible; assessment and evaluation strategies that have been used with the students; and the record of student assessment and evaluation. The Ministry inspector generally will observe the teacher in a classroom setting for a full 70-75 minute period.

In conducting an inspection of teachers for certification purposes, the Ministry employs the following criteria:[20]

1) Planning and Preparation: The teacher has developed appropriate long range plans (courses of study), unit and lesson plans to guide instruction;
2) Classroom Organization: The teacher has developed a safe, functional and inviting classroom environment, with pupil work appropriately displayed;
3) Classroom Management: The teacher has developed effective techniques and skills to manage student activities and behaviour in the classroom;
4) Methodology: The teacher employs a variety of instructional approaches that recognize and accommodate the learning strengths, needs and styles of individual pupils;
5) Assessment and Evaluation: The teacher employs a variety of techniques to systematically monitor student performance relative to intended outcomes and maintains an appropriate record keeping system for tracking the performance; and
6) Rapport: The teacher has developed a positive and constructive working relationship with the class.

After the inspector has observed the teacher in the classroom, the inspector will usually try to meet with the teacher to review the teacher's performance in light of these criteria. If the inspector determines that the teacher's performance is satisfactory, the teacher's application will be signed and submitted by the Min-

---

[18] O. Reg. 184/97, s. 15.
[19] Section 17.
[20] *Private School Manual* (August, 1997) at pp. 36-7.

istry of Education and Training to the Ontario College of Teachers for processing.

Membership in the Ontario College of Teachers

Every teacher who holds a certificate of qualification and registration is a member of the Ontario College of Teachers, subject to any term, condition or limitation to which the certificate is subject.[21] The College has a Council which acts as its governing body and board of directors. A majority of the members to the Council are elected by members of the College, and one of the elected positions is designated for a representative of independent schools.[22] While logic would dictate that only members of the College who teach in independent schools should vote for the independent school representative on the Council, the regulation made under the *Ontario College of Teachers Act, 1996*, very strangely permits any teacher in Ontario to vote for the independent school representative on the Council.[23] The regulation does require any person standing for election as the independent school representative to be employed at an independent school that has submitted a current Notice of Intention under section 16 of the *Education Act*.[24]

Members of the College must pay an annual membership fee as set by the College in its by-laws. Where an independent school employs a member of the College who contributes to the Ontario Teachers Pension Plan, the school is required to deduct the amount of the annual membership fee payable each year by the member, from the member's salary and submit the fee to the College.[25] This obligation applies only if the school has received notice that the member contributes to the Ontario Teachers Pension Plan.[26] Any amounts which the school must deduct must be submitted to the College no later than 35 days after the annual due date of the membership fees.[27] Prior to the due date an independent school may request an extension from the College of the date for the submission of fees, but if the school is otherwise late in submitting the fees, interest will be charged on the amount in arrears.[28]

The *Ontario College of Teachers Act, 1996*, establishes a procedure by which the College investigates complaints about the conduct or actions of a member,[29] and reviews a member's conduct before the Discipline Committee

---

[21] *Ontario College of Teachers Act, 1996*, s. 14(1).
[22] *Ibid.*, s. 4 and First Election, O. Reg. 344/96, s. 2.
[23] O. Reg. 344/96, s. 7.
[24] Section 14.
[25] O. Reg. 72/97, s. 2(3).
[26] Section 2(4).
[27] Section 2(5).
[28] Sections 3 and 4.
[29] *Ontario College of Teachers Act, 1996*, s. 26.

and Fitness to Practice Committee.[30] These procedures would apply to any teacher in an independent school who is a member of the College.

In order to carry out its task, the College may require an independent school to provide it with information, including personal information, about members of the College.[31] While the Act imposes on school boards obligations to promptly notify the College when the board becomes aware that a member has been convicted of a criminal offence involving sexual conduct with minors, or indicates that students may be at risk of harm or injury, as well as any conduct or actions of a member which in the opinion of the board should be reviewed by the College, similar obligations are not imposed by the Act on independent schools.[32] Prudent management of an independent school, however, should prompt a school to report such circumstances to the College.

TEACHERS' CONTRACTS OF EMPLOYMENT

General Principles

Teachers in most independent schools are not members of a union. As a result, the employment relationship between an independent school and a teacher usually is based on individual contracts of employment governed by the common law of contracts, and not by labour law governing collective agreements. Although a teacher may enter into an individualized contract with a school, prudent management suggests that a school should standardize the main terms and conditions of its teachers' employment contracts so that they are consistent for the entire school faculty.

Categories of Contract Positions

A school may employ several different classes of teachers: regular (or full-time), part-time, interim and probationary teachers. Since the duties of each class of teacher may vary, as will the nature of the school's financial obligations to the teacher, the contract of employment must reflect the specific terms and conditions relating to the particular class of teacher.

Specification of the Duties of the Teacher

Any teacher employment contract should clearly spell out the duties and obligations of the teacher. A list of duties for a teacher should form part of the main body of the contract, or be attached as a schedule to the contract. The list would enumerate such areas of a teacher's responsibilities as the number of

---

[30] *Ibid.*, Parts IV and V.
[31] *Ibid.*, s. 47(1); O. Reg. 72/97, s. 26.
[32] *Ibid.*, s. 47(2), (3).

classes to be taught; classroom responsibilities; planning; testing and evaluation; program development; the maintenance of order and discipline within the classroom; a commitment to professional growth and development; and requirements to attend staff and school meetings. The contract might also include general agreements by the teacher to perform all the normal duties of a teacher, subject to the authority of the principal and board of directors, and to uphold and to promote the objects and purposes of the school.

Length of the Employment Contract

A critical component of any employment contract is the period of time during which the employee is to provide services. The law does not place a minimum or maximum period of time on the term of an employment contract. As a practical matter, unless a teacher is hired to teach for only part of the year, or is hired part way through a school year, the contract of employment will run for at least one academic year. Whether a school offers teachers employment contracts for a term of more than one year, or negotiates renewals of each teacher's contract on an annual basis, is a matter of policy for each school to consider and decide on. Many independent schools prefer to negotiate teachers' contracts on an annual basis.

Where contracts are negotiated annually, fairness and common sense dictate that a school should provide each teacher with notice of the school's intention for the next academic year far enough in advance to permit the teacher whose contract will not be renewed a reasonable period of time in which to seek alternate employment for the next academic year. For many schools, the ability to renew teachers' contracts depends on the projected levels of enrolment for the next academic year and the resulting budget which flows from the projections. Since these numbers often are not available until towards the end of a school year, decisions to renew contracts may not be able to be made until that time. More established schools, for which the steady demand for enrolment allows greater certainty in their budget setting process, could fix the time to decide on the renewal of contracts earlier in the school year. Whatever time a school decides on, its contract of employment with a teacher should clearly state the date by which the school must notify a teacher that it does not intend to offer the teacher a contract for the subsequent academic year. To avoid confusion or misunderstanding, the school should notify the teacher in writing of its decision whether or not to renew the contract.

By the same token, the contract should specify the deadline for a teacher to advise the school that he or she intends to change employment at the end of the school year. The insertion of a clear deadline for such notice will afford the school the opportunity to appropriately plan its staffing requirements for any academic year.

Salary and Benefits

The contract of employment with a teacher must state the salary to be paid to the teacher during the term of the contract. The level of teachers' salaries should be set by the board of directors on a consistent basis. A school should formulate clear guidelines for the calculation of a teacher's salary based on: categories of teacher's duties (full-time, sessional or part-time), the course load required of a teacher, and experience (length of service, together with academic experience). The complexity and detail of any salary grid adopted by a board of directors will vary with the circumstances of the school. Whatever salary grid is adopted, it should contain a clear statement of the method by which salaries are calculated, and the frequency and timetable for a review of the levels contained in the salary group.

A school should provide its teachers with individual written confirmation of their salary and benefits for each academic year.

A school should adopt clear policies regarding sick leave, compassionate leave and maternity leave which must comply with all applicable Canadian and provincial labour laws. Whether a school offers disability and medical benefits will depend on the financial means of the school. Any contract of employment should specify which, if any, employment benefits are made available to the various categories of teachers. The availability of some benefits, such as medical and dental, may depend on the underwriting policies of the insurance companies and their criteria for benefit eligibility. A contract of employment should also specify any pension benefits made available to school employees, contributions to provincial and federal unemployment insurance programs, as well as professional development days.

Termination of the Contract

A contract of employment should specify when and for what reasons the contract can be terminated and the procedure for terminating the contract. If the contract does not contain such information, then common law principles of reasonable notice and cause will govern the termination of a contract.[33] Under the common law, a contract of employment for an indefinite term can be terminated without notice, or pay in lieu of notice, only if the school has cause to terminate the employment — for example, the teacher has engaged in serious misconduct which merits immediate termination. If cause does not exist, the school must provide the teacher with reasonable notice of the termination, or pay in lieu of the period of reasonable notice. What constitutes reasonable notice will depend on the facts of any particular case. A large body of case law

---

[33] For a full discussion of these principles and their application, see David Harris, *Wrongful Dismissal* (Toronto: Carswell, 1989) or Ellen E. Mole, *Wrongful Dismissal Practice Manual* (Toronto: Butterworths, 1984).

has developed over the years to provide guidelines regarding the appropriate notice periods which will vary with the length of employment and the amount of responsibility assumed by the employee.

When the contract of employment is for a fixed term, a school cannot terminate the teacher's employment without cause unless it pays the teacher the amount owing for the remainder of the contract's term.

In addition to the common law, provincial employment standards legislation sets out minimum periods of notice, or pay in lieu of notice, which must be given to an employee on termination of an employment contract.[34]

In order to avoid the uncertainty associated with applying the common law principles of cause and reasonable notice, a school's contract of employment should state that the school may terminate the contract without notice if it has cause to do so, and it often is useful to identify the circumstances constituting cause for dismissal without notice. A contract also should specify the amount of notice, if any, a teacher is entitled to receive if the school decides to terminate the teacher's employment for cause, or for reasons of poor performance or breach of school rules and regulations. As well, the contract should specify the amount of notice, or pay in lieu of notice, the school will give the teacher in the event the school terminates the employment without cause.

A contract of employment can be terminated on the mutual consent of the parties. This should be spelled out in the contract. If a teacher wishes to terminate a contract at the end of a school year, or does not wish to be considered for re-employment in the following school year, the contract should specify the date by which the teacher must provide the school with such notice.

As a school increases in enrolment, with a corresponding increase in the number of faculty, changes may be required in the school's approach to teacher employment contracts. Simple contracts of employment appropriate for a school with a faculty of five teachers may be inappropriate for a school with a faculty of fifty. The larger the size of the faculty, the greater the potential for the faculty to consider forming a bargaining unit to negotiate a collective agreement with the school. In order to avoid the confrontation and rigidity which often accompanies collective agreements and the associated collective bargaining and grievance procedures, some schools have developed highly sophisticated contracts of employment which incorporate some of the procedural features of a collective agreement, without actually having a union present in the school.

A key feature of such contracts is a detailed, formal procedure governing the discipline and termination of teachers. An employment contract can contain a variety of approaches to ensuring that any procedure for teacher discipline is conducted in accordance with the principles of fairness, and that decisions to

---

[34] *Employment Standards Act*, R.S.O. 1990, c. E.14, s. 57.

terminate a teacher are accompanied by an opportunity for a teacher to respond to any charges or complaints made against him. Some of these contracts provide that informal hearings be held in respect of any decision to discipline a teacher. At the end of the hearing, the board, or appropriate committee of the board, would render its decision on discipline. The decision of the board would be final. In the event the board decides to terminate a teacher's contract, the contract provides for an arbitration procedure in the event the teacher disputes the termination.

Such a style of employment contract has the benefit of providing the school with flexibility in disciplining and terminating teachers when necessary, but at the same time affording teachers procedural protection in the event the board decides to terminate the contract of employment. Under such contracts, a school enjoys more flexibility than under a collective agreement entered into with a union bargaining unit, yet gives greater security to the teacher than would be found in a simple contract of employment.

Reviews of Teacher Performance

A school should develop and implement a consistent policy for the evaluation of teacher performance. Teacher evaluations should be conducted at least once a year. In the case of newly hired teachers, an evaluation should be performed before the end of the teacher's probation period.

The development of criteria by which to evaluate teachers, and the actual performance of teacher reviews are separate, albeit interrelated, functions. A board of directors certainly can play a legitimate role in developing and articulating the criteria on which a teacher will be evaluated, as well as ensuring that such evaluation criteria advance the educational objectives of the school. Some boards find it useful to hire outside consultants to assist in the development of teacher evaluation criteria. Once the performance indicators have been established, the conduct of the evaluations generally should be left in the hands of the school's principal. A principal usually is best placed to monitor the performance and professional development of the school's teachers. The periodic appraisal of teachers forms an integral part of a principal's duties. Boards should resist the temptation to micro-manage schools to the extent of conducting teacher evaluations, for such an approach will only undermine the authority of the principal in relation to the teaching staff. If a board is viewed by teachers as a court of ultimate appeal from any review, a principal's ability to implement board policy will be severely hampered.

The actual performance indicators adopted by a school for the evaluation of teachers will be tied closely to the school's educational philosophy. Whatever criteria a school adopts, they should be clearly articulated, communicated to the teaching staff, and consistently and fairly applied across the teaching staff.

During the course of any evaluation process, adverse comments inevitably may be made by the school's administrative officers or principal about the performance of some of the teaching staff. Some teachers may feel offended by such remarks and consider them defamatory. The law recognizes that the proper functioning of a school requires a candid exchange of information about the character, qualifications, behaviour and performance of a school's staff. A qualified privilege consequently protects communications among school officers and staff regarding the behaviour and performance of staff. A principal is privileged to comment on a teacher's performance, either orally or in any records and files recording such information, as long as the statements which are made are pertinent to the function of the education institution, are made within normal channels of communication, and are not published with actual malice.[35]

Teachers who have worked in a public or separate school environment may be familiar with a section of the Regulation Made Under the *Teaching Profession Act* which requires any member of the Ontario Teachers' Federation who makes an adverse report on another member to furnish the other member with a written statement of the report at the earliest possible time, and not later than three days after making the report.[36] In most circumstances this requirement will not apply to teachers employed by independent schools. The *Teaching Profession Act*[37] provides that every "teacher" is a member of the Ontario Teachers' Federation, but amendments made by Bill 160 to that Act define "teachers" as persons who are members of the Ontario College of Teachers *and* are employed by a board as a teacher.[38] Consequently, the regulation does not apply to independent school teachers.

CODES OF CONDUCT

As a Term of Employment

Many independent religious schools require their teachers to act as living examples of their faiths and to serve as role models to students on how to lead their lives. Such schools often restrict the hiring of teachers to those who are members of their faith, and also require teachers, as a condition of their employment, to follow a code of conduct based on the precepts of their faith. As a general rule, such requirements are permitted by Ontario law, but the permissi-

---

[35] See Raymond E. Brown, *Law of Defamation*, 2nd ed. (Toronto: Carswell, 1994) at pp. 13-137 to 13-139 (March 1998, looseleaf).
[36] Regulation Made Under the *Teaching Profession Act*, s. 18(1)(b).
[37] R.S.O. 1990, c. T.2, s. 4(1).
[38] *Education Quality Improvement Act, 1997*, s. 180(2) amending s. 1 of the *Teaching Profession Act*.

ble scope of such requirements requires an understanding of the *Human Rights Code*.[39]

The *Human Rights Code* states that every person has a right to equal treatment with respect to employment without discrimination because of "race, ancestry, place of origin, colour, ethnic origin, citizenship, creed, sex, sexual orientation, age, record of offences, marital status, family status or handicap".[40] The Code prohibits any infringement of this right,[41] and establishes an inquiry process to investigate and remedy any breach of this guarantee of equal treatment.[42]

On its face, this guarantee of equal treatment in employment would prevent an independent school from imposing conditions of employment based on religion, or any of the other enumerated prohibited grounds of discrimination. Section 24(1) of the Code, however, creates a partial exemption from the general requirement. Section 24(1) reads as follows:

> 24(1) The right under section 5 to equal treatment with respect to employment is not infringed where,
> (a) a religious, philanthropic, educational, fraternal or social institution or organization that is primarily engaged in serving the interests of persons identified by their race, ancestry, place of origin, colour, ethnic origin, creed, sex, age, marital status or handicap employs only, or gives preference in employment to, persons similarly identified if the qualification is a reasonable and *bona fide* qualification because of the nature of the employment;

This provision of the Code permits independent schools to employ only, or give preference to, teachers who are members of the group primarily served by the school. Thus, an independent Catholic school could employ only Catholic teachers, as could a Muslim school give preference to Muslims as teachers.

To qualify for this exception the Code requires an independent school to meet the two key conditions contained in section 24(1)(a). First, the school must be "primarily engaged in serving the interests of persons identified" by one of the personal characteristics listed in the section. A school which originated many decades ago as a religious school serving a specific faith, but which over the years has changed its mandate to provide non-denominational, or secular education, likely would not qualify for the exemption because it no longer is "primarily engaged" in serving a specific group. On the other hand, an independent school whose objectives are clearly defined as providing an education in accordance with the principles of a specific faith does not lose the protection of the exception simply because it admits students of other faiths. As

---

[39] R.S.O. 1990, c. H.19.
[40] Section 5(1).
[41] Section 9.
[42] Part IV.

long as the school is "primarily", although not exclusively, engaged in serving a particular faith, it would qualify for the exemption.

Second, the school must be able to demonstrate that the decision to employ only, or give preference in employment to, persons of the faith served by the school is "a reasonable and *bona fide* qualification because of the nature of the employment". In the seminal 1984 case of *Caldwell v. Stuart*[43] the Supreme Court of Canada commented extensively on the requirement of a "reasonable and *bona fide* qualification" in the context of the employment of teachers. The case concerned a private Catholic school in British Columbia which had hired Caldwell to teach commercial subjects and mathematics. Caldwell, a Roman Catholic, did not give any form of religious instruction in the school, but she led prayers in her classroom each morning as did the other teachers in the school. After teaching for several years in the school, Caldwell married a divorced man in a civil ceremony, in contravention of the rules of the Roman Catholic Church. When the school administration learned this information several months later, they advised Caldwell that her teaching contract for the following year would not be renewed. Caldwell filed a complaint under the British Columbia *Human Rights Code* alleging discrimination in employment on the basis of marital status and religion.

The school's employment contract required teachers to exhibit the highest model of Christian behaviour, and the periodic appraisals of teachers included consideration of whether the teacher taught in the spirit of the Catholic school, its character and mission.

The Board of Inquiry struck under the British Columbia *Human Rights Code* concluded that Mrs. Caldwell's employment contract was a case where religion and marital status could be considered as *bona fide* qualifications for employment. The Supreme Court of Canada upheld the decision of the Board, and discussed the special character of religious schools against which any claim of discrimination has to be considered:

> As has been pointed out, the Catholic school is different from the public school. In addition to the ordinary academic program, a religious element which determines the true nature and character of the institution is present in the Catholic school. To carry out the purposes of the school, full effect must be given to this aspect of its nature and teachers are required to observe and comply with the religious standards and to be examples in the manner of their behaviour in the school so that students see in practice the application of the principles of the Church on a daily basis and thereby receive what is called a Catholic education. Fulfillment of these purposes requires that Catholics observe the Church's rules regarding marriage. It must be celebrated in the Church and the marriage of divorced persons is not recognized. The Board found that Mrs. Caldwell knew this when she was employed, that inquiries were made respecting these matters before she was hired to insure her eligibility for employment in this respect. It was

---

[43] (1984), 15 D.L.R. (4th) 1, [1984] 2 S.C.R. 603.

therefore open to the Board to find that when Mrs. Caldwell in contravention of the Church's requirements married a divorced man in a civil ceremony, she deprived herself of a *bona fide* qualification for the employment. In my view the Board made no error in so finding and in concluding that the provisions of s. 8 [of the *Human Rights Code*] were not operative to protect her.[44]

In considering whether a requirement of religious conformance by Catholic teachers was reasonably necessary to ensure the accomplishment of the objectives of a Catholic school, the Supreme Court of Canada stated:

> The Board found that the Catholic school differed from the public school. This difference does not consist in the mere addition of religious training to the academic curriculum. The religious or doctrinal aspect of the school lies at its very heart and colours all its activities and programs. The role of the teacher in this respect is fundamental to the whole effort of the school, as much in its spiritual nature as in the academic. It is my opinion that objectively viewed, having in mind the special nature and objectives of the school, the requirement of religious conformance including the acceptance and observance of the Church's rules regarding marriage is reasonably necessary to assure the achievement of the objects of the school. It is my view that . . . the requirement of conformance constitutes a *bona fide* qualification in respect of the occupation of a Catholic teacher employed in a Catholic school, the absence of which will deprive her of the protection of . . . the *Human Rights Code*. It will be only in rare circumstances that such a factor as religious conformance can pass the test of *bona fide* qualification. In [this] case . . . the special nature of the school and the unique role played by the teachers in the attaining of the school's legitimate objects are essential to the finding that religious conformance is a *bona fide* qualification.[45]

The Supreme Court of Canada concluded by making the following comments which would apply to any religious independent school:

> The purpose of the section [of the British Columbia *Human Rights Code*] is to preserve for the Catholic members of this and other groups the right to the continuance of denominational schools. This, because of the nature of the schools, means the right to preserve the religious basis of the schools and in so doing to engage teachers who by religion and by the acceptance of the Church's rules are competent to teach within the requirements of the school. This involves and justifies a policy of preferring Roman Catholic teachers who accept and practice the teachings of the Church. In failing to renew the contract of Mrs. Caldwell, the school authorities were exercising a preference for the benefit of the members of the community served by the school and forming the identifiable group by preserving a teaching staff whose Catholic members all accepted and practised the doctrines of the Church. In my opinion then, the dismissal of Mrs. Caldwell may not be considered as a contravention of the Code and the appeal must fail.[46]

---

[44] *Supra*, at pp. 618-19.
[45] *Supra*, at pp. 624-5.
[46] *Supra*, at p. 628.

A 1997 decision of an Ontario court reinforced the reasonableness of requiring teachers in a religious school to be members of the faith (in the particular case members of the Roman Catholic Church). The court stated:

> The argument that a non-Catholic could acquire knowledge of the Catholic perspective on these matters and convey that knowledge to the students seems to me entirely to miss the point of such a course and to overlook the central objective of Catholic education . . . A non-believer would necessarily teach the subject from an intellectual rather than faith-based perspective. Separate schools do not aim to teach their students about these matters from a neutral or objective point of view. Separate schools explicitly reject that secular approach and have consistently defined their mission to be the inculcation of a particular religious faith as the appropriate way for students to confront these issues in their lives. Given those objectives, it is difficult to see how the non-Catholic teacher's lack of belief could remain concealed from students. Even if the teachers were able to hide the fact that he or she did not embrace the Catholic faith, how could the teacher effectively urge a faith-based approach upon students? The very notion of religious faith involves an acceptance of the limits of the human intellect and of the need to accept, on faith, certain fundamental precepts as a guide to life.[47]

The approach adopted by the Supreme Court of Canada in the *Caldwell v. Stuart* case has been applied in cases involving non-Catholic religious schools. In *Garrod v. Rhema Christian School*[48] an independent Christian school dismissed a teacher when it discovered that she was living in a common law relationship. The Board of Inquiry under the Ontario *Human Rights Code* found that the school's proscription of common law relationships for their teachers was a *bona fide* occupational qualification in light of the need for religious conformance in the independent school.[49] In reaching that decision, the Board of Inquiry paid careful attention to the emphasis placed by the Rhema Christian School in its corporate and contractual documents on the necessity of teachers adhering to and living their lives in accordance with specific religious principles. The school corporation had passed a by-law requiring teachers to declare their unconditional agreement with the doctrinal basis of the school, attend at a church whose doctrine was in agreement with the school's doctrinal principles, and be "scripturally sound in their teaching and lead exemplary lives". The school's by-law specifically provided for the dismissal of a teacher "who proves to be unfit for the work or because such teacher's instructions with personal life conflict with the basis and purpose of this society". The school's parent handbook stated that a "teacher's life commitment gives our children a sense of cultural meaning and wholeness or meaninglessness. It is of vital importance, therefore, that our children are taught by teachers whose ideas on life we clearly know, whose life commitment we share, and whose life style

---

[47] *Daly v. Ontario (Attorney General)* (1997), 154 D.L.R. (4th) 464 (Ont. Ct. (Gen. Div.)) at p. 496.
[48] (1991), 15 C.H.R.R. D/477, 92 C.L.L.C. ¶ 17,003 (Ont. Bd. Inq.).
[49] *Supra*, at p. D/499, para. 141.

our children may follow."[50] The school's teaching contract also specifically provided that a teacher might be "dismissed by the board for fundamental breach of contract only", and that "fundamental breach of contract includes, *inter alia*, conduct that is in flagrant conflict with Christian ethics and morals".[51] The school gave copies of its by-laws and the parent handbook to the teacher when she signed her contract of employment and began teaching.

Finally, in *Kearley v. Pentecostal Assemblies Board of Education*[52] a Pentecostal school fired a teacher who divorced and then remarried. The teacher's complaint of discriminatory treatment in employment was dismissed. The Board of Inquiry under the Newfoundland *Human Rights Code* followed the principle in the *Caldwell* case that religious conformance by the teacher to the precepts of the faith was a *bona fide* occupational requirement. It is noteworthy that the by-laws of the Pentecostal Assemblies Board of Education contained detailed provisions regarding the precepts of the Pentecostal Church, the objectives of the school to preserve and to promote the interest of Pentecostal education, and the role of the Christian teacher in achieving those objectives. The by-laws, for example, described the role of the Pentecostal teacher as "one of the most important factors in the school. Every teacher influences the development of the child by behavior, attitudes, philosophy of life, knowledge and skills, and by understanding and guidance. The teacher's position of the group should be one of service and guidance, teaching by precept and example."[53] The by-laws continued by setting out guidelines which required teachers to support and uphold the basic doctrines of the Pentecostal Assemblies. These detailed provisions and guidelines in the by-laws readily enabled the Board of Inquiry to conclude that there was a ubiquitous religious framework in the Pentecostal schools, and that great emphasis was placed on the role of the teacher in achieving the aims of the Pentecostal school system.[54]

In light of these decisions, independent religious schools which plan to engage in the preferential hiring of teachers should take great care to include in their by-laws references to the principles and precepts of their faith and the important role of the teacher in promoting the principles of the faith, both through teaching and through the example of living his or her life. The school should bring these principles to the attention of any prospective teacher during the hiring process, and clearly make adherence to such principles a term of the teacher's employment contract. The contract should also state clearly that the failure by the teacher to follow the school's code of conduct constitutes grounds for termination of the contract.

---

[50] *Supra*, at p. D/481, para. 15.
[51] *Supra*.
[52] (1993), 19 C.H.R.R. D/573 (Nfld. Bd. Inq.).
[53] *Supra*, at p. D/483, para. 54.
[54] *Supra*, at p. D/484, para. 54.

A Recent Challenge to Codes of Conduct

A recent case involving the British Columbia College of Teachers potentially poses a long-term challenge to independent religious schools which require their staff and students to observe codes of conduct consistent with the religious precepts of the school. In *Trinity Western University v. British Columbia College of Teachers*,[55] Trinity Western University, a liberal arts university in British Columbia, required all members of the university community, students and faculty, to live by a set of community standards at the heart of which rested four core values: responsible citizenship, pursuit of biblical holiness, Christian leadership and placing community welfare above self-interest. Trinity Western faculty and students had to agree to abide by this code of conduct and to refrain from biblically condemned practices including drunkenness, swearing, dishonesty, abortion and sexual sins including "viewing of pornography, premarital sex, adultery and homosexual behaviour".

When Trinity Western applied to the British Columbia College of Teachers ("BCCT") in 1995 for accreditation of its four-year teacher education program, the BCCT raised several concerns about the school's program, especially its student code of conduct. The BCCT found "an inherent contradiction" between the necessity of preparing teachers to go out into public schools to work with colleagues and students from diverse ethnic and values background and Trinity Western's biblical code of conduct. An inspection team sent to Trinity Western by the BCCT recommended approval of the teacher education program on an interim five-year basis, but the BCCT's governing council rejected Trinity Western's application outright, deciding that it "is contrary to the public interest" because it appears "to follow discriminatory practices that public institutions are, by law, not allowed to follow".[56] The BCCT's governing council specifically pointed to the requirement in the student code of conduct to refrain from "sexual sins including . . . homosexual behaviour" as discrimination on the basis of sexual orientation. Arguing that it had to make decisions about "suitable and appropriate preparation" for teaching in a public school system, the governing council speculated that Trinity Western's position on homosexual behaviour might have a detrimental effect on the learning environment of public schools because a "teacher's ability to support all children regardless of race, colour, religion or sexual orientation within a respectful and non-judgmental relationship is considered by the college to be essential to the practice of the profession".[57]

The British Columbia Supreme Court overturned the governing council's rejection of Trinity Western's application and ordered the BCCT to accredit the

---

[55] (1997), 41 B.C.L.R. (3d) 158, 47 C.R.R. (2d) 155 (S.C.).
[56] *Supra*, at p. 177, para. 50.
[57] *Supra*, at p. 181, para. 55.

university's education program. The court considered that a teacher's governing college could legitimately assess the standards for the education, professional responsibility and competence of teachers, but not a teacher's religious beliefs. Tolerance, according to the court, requires people to respect others and their views, and the BCCT could not refuse to allow a qualified teacher to teach in British Columbia because of a religious belief that homosexual behaviour is a sin. The court concluded that it was legitimate for a college of teachers to expect appropriate conduct of teachers, and therefore it was legitimate for the BCCT to see how Trinity Western's graduates were conducting themselves in public schools. If any of the graduates engaged in inappropriate conduct, the court stated that the BCCT could look to see whether such conduct was related back to Trinity Western's student code of conduct. On the facts of the case, the court stated that there was simply no evidence that Trinity Western's graduates were engaged in unsuitable conduct in the public schools; on the contrary, the evidence showed that Trinity Western could not satisfy the demand by public schools for its graduates, and many of its graduates made a contribution to society by going to teach in poor neighbourhoods or on Indian reserves.

The BCCT has appealed the decision to the British Columbia Court of Appeal, and at the time of writing, the appeal had not yet been heard.

NON-TEACHING STAFF: CODES OF CONDUCT

Courts and boards of inquiries under provincial human rights legislation have distinguished between the role of teaching and non-teaching staff in a religious school. In the *Gore* case[58] a Catholic school board refused to engage a non-Catholic as a secretary for clerical duties in the school's administration. The Board of Inquiry sustained the complaint and in so doing drew a clear distinction between the position of a teacher and that of an administrative worker:

> I think it would be reasonable for the Separate School Board to refuse to hire a secretary who was hostile to the Catholic faith or to the aims of the Separate School system, regardless of her religious upbringing, but I cannot see how a secretary can be expected to provide an example for the children. This is surely the responsibility of the teachers, and the religious aspect is the responsibility of the ecclesiastics as well as most of the teachers. The secretary performs secretarial and clerical functions (and only for half a day), under directions from, and subject to supervision by, the principal. Requiring that she be a Roman Catholic is not, in my opinion, a "reasonable occupational qualification" within the meaning of s. 4(4)(b) of the Ontario *Human Rights Code*.[59]

---

[58] *Ontario Human Rights Code 1961-62 and Gore (Re)* (unreported, December 7, 1971, Ont. Bd. Inq.).

While this decision may have been correct on the facts of the case, an argument certainly can be made that in many schools the close daily contact which occurs between the administrative staff and students reasonably requires the staff to observe the precepts of the school's faith. Whether a school may employ preferential hiring practices for non-teaching staff no doubt will depend upon the specific circumstances of the school and the interaction between students and non-teaching staff.

---

[59] Quoted in *Caldwell v. Stuart* (1984), 15 D.L.R. (4th) 1, [1984] 2 S.C.R. 603 at p. 619.

8
Student Records

GENERAL REQUIREMENTS

The proper operation and organization of any independent school requires the school to maintain two kinds of records for each student: a record containing personal information about the student and a record tracking the student's academic performance while at the school.

The *Education Act* requires principals of public or separate schools to collect information for inclusion in a record in respect of each pupil enrolled in the school and to establish, maintain, retain, transfer and dispose of the records in accordance with the Act and the guidelines issued by the Minister.[1] Guidelines issued by the Ministry require that an Ontario Student Record ("OSR") be established for each student who enrols in a school operated by a board. The OSR is the record of a student's educational progress through schools in Ontario.[2] The OSR Guideline specifies in considerable detail the format and content of the OSR which must be maintained for each student.

The OSR Guideline does not apply to independent schools with one significant exception — the transfer of students from public to independent schools. The OSR Guideline provides that before a public or separate school principal transfers an original OSR to an independent school in Ontario, the principal shall have received a written request for the information from the independent school and a written statement signed by the parents or guardians of a student indicating their consent to the transfer of the OSR.[3] The OSR Guideline sets out the request form which the independent school must use, part of which requires the independent school to agree to accept responsibility for the OSR and to maintain, retain, transfer and dispose of the OSR in accordance with the guideline.

---

[1] *Education Act*, R.S.O. 1990, c. E.2, s. 265(d).
[2] *Ontario Student Record (OSR): Guideline 1989* (Ministry of Education and Training) at p. 2.
[3] *Ibid.*, s. 6.2.

Although the OSR Guideline does not apply to independent schools, except in the case of transferring students, the components of the OSR are a useful guide to assist independent schools in developing their own student records. An OSR folder contains: biographical data, information on the schools attended by the student and the highest grade completed at each school, names of parents or guardians, a summary of any student's special health conditions, photographs, information on school activities and, in the case of secondary school students, the Ontario Student Transcript ("OST"). Where the parents of a child are separated or divorced, a school should have on file a clear record of the custody arrangement regarding the child.

Many of the larger independent schools use the OSR as their student record. Given the continuous transfer of students into and out of independent schools, use of the OSR often provides a simple, consistent and cost-effective method to maintain student records. Use of the OSR may also allay any parental concerns about the ease of transferring their children back into the public system if they so decide at some future date.

ONTARIO EDUCATION TRANSCRIPT

As a matter of proper organization, an independent school should maintain some record or transcript of each student's academic progress in the school. The *Education Act* does not impose any specific requirements for the form of transcript used in independent elementary and secondary schools which do not offer an Ontario secondary school diploma ("OSSD").

In the case of inspected secondary schools which do offer a program of study leading to an OSSD, such schools usually use the Ontario Student Transcript ("OST"). An OST records the courses taken by a student in each grade, the Ministry of Education and Training course code for each course, the final mark achieved in the course, the credits granted for the course, whether the course is compulsory, the level of difficulty of the course, and whether the course is an OAC course.[4] OS:IS only permits percentage marks to be recorded on the OST, although either percentages or grade letters are acceptable methods of reporting student achievement on report cards.[5]

It must be recalled that when an inspected independent secondary school files its annual Notice of Intention to Operate, it expressly agrees to adopt the OST Common Course Coding. Accordingly, an inspected independent secondary school must use the Common Course Coding developed by the Ministry of Education and Training.[6]

---

[4] *Ibid.*, Appendix "D".
[5] OS:IS, s. 4.14.
[6] *Manual for the Common Course Code, 1986* (Toronto: Ministry of Education and

REPORT CARDS

Independent elementary schools may develop and use report cards which best reflect the schools' pedagogical principles. The provincial report cards introduced in September, 1997, for public and separate elementary schools are not required to be used in independent elementary schools.

At the secondary level, less flexibility exists. Although OS:IS does not require a specific form of report card to be used for those schools which offer an OSSD, the requirements of the OSR impose some limitations. Since the OSR Guideline requires both inspected and non-inspected independent schools to which public school students have transferred to maintain the student's OSR in accordance with the guideline,[7] some regard must be had to the provisions of the OSR dealing with report cards.[8] Most of the OSR Guideline requirements for report cards are matters of common sense and should be followed simply as a matter of good record keeping. The OSR Guideline requires a copy of each completed report card to be filed in the OSR folder for each student.[9] The report card should contain the full name of the student, the name and address of the school, the name and signature of the principal, the grade in which the student is placed, the grade to which the student is promoted, the record of attendance of the student at the school, the date the report card is issued and the student's level of achievement in each course.[10]

The OSR Guideline provides that a report card should also contain a concise statement of the program of study undertaken by the student sufficient to enable a person to understand the objectives, contents and degree of difficulty of the courses included in the program of study.[11] Given that a school's course catalogue usually will contain such information, it seems redundant to place that information on the report card. The title of the course, together with the common course code, should be sufficient. In the case of secondary school courses, the value of the credits assigned to the course should also be shown on the report card.

ONTARIO EDUCATION NUMBERS

The *Education Quality Improvement Act, 1997*, introduced a new feature to Ontario student records — Ontario education numbers. Under this new

---

Training). The list of common course codes is posted on the Ministry's website at www.edu.gov.on.ca.

[7] OSR Guideline, *op. cit.*, footnote 2, s. 6.2.
[8] Section 3.2.
[9] Section 3.2.1.
[10] Section 3.2.2.
[11] Section 3.2.2.

scheme, the Ministry of Education and Training may assign an Ontario education number to each person enrolled in a prescribed educational or training institution and the number will then follow the student as he or she progresses through the educational system. Since at the time of writing this book no regulation had been passed prescribing which educational institutions must use Ontario education numbers, it is unclear whether independent schools will be affected by this new system. Given the continual transfer of students between the public and independent school sectors, it is likely that the Ontario education numbers system will apply in some circumstances to independent schools, but the precise scope of its application must await the publication of a regulation.[12]

If the Ontario education numbers scheme applies to independent schools, great care will have to be taken in the use of Ontario education numbers. Under the new system, prescribed educational institutions will be authorized to collect personal information about each student for the purpose of assigning an Ontario education number.[13] A prescribed educational institution will be permitted to collect, use, disclose or require the production of a person's Ontario education number for purposes related to the provision of educational services to that person. A further group of persons to be prescribed by regulation may use Ontario education numbers for purposes relating to education administration, funding, planning or research.[14] Except as permitted by the *Education Act*, no other person may collect, use, disclose or require the production of another person's Ontario education number. Any person who violates the requirements of the Act is guilty of an offence.[15]

CONFIDENTIALITY OF AND ACCESS TO STUDENT RECORDS

The *Education Act*[16] and the *Municipal Freedom of Information and Protection of Privacy Act*[17] create a regime to ensure the confidentiality of student records for public and separate school students, as well as establishing a mechanism by which a person can access personal information in his or her student record. This regime does not apply to independent schools.[18] Neverthe-

---

[12] *Education Act*, s. 266.2, as amended by the *Education Quality Improvement Act, 1997*, S.O. 1997, c. 31, s. 121.
[13] Section 266.2(2).
[14] Section 266.3(2) and (3).
[15] Sections 266.3(1) and 266.4(1).
[16] Section 266.
[17] R.S.O. 1990, c. M.56.
[18] Section 266 of the *Education Act* applies only to "schools"; the *Municipal Freedom of Information and Protection of Privacy Act* applies to "institutions" which includes a "school board". Independent schools do not fall within either definition.

less, the principle of confidentiality embodied in section 266 of the *Education Act* reflects the common law principle that personal information usually is provided to an institution in circumstances of confidentiality and that the misuse of confidential information may be actionable. Canadian common law principles treat information as confidential where the information itself possesses the necessary quality of confidence about it, and the information was imparted in circumstances importing an obligation of confidence.[19]

Although the matter has not been subject to court comment, common sense suggests that most of the information provided by parents to an independent school about their children when applying for admission to a school, together with most of the information maintained by the school on a student in its records, likely possesses the "necessary quality of confidence about it, consisting as it does of personal information", and likely was imparted in circumstances importing an obligation of confidence. Although the *Municipal Freedom of Information and Protection of Privacy Act* does not apply to independent schools, the Act's definition of "personal information" provides some guidance about the type of information the common law likely would treat as confidential. The Act considers the following information to be personal information about an individual, and therefore confidential: information relating to the race, national or ethnic origin, colour, religion, age, sex, sexual orientation or family status of the individual; information relating to the education or medical history of the individual; the address, telephone number and blood type of the individual; and correspondence sent to a school by the individual that is implicitly or explicitly of a private or confidential nature as well as responses to that correspondence.

If an independent school intends to make public personal information about a student which is obtained during the application and registration process, this fact should be communicated clearly to parents in the school's literature. A common example involves the use of telephone numbers for school-related activities, such as the school's parent association, or grade telephone trees which are used in a variety of circumstances. To remove any confidentiality from the information, a school need simply include on its application materials a statement that the school intends to make available a student's telephone number to the parent association or for other school uses. Alternatively, a school's application form could provide parents with a negative option regarding telephone numbers — *i.e.*, unless they indicate in writing to the contrary, the school will be authorized to provide their telephone numbers to the parent association or other school organizations.

---

[19] *Coco v. A. N. Clark (Engineers) Ltd.*, [1969] R.P.C. 41 (Ch.) *per* Megarry J. at p. 47, quoted with approval by the Supreme Court of Canada in *Lac Minerals Ltd. v. International Corona Resources Ltd.* (1989), 61 D.L.R. (4th) 14, [1989] 2 S.C.R. 574 at p. 635.

An independent school should develop and implement a consistent policy regarding the confidentiality of students' records and access to them. Since the common law likely would regard most personal information about a student as cloaked with confidentiality, any exception to this principle should be spelled out clearly in a school's policy and communicated to parents. The provisions of the *Education Act* offer some guidance to an independent school in developing a policy about access to student records. A standard policy would permit the use of a student's record by the principal and teachers of the school for the improvement or instruction of the pupil.[20] As well, a parent should be entitled to examine the record of his or her child and, if the pupil is above the age of majority, the pupil should be entitled to examine his or her record.[21] The Act also provides some common sense exceptions to confidentiality which an independent school may wish to consider for its school records policy. For example, the Act does not prevent the principal from using a student record to assist in the preparation of a report for an application in respect of further education by the pupil, or an application for employment by the pupil where the pupil requests such a report.[22]

In the case of public and separate schools, the *Education Act* authorizes the local medical officer of health to obtain from a school principal a pupil's name, address, telephone number, birth date and the name, address and telephone number of the pupil's parent or guardian. While this provision of the *Education Act* does not apply to independent schools, it is worth noting that the *Immunization of School Pupils Act*[23] requires the person operating an independent school to notify the local medical officer of health of the names of any pupils transferring from its school.[24] An independent school's student record policy should indicate whether as a matter of course the school will provide personal information about a student at the request of the local medical health officer, or whether the school will first seek the consent of the parent before releasing the information.

Finally, a school's policy should indicate the extent of access which members of the school's board of directors may have to students' records. Since members of the board of directors usually are not directly involved in the education of the schools' students, there would be fewer circumstances necessitating their access to students' records compared to the need for the school's principals and teachers to look at students' records. Where a board of directors plays a review or appeal role in a school disciplinary process, there likely would be some need for members to obtain access to student records.

---

[20] *Education Act*, s. 266(2).
[21] Section 266(3).
[22] Section 266(6).
[23] R.S.O. 1990, c. I.1.
[24] Section 14(1).

DEFAMATORY STATEMENTS IN STUDENT RECORDS

A student's record inevitably will contain comments made by the school's staff and administration about the performance and conduct of the student. Some of the comments may reflect adversely on the student's ability or character. The common law regards as defamatory any statement made about a person which tends to lower the person's reputation in the eyes of others. Some defamatory statements may find their way into a school's student records. Given that the operation of any school requires an ability on the part of the school to monitor the student's performance, to communicate with parents regarding the performance and conduct of students, as well as to communicate such information to students, the law affords some protection to defamatory statements found in a school's student records. In the case of public and separate schools, the *Education Act* provides that no legal action shall be brought against any person in respect of the content of a student record.[25] Although this broad statutory protection does not extend to independent schools, the common law of defamation recognizes that a defence of qualified privilege or immunity, arises in circumstances where administrative officers and school staff make comments about a student's performance to parents, to the student or, indirectly, in the student records. Accordingly, there is a qualified privilege on the part of the school to record or communicate reasons why a student cannot continue at the school, why the grades on a report card were low, or to criticize the conduct of a student which deleteriously affects the well-being of other children. As long as the statements which are made are pertinent to the functioning of the educational institution, are made in the normal channels of communication and are not published with actual malice, then the school and its staff enjoy a qualified immunity from any legal action in respect of such statements.[26]

---

[25] *Education Act*, s. 266(8).
[26] For a full discussion, see Raymond E. Brown, *Law of Defamation*, 2nd ed. (Toronto: Carswell, 1994) at pp. 13-137 to 13-141 (March 1998, looseleaf).

9

Student Discipline

THE LEGAL SOURCE OF THE POWER TO DISCIPLINE

The legal power of independent schools to discipline, suspend or expel pupils, flows from a different source than that of public schools. Statute provides public schools with their disciplinary power. Section 265(a) of the *Education Act* imposes a duty on a principal to maintain proper order and discipline in a school, while section 23 of the *Education Act* vests in "principals" and "boards" the power to suspend or expel students. Section 23(3) of the Act establishes the procedure which a board must follow when expelling a student, a procedure which includes a hearing to which the parents of the pupil are parties. This statutory requirement for an expulsion hearing, in turn, invokes the procedures set out in the *Statutory Power Procedures Act*.[1]

Independent schools are not subject to the statutory procedures governing the suspension and expulsion of students contained in section 23 of the *Education Act*, nor do independent school principals fall within the definition of "principal" in section 265 of the Act. Instead, the source of independent schools' power to discipline, suspend or expel their students, rests in, and is subject to, the terms and conditions of the contract of instruction.[2] As already pointed out, the precise terms and conditions of the contract of instruction may be set out in a variety of documents, including the school's prospectus or catalogue, the student's application for enrolment, student handbook and other documents provided by the school to the student or his parents.[3] As long as these rules or regulations are known by, or brought to the attention of, the student or his parents at the time of entering into the contract of instruction,[4] or

---

[1] R.S.O. 1990, c. S.22.
[2] *Wisch v. Sanford School, Inc.*, 420 F. Supp. 1310 (1976) at p. 1315.
[3] *Corpus Juris Secondum*, Vol. 78A (St. Paul, Minn.: West Publishing Co., 1995) s. 815.
[4] *Ibid.*, s. 816.

at the start of the school year,[5] they form part of the contract of instruction. In order to bind a student and his parents any rules or regulations contained in a school catalogue, or other document, must be stated in terms sufficiently specific to convey to a reader their compulsory character.[6] A parent or student who has received the school's catalogue or rules will be taken to have read and understood them.[7] Terms of the contract of instruction also may be implied from the nature of the relationship.[8]

REASONABLENESS OF DISCIPLINARY RULES: IN LOCO PARENTIS

An independent school may adopt suitable rules and regulations for the governance and management of the school and its pupils, and the school may require, as a matter of contract, that these rules and regulations be obeyed by the pupils.[9] Indeed, it is an implied term of any contract of instruction that a student who enters a school will comply with its reasonable rules and regulations.[10] There is a dearth of Canadian jurisprudence on the permissible nature and scope of disciplinary rules which independent schools may adopt, United Kingdom and American cases however, provide some guidance. Rules and regulations regarding student discipline must be reasonable,[11] but the reasonableness of their content will vary according to the nature of the education offered by the independent school. For example, the rules of discipline applicable to an academic school will differ from those employed by a military-like academy.

Since the school stands *in loco parentis*, or in the position of the parent, the reasonableness of the rules will be measured in terms of rules which parents would formulate for their children. As put by one court:

> College authorities stand *in loco parentis* concerning the physical and moral welfare, and mental training of the pupils, and we are unable to see why, to that end, they may not make any rule or regulation for the government, or betterment of their pupils that a parent could for the same purpose. Whether the rules or regulations are wise or their aims worthy is a matter left solely to the discretion of the authorities or parents, as the case may be, and, in the exercise of that

---

[5] *Kentucky Military Institute v. Bramblet*, 164 S.W. 808 (Ky. Ct. App., 1914) at p. 809.
[6] *Miami Military Institute v. Leff*, 220 N.Y.S. 799 (1926) at p. 807.
[7] *Teeter v. Horner Military School*, 81 S.E. 76 (1914) at pp. 769 and 771; see also *Sutcliffe v. Acadia University (Governors)* (1978), 95 D.L.R. (3d) 95 (N.S.C.A.).
[8] *Wisch, supra,* footnote 2, at p. 1315.
[9] *Corpus Juris Secondum, op. cit.,* footnote 3, s. 816.
[10] *Teeter, supra,* footnote 7, at p. 770.
[11] *Miami Military Institute, supra,* footnote 6, at p. 804; *Fitzgerald v. Northcote* (1865), 4 F. & F. 656, 176 E.R. 735 at p. 750 (Q.B.).

discretion, the courts are not disposed to interfere, unless the rules and aims are unlawful or against public policy.[12]

Consequently a large degree of discretion must be allowed to the head, or principal, of an independent school to discipline students,[13] but a principal cannot act arbitrarily, maliciously, unfairly or from some improper purpose.[14]

The concept of *in loco parentis* was explained by another court in the following terms:[15]

> This concept in its educational context apparently originated as a means whereby a teacher or tutor might exercise the powers of restraint and correction over a minor which a parent could exercise without fear of criminal proceedings or civil action being brought against him by the parent. The matter was put thus by Doull, J., in *Murdock v. Richards et al.*, [1954] 1 D.L.R. 766 (N.S.S.C.), at p. 769:
>
>> "As to whether there was any cause of action at all, it may be useful to first consider the position of a teacher in charge of the pupils in a school. The statement in Salmond on Torts, 11th ed., p. 381, is, I think, accepted by both sides. It is as follows: 'When a father sends his child to school he delegates to the schoolmaster all his own authority, as far as is necessary for the welfare of the child, and a school master therefore is entitled to administer reasonable chastisement to the child.' And continuing and quoting from Lord Hewart C.J. in *R. v. Newport (Salop) Justices*, [1929] 2 K.B. 416 at p. 428: 'Any parent who sends a child to school is presumed to give to the teacher authority to make reasonable regulations and to administer to the child reasonable corporal punishment for breach of those regulations.'
>>
>> "The editor of the 11th edition of Salmond says in a note that Prosser gives a sounder reason for the rule than in the statement of Lord Hewart. Prosser on Torts, 1949, p.167, states the rule as follows: 'A parent or one who stands in a place of a parent, may use reasonable force, including corporal punishment, for discipline and control. A school teacher has the same authority. It is sometimes said that the parent, by sending the child to school, has delegated his discipline to the teacher; but since many children go to public schools under compulsion of law, and the child may well be punished over the objection of the parent, a sounder reason is the necessity for maintaining order in and about the school.'"

While the concept of *in loco parentis* has fallen into disfavour within sections of the education community, the Supreme Court of Canada recently reaffirmed the delegated nature of authority from parents to teachers.[16]

---

[12] *Gott v. Berea College*, 161 S.W. 204 (1913) at p. 206.
[13] *Fitzgerald, supra*, footnote 11, at p. 750.
[14] *Corpus Juris Secondum*, Vol. 78A (St. Paul, Minn.: West Publishing Co., 1995) s. 816; *Fitzgerald, supra*, footnote 11, at p. 750.
[15] *Sutcliffe, supra*, footnote 7, at pp. 99-100.
[16] *R. v. Audet* (1996), 135 D.L.R. (4th) 20, [1996] 2 S.C.R. 171.

PROCEDURAL FAIRNESS IN DISCIPLINE

A contract between a school and parents also gives rise to an implied contractual term that the school will adhere to the basic requirements of procedural fairness in disciplinary matters.[17] A recent Ontario case held that any contract of instruction with an independent school contains an implied term of procedural fairness as a condition precedent to the right of expulsion.[18] Subject to the requirements of procedural fairness, independent schools are afforded broad discretion in conducting their programs including decisions involving the discipline, suspension and expulsion of their students.[19]

Although the fairness of any disciplinary process must be determined in light of the particular circumstances of each school and the contract of instruction entered into with parents, the requirement of procedural fairness contains several necessary elements.[20] First, the school should clearly identify the types of conduct which will attract discipline and specify the disciplinary action which may result from an infraction of the rules.[21] The rules of discipline and the steps in the discipline process should be set out in a code of behaviour, or book of rules and regulations, so that both the parents and the students are aware of the standard of conduct expected by the school.[22] When a student commits a serious infraction, the school should promptly confront the student and his parents with a description of the infraction.[23]

Where a school moves to expel a student for his conduct, the school should provide the student and his parents with an opportunity to explain the student's conduct or counter the allegation,[24] and afford the parents an opportunity to be heard on the merits of the expulsion.[25] This would include the opportunity to present proof and arguments in support of the student's position,[26]

---

[17] *Wisch v. Sanford School, Inc.*, 420 F. Supp. 1310 (1976) at p. 1315.
[18] *D. (C.) (Litigation Guardian of) v. Ridley College* (1996), 140 D.L.R. (4th) 696 at p. 708, 44 Admin. L.R. (2d) 108 (Ont. Ct. (Gen. Div.)).
[19] *Hutcheson v. Grace Lutheran School*, 517 N.Y.S.2d 760 (1987) at p. 761.
[20] For a description of the general principles of procedural fairness see *Lakeside Colony of Hutterian Brethern v. Hofer* (1992), 97 D.L.R. (4th) 17 at pp. 36-7, [1992] 3 S.C.R. 165.
[21] *Wisch, supra*, footnote 17, at p. 1316.
[22] *Hutcheson, supra*, footnote 19, at p. 762; *Wisch, supra*, footnote 17, at p. 1316 where the court noted that the existence of a promulgated code of disciplinary rules would greatly facilitate a court's evaluation of the fairness of the school's conduct, but the absence of a written code "does not *ipso facto* require a conclusion that the procedures followed in this case were unfair".
[23] *Wisch, supra*, footnote 17, at p. 1316; *Ridley College, supra*, footnote 18, at p. 705.
[24] *Wisch, supra*, footnote 17, at p. 1316.
[25] *Burke v. Yeshiva Beit Yitzchak of Hamilton* (1996), 90 O.A.C. 81 (Div. Ct.) at p. 82.
[26] David J. Mullan, *Administrative Law*, 3rd ed. (Toronto: Carswell, 1996) at §168.

although some flexibility exists under the common law in the scope of the requirement to be given an opportunity to make representations.[27]

More difficult are the questions of legal representation and the ability to cross-examine during the expulsion process. While in a recent case an Ontario court found that the parents and student, or their legal representative, should have been permitted the opportunity to test the evidence of the accusing students by means of cross-examination during an expulsion hearing at an independent school,[28] at common law there does not exist a universal right to legal representation at hearings[29] or to cross-examine witnesses.[30] While the procedures for expelling students from public and separate schools (subject as they are to the *Statutory Powers Procedures Act*[31]) permit the student to be represented by counsel[32] and to conduct cross-examinations reasonably required,[33] as noted above, those provisions of the *Education Act* do not apply to independent schools.

The requirement of an unbiased tribunal is also one of the central requirements of natural justice. The structure of an independent school, particularly the central role played by the principal, often may result in the principal having had some previous contact with the student or issue in question.[34] A school therefore should develop a disciplinary process which ensures that the person making the allegations against the student is not acting as a decision-maker in the case.[35] Where a teacher or student makes the allegation, the principal can make the disciplinary decision; but where the principal makes the allegation, the school's board of directors, or a committee of the board, should consider the allegation and make the decision about expulsion.

Two recent Ontario cases illustrate pit-falls which may confront independent schools which do not develop suspension and expulsion policies which incorporate the rules of procedural fairness. In the first case, *Burke v. Yeshiva Beit Yitzchak of Hamilton*,[36] an independent school in Hamilton expelled a student for absenteeism, insubordination and non-observance of the decorum man-

---

[27] *Lakeside Colony of Hutterian Brethern, supra*, footnote 20, at p. 37.
[28] *Ridley College, supra*, footnote 18, at pp. 708-9.
[29] *Administrative Law, op. cit.*, footnote 26, at §128; *Irvine v. Restrictive Trade Practices Commission* (1987), 41 D.L.R. (4th) 429, [1987] 1 S.C.R. 181 at p. 231.
[30] *Administrative Law, op. cit.*, footnote 26, at §153.
[31] See also Anthony F. Brown, *Legal Handbook for School Administrators*, 3rd ed. (Toronto: Carswell, 1995) at p. 43.
[32] *Statutory Powers Procedure Act*, s. 10.
[33] Section 10.1.
[34] As to the problems this creates, see *Lakeside Colony of Hutterian Brethern v. Hofer* (1992), 97 D.L.R. (4th) 17 at p. 37, [1992] 3 S.C.R. 165.
[35] 46 C.E.D. (Ont. 3rd), "Associations".
[36] (1996), 90 O.A.C. 81 (Div. Ct.). These cases are examined in detail in David Brown, "Are Private Schools Really Private? Judicial Review of Discipline Decisions in Private Schools" (1998), 8 E.L.J. 453.

dated by the school's rules. Although the reported judicial decision recites few facts about the expulsion process undertaken by the school, the court set aside the expulsion because the school had failed to give the student's parents sufficient details of the grounds for his expulsion, nor did the school give the parents an opportunity to be heard before their child was expelled. The court ordered the school to allow the student to complete his current academic year, with the school to make reasonable efforts to accommodate the student, and the student to make reasonable efforts, with the assistance of his parents, to comply with disciplinary and academic requirements of the school.[37]

In the second case, *D. (C.) (Litigation Guardian of) v. Ridley College*,[38] two grade 9 students alleged that a grade 11 student had supplied them with marijuana on a school trip to Quebec City. A department head initially questioned the grade 11 student about the allegations, and the student denied them. The following day, the residence head asked the student to be present that afternoon at the library for a meeting. When the student arrived at the library, the residence head told him to "stick around" because a meeting was going on in an adjacent room. Some time later the residence head came out of the meeting, spoke to the student, and advised him that two grade 9 boys had gone before a committee to state that they had purchased marijuana from him. When asked whether he wanted to go before the committee himself, or have the residence head relay his views to the committee, the student opted for the latter and denied any involvement in the matter. Unknown to the student, the meeting was one of the school's full discipline committee. That evening, the residence head telephoned the student's father to advise him that the student "had either advertently or inadvertently been linked to a two way supply chain of marijuana . . . that the matter could be serious or may not be". The father was told that there would be a discipline committee meeting and the father would be kept informed.

Two days later, the student was awakened by the residence head early in the morning and told to go the head master's office. The head master accused the student of being a "drug pusher" and stated that there was no place for him at the school. The head master then announced in Chapel to the assembled Ridley College student body that the student was a drug pusher. At 8:15 a.m. that morning, the residence head telephoned the father to advise him that the student had been expelled and that the child had to leave Ridley College immediately.

On an application by the parents to the court, the court found that the school's expulsion process was not fair. Ridley College should not have held an expulsion hearing without giving notice to one of the parents, and the parents, or their legal representative should have been permitted the opportunity to

---

[37] *Supra*, at p. 82.
[38] (1996), 140 D.L.R. (4th) 696, 44 Admin. L.R. (2d) 108 (Ont. Ct. (Gen. Div.)).

test the word of the accusers by means of cross-examination. The court ordered Ridley College to readmit the student to complete his grade 11 studies and to provide all academic instruction, testing and examinations that he had lost as a result of his expulsion. The court also ordered the school to provide the student's parents with all notes, records and documents in their possession relating to the allegations made against the student, the disciplinary proceedings taken and the decision to expel the student.[39]

Where a student's conduct results in both criminal charges and disciplinary proceedings, a school may proceed with an expulsion hearing before the courts dispose of the criminal charges. Although the provisions of the *Young Offenders Act*[40] placing a publication ban on any information relating to any offence or proceeding which might identify the young offender initially led some courts to question whether a school could hold an expulsion hearing while the charges were pending, recent case law has clarified that an expulsion hearing does not constitute the publication of a report of an offence in contravention of the *Young Offenders Act*.[41] However, any school conducting an expulsion hearing in such circumstances should ensure that the hearing is held in private.

REMEDY FOR BREACH OF THE PRINCIPLES OF FAIRNESS

In light of the contractual basis for the application of the rules of fairness in independent school disciplinary matters, any remedy for their breach should be by way of an action for breach of contract,[42] seeking, if required, interlocutory and permanent injunctive relief, declarations and damages.[43]

---

[39] *Supra*, at pp. 708-9 D.L.R.
[40] R.S.C. 1985, c. Y-1, s. 38.
[41] *G. (F.) v. Scarborough Board of Education* (1994), 68 O.A.C. 308 (Div. Ct.). See also the detailed discussion in Eric M. Roher, *An Educator's Guide to Violence in Schools* (Aurora: Aurora Professional Press, 1997) at pp. 95-8.
[42] Two decisions of Ontario courts, *Burke*, *supra*, footnote 36, and *Ridley College*, *supra*, footnote 39, granted relief by way of judicial review of private schools' decisions to expel students. While the courts probably reached the right decision, they did so for the wrong reasons. The remedy of judicial review should not be against a private school; instead any claim for procedural unfairness should be brought by action for breach of contract.
[43] *Parks (Guardian ad Litem of) v. B.C. School Sports* (1997), 145 D.L.R. (4th) 174 (S.C.) at para. 4.

SEARCH AND SEIZURE

Section 8 of the *Canadian Charter of Rights and Freedoms* provides that: "Everyone has the right to be secure against unreasonable search or seizure". While this section has spawned some litigation over the power of public school principals to conduct searches of students or their lockers, the requirements of the Charter do not apply to independent schools since they are not a part of "government", a precondition to the application of the Charter. Nevertheless, it should be noted that in the public school context, courts have upheld the power of a principal to search a pupil where the principal had a "reasonable suspicion" that the student had violated the law and the school's code of conduct.[44]

To avoid any legal problems which may arise from conducting searches, an independent school should take two precautionary steps. First, the school's contract of instruction should clearly state that the school reserves the power to search students, lockers and desks, thereby negating any argument that the student enjoyed some expectation of privacy. Second, the school's policy manual should address directly the issue of searches, limiting the power to search to the principal or his delegate and stipulating that the scope of any search must be reasonable to the particular circumstances giving rise to the search.

USE OF REASONABLE FORCE FOR CORRECTIVE PURPOSES

Although corporal punishment plays a much reduced role in most Canadian schools, circumstances may still arise where physical contact takes place between a teacher and a student in a disciplinary context. Under Canadian criminal law, a person commits an assault when, without the consent of another person, he applies force intentionally to that person, directly or indirectly.[45] The *Criminal Code* provides a defence to a charge of assault for school teachers and parents. Section 43 of the *Criminal Code* provides:

> 43. Every schoolteacher, parent or person standing in the place of a parent is justified in using force by way of correction toward a pupil or child, as the case may be, who is under his care, if the force does not exceed what is reasonable under the circumstances.

This section authorizes the use of force only where it is by way of correction — *i.e.*, for the benefit or the education of the child. Where a child is incapable of appreciating correction, as when the child is mentally retarded, this section

---

[44] *R. v. G. (J.M.)* (1986), 33 D.L.R. (4th) 277, 56 O.R. (2d) 705 (C.A.), leave to appeal to S.C.C. refused 59 O.R. (2d) 286*n*, 21 O.A.C. 239*n*.
[45] *Criminal Code*, R.S.C. 1985, c. C-46, s. 265(1)(a).

does not justify the use of force by a school teacher.[46] In determining whether the force used exceeds what is reasonable under the circumstances, a court will consider such matters as the nature of the offence calling for correction, the age and character of the child, the likely effect of the punishment on the child, the degree of gravity of the punishment, the circumstances under which it was inflicted, and the injuries, if any, suffered.[47] A court will look to the customs of contemporary Canadian society in determining whether the force used was reasonable under the circumstances.[48] One judge has commented that the word "reasonable" in this section of the *Criminal Code* means moderate, or not excessive, and that whether punishment is or is not excessive should depend solely upon the age and physical condition of the child.[49]

Two recent cases illustrate the application of section 43 of the *Criminal Code*. In the first, a student with a history of violence began to act in a physically violent way. The teacher put him into a wrist restraint and forced the student to sit down at a desk by applying a downward push. Both the student and the teacher fell to the floor, whereupon the teacher again applied a wrist restraint to control the screaming, swearing, thrashing, pushing and kicking student. The student suffered a broken wrist and the teacher was charged with assault. The teacher was acquitted, invoking section 43 of the *Criminal Code* as a defence. The court concluded that given the nature of the child and his history, the degree of force used by the teacher in the circumstances was reasonable.[50]

In the other case, a teacher was charged with several counts of assault against her students. The counts related to pulling and grabbing a student by his shirt, hitting a student on the top of the head with her hand and on the leg with a classroom pointer, pinching and hitting his nose on two occasions, hitting another student on the face with her hand, shaking a student's head with her hands, and slapping another student on the face, pulling his hair and pushing him into the classroom. In each case the punishment related to minor misbehaviour. The court dismissed the charge relating to the pulling and grabbing a student's shirt as *de minimus*, as well as the charge involving shaking the student's head while he was talking in class and hitting the desk with her ruler.

---

[46] *R. v. Ogg-Moss* (1984), 11 D.L.R. (4th) 549, [1984] 2 S.C.R. 173.
[47] *R. v. Dupperon* (1984), 16 C.C.C. (3d) 453, [1985] 2 W.W.R. 369 (Sask. C.A.).
[48] *R. v. Baptiste* (1980), 61 C.C.C. (2d) 438 (Ont. Prov. Ct.).
[49] *R. v. Halcrow* (1993), 80 C.C.C. (3d) 320 at p. 333, 40 W.A.C. 197 (B.C.C.A.), affd [1995] 1 S.C.R. 440, 95 C.C.C. (3d) 94.
[50] *R. v. Collins* (1986), 192 A.R. 71 (Prov. Ct.) as reported in The *Education Law Reporter*, Vol. 8, No. 6, Feb. 1997, at p. 42. See also: *R. v. Cyr* (1991), 138 N.B.R. (2d) 252 (Q.B.). — teacher used a headlock to remove abusive child from class; *R. v. Plourde* (1993), 140 N.B.R. (2d) 273 (Prov. Ct.) — teacher physically removing student from class; *R. v. Godin* (1996), 172 N.B.R. (2d) 375 (Q.B.) — teacher using force to stop students from fighting.

The court dismissed as reasonable force by way of correction the counts where the teacher had slapped the student on the head which hurt for a few seconds with no residual bump or sore, pulled the student's nose, hit the student's nose with a book and slapped the face for talking while going down the stairs. In the instance where the teacher slapped the student on the face after the student angrily threw a baseball bat down on the ground near the teacher, the court dismissed the charge as a reflex response by the startled teacher who lacked the intent to use unreasonable force. However, the teacher was convicted of assault where she had slapped the student, pulled his hair and pushed him into the classroom, causing him to cry, because he had run down the stairs to get into line outside of the classroom. The court found that the teacher had "lost it", and acted impulsively and not for the purpose of correcting a student's behaviour.[51]

If a school permits the use of corporal punishment, its policy should clearly indicate the circumstances when teachers may use reasonable force for corrective purposes and the school should instruct its teachers on the limits of the policy.

RESTRICTING ACCESS TO SCHOOL PREMISES

In some cases a school may encounter problems with expelled students who return to the school's premises without permission. The school can resort in these circumstances to the *Trespass to Property Act*,[52] which makes it an offence for a person to enter premises when entry is prohibited or to remain on premises after being directed to leave.

---

[51] *R. v. Ocampo* (1997), 36 W.C.B. (2d) 479 (Ont. Ct. (Prov. Div.)) as reported in *Education Law Reporter*, Vol. 9, No. 7, March, 1998 at pp. 49-50. See also *R. v. Whalen* (1994), 118 Nfld. & P.E.I.R. 331 (Nfld. Prov. Ct.).
[52] R.S.O. 1990, c. T.21, s. 2.

10

Liability for Student Injuries

GENERAL PRINCIPLES OF NEGLIGENCE

Independent schools owe a duty of care to protect their students, employees and visitors from reasonably foreseeable risks of harm. The law of negligence governs the potential liability of a school for the acts or omissions of its staff which result in injury to another person. As a matter of law, if a person is negligent and causes harm to another, then that person will be liable for any foreseeable damages suffered by the other caused by the negligence. The principles of negligence usually are considered by asking the following questions:

1. Does the defendant owe a duty of care to the plaintiff?
2. Did the defendant breach this duty of care by acting, or failing to act, in accordance with the required standard of care?
3. Did the defendant's breach cause the plaintiff's injury and loss?

Duty of Care

Under Canadian common law, every person owes a duty to take reasonable care to avoid acts or omissions which one can reasonably foresee would be likely to injure one's "neighbour". In law one's "neighbour" is any person who is so closely and directly affected by one's act that one ought reasonably to have him in contemplation as being so affected when one directs one's mind to the acts or omissions which are called in question.[1] The law has long imposed on schools a duty of care to ensure the safety and well being of students placed in their care.

Whether a duty of care arises in any particular circumstance generally falls to be decided by the common law, or judge-made law, on a case-by-case basis. Statutes may provide some guidance as to whether a duty of care exists. For example, the *Education Act* contains several provisions which impose on

---

[1] *Donoghue v. Stevenson*, [1932] A.C. 562 (H.L.) at p. 580.

146   An Educator's Guide to Independent Schools

school boards, principals and teachers, a duty of care to ensure their pupils' safety. Although these specific provisions do not apply as a matter of statutory interpretation to independent schools, there can be no doubt that the general principles which they express would be followed by any court called on to consider the conduct of an independent school or its staff. Section 170 of the *Education Act* provides:

> 170(1) Every board shall,
>
> . . . . .
>
> 8. keep the school buildings and premises in proper repair and in a proper sanitary condition, provide suitable furniture and equipment and keep it in proper repair, and protect the property of the board;
> 9. make provision for insuring adequately the buildings and equipment of the board and for insuring the board and its employees and volunteers who are assigned duties by the principal against claims in respect of accidents incurred by pupils while under the jurisdiction or supervision of the board;

Section 265 of the *Education Act* requires the principal of a public school:

> 265(a) to maintain proper order and discipline in the school;
>
> . . . . .
>
> (j) to give assiduous attention to the health and comfort of the pupils, to the cleanliness, temperature and ventilation of the school, to the care of all teaching materials and other school property, and to the condition and appearance of the school buildings and grounds;

In the case of teachers, section 264(1) of the *Education Act* requires them "to maintain, under the direction of the principal, proper order and discipline in the teacher's classroom and while on duty in the school and on the school ground".[2] Regulations under the *Education Act* require a teacher to be responsible for the management of the classes assigned to the teacher, to carry out the supervisory duties assigned to the teacher by the principal, to ensure that all reasonable safety procedures are carried out in courses and activities for which the teacher is responsible, and to co-operate with the principal and other teachers to establish and maintain consistent disciplinary practices in the school.[3]

Although the breach of any of these statutory requirements does not automatically result in a finding of negligence, since all three of the elements of negligence must be established in order to make a finding of liability, a court likely would be closely guided by these statutory provisions in determining whether a duty of care arose in specific circumstances.

While these provisions of the *Education Act* do not apply as a matter of interpretation to independent schools, the provisions of the *Occupiers' Liability*

---

[2] R.S.O. 1990, c. E.2, s. 264(1)(e).
[3] Operation of Schools — General, R.R.O. 1990, Reg. 298, s. 20(a), (b), (g), and (h).

Act[4] do bind independent schools and create a statutory duty of care. The *Occupiers' Liability Act* provides that any occupier of premises owes a duty to take such care "as in all the circumstances of the case is reasonable to see that persons entering on the premises, and the property brought on the premises by those persons are reasonably safe while on the premises".[5] As a result, any independent school must ensure that anyone who enters onto the school premises — student, parent, teacher or visitor — is reasonably safe while on the premises and the school must take reasonable steps to eliminate any dangers to the safety of a person which may be caused either by the condition of the premises or by an activity carried out on the premises.[6]

Standard of Care: The Careful or Prudent Parent

Whenever a plaintiff alleges that a defendant has been negligent, a court must determine whether the defendant's conduct met the required legal standard of care in the particular case. The legal standard of care owed by schools, principals and teachers toward their pupils has been expressed as that of a "careful or prudent parent". The classic formulation of the standard of care for teachers was made in 1893 by the English Court of Appeal in the case of *Williams v. Eady*,[7] where the court stated:

> The school master was bound to take such care of his boys as a careful father would take of his boys, and there could not be a better definition of the duty of a school master. Then he was bound to take notice of the ordinary nature of young boys, their tendency to do mischievous acts, and the propensity to meddle with anything that came in their way.

The Supreme Court of Canada applied the standard of care of a prudent parent in its 1981 decision in *Myers v. Peel County Board of Education.*[8] The Supreme Court of Canada stated:

> The standard of care to be exercised by school authorities in providing for the supervision and protection of students for whom they are responsible is that of the careful or prudent parent, described in *Williams v. Eady* . . . It has, no doubt, become somewhat qualified in modern times because of the greater variety of activities conducted in schools, with probably larger groups of students using more complicated and more dangerous equipment than formerly . . . but with the qualification expressed in the *McKay* case and noted by Carrothers J.A. in *Thornton supra*, it remains the appropriate standard for such cases. It is not, however, a standard which can be applied in the same manner and to the same extent in every case. *Its application will vary from case to case and will depend upon the number of students being supervised at any given time, the nature of the exercise*

---

[4] R.S.O. 1990, c. O.2.
[5] Section 3(1).
[6] Section 3(2).
[7] (1893), 10 T.L.R. 41 (C.A.) at p. 42.
[8] (1981), 123 D.L.R. (3d) 1, [1981] 2 S.C.R. 21.

or activity in progress, the age and the degree of skill and training which the students may have received in connection with such activity, the nature and condition of the equipment in use at the time, the competency and capacity of the students involved, and a host of other matters which may be widely varied but which, in a given case, may affect the application of the prudent-parent standard to the conduct of the school authority in the circumstances.[9]

The highlighted passage in the *Myers* decision points out the variety of factors which any court must take into account in ascertaining whether the required standard of care was or was not met in particular circumstances. While the standard of the "careful and prudent parent" has been the subject of some debate, it remains the standard applied by the courts in negligence actions brought against schools and their teachers.[10] Recognizing that in a school context a teacher normally takes care of a larger number of children than does a parent, the "careful and prudent parent" standard of care allows "for the larger-than-family size" of many classrooms or activities in a school.[11]

Physical Education Classes

Canadian courts frequently have been faced with claims of negligence arising from injuries suffered by students during physical education classes, in particular gymnastic classes. Since many physical education activities involve an element of inherent danger, the courts have tended to impose a higher standard of care on teachers supervising such activities. For example, in the *Thornton* case, a 15-year-old pupil was seriously injured in a gymnastic class when he jumped off a vaulting box onto a spring board and attempted an aerial somersault. The student overshot the landing pit and landed on his head on a fitter mat on the periphery of the pit. In commenting on the standard of care applicable to gymnastic classes, the British Columbia Court of Appeal stated that students may be permitted to participate in gymnastic activities provided that the following criteria of the standard of care are adhered to:

(a) the activity must be suitable to the pupil's age and mental and physical condition;

(b) the pupil must be progressively trained and coached to do the activity properly and avoid the danger;

---

[9] *Supra*, at p. 10 (emphasis added) referring to *McKay and Govan School Unit No. 29 (Re)* (1968), 68 D.L.R. (2d) 519, [1968] S.C.R. 589 and *Thornton v. School District No. 57* (1975), 57 D.L.R. (3d) 438, [1975] 3 W.W.R. 622 (B.C.S.C.), vard on other grounds 73 D.L.R. (3d) 35, [1976] 5 W.W.R. 240 (C.A.), vard on other grounds 83 D.L.R. (3d) 480, [1978] 2 S.C.R. 267. *Myers* was followed recently by the Ontario Court of Appeal in *Thomas v. Hamilton (City) Board of Education* (1994), 20 O.R. (3d) 598, 85 O.A.C. 161 at p. 168.

[10] For a discussion of the debate see Eric Roher, *An Educator's Guide to Violence in Schools* (Aurora: Aurora Professional Press, 1997) at pp. 31-2.

[11] *Thornton, supra*, footnote 9, 73 D.L.R., at p. 57.

(c) the equipment must be adequate and suitably arranged; and
(d) the performance of the activity must be properly supervised.[12]

Chemistry Classes and Industrial Arts

Many chemistry experiments are inherently dangerous and accordingly require that teachers properly instruct, caution and supervise students as well as ensure that they wear proper protective devices.[13] The same strict duty of care applies when students operate dangerous machinery.[14]

Sports

While the inherent danger of any activity imposes greater demands on the part of the school, a school is not negligent simply by allowing students to participate in dangerous activities or activities involving some risk.[15] Football, for example, is an inherently dangerous sport and is known by parents to be such.[16] A school should ensure that a parent consents to his child participating in a dangerous sport such as football, and to that end should require parents to sign participation consent forms and to obtain medical certificates stating that the students are fit to participate. A signed parental consent serves as evidence that the parent was aware of the risks involved in the activity and was afforded the opportunity to refuse permission for his child to participate.

Where an activity involves a risk of danger not generally known by parents, a consent to participation may not be sufficient to absolve a school from liability. As stated by the Ontario Court of Justice:

> The consent in itself does not absolve the Board because if the Board knew of, or had reason to believe that there were dangers involved that a reasonable parent would not know, or that if [the student] was the subject of a particular risk, then

---

[12] For a good summary of this case see Anthony Brown and Marvin Zuker, *Education Law* (Toronto: Carswell, 1994) at pp. 60-61. Liability for negligence has also been found where: the method of holding gym mats together was dangerous (*Piszel v. Etobicoke (Board of Education)* (1977), 77 D.L.R. (3d) 52, 16 O.R. (2d) 22 (C.A.)); a 7 foot jump was not properly supervised (*Boese v. St. Paul's Roman Catholic Separate School District No. 20* (1979), 97 D.L.R. (3d) 643 (Sask. Q.B.)); a gymnastic springboard was put to an inherently dangerous use (*Thornton, supra*, footnote 9).

[13] *James v. River East School Division No. 9* (1975), 58 D.L.R. (3d) 311, [1975] 5 W.W.R. 135 (Man. Q.B.), affd 64 D.L.R. (3d) 338, [1976] 2 W.W.R. 577 (C.A.).

[14] *Dziwenka v. Alberta* (1971), 25 D.L.R. (3d) 12, [1972] S.C.R. 419; *Hoar v. Board of School Trustees, District No. 68*, [1984] 6 W.W.R. 143 (B.C.C.A.).

[15] *Murray v. Belleville (City) Board of Education*, [1943] 1 D.L.R. 494, [1943] O.W.N. 44 (H.C.J.); *Hall v. Thompson*, [1952] 4 D.L.R. 139, [1952] O.W.N. 133 (H.C.J.), affd [1952] 4 D.L.R. 139 at p. 142, [1952] O.W.N. 478 (C.A.); *Gard v. Duncan Board of School Trustees*, [1946] 2 D.L.R. 441, [1946] 1 W.W.R. 305 (B.C.C.A.).

[16] *Thomas v. Hamilton (City) Board of Education* (1990), 19 A.C.W.S. (3d) 602 (H.C.J.), vard 20 O.R. (3d) 598, 85 O.A.C. 161 (C.A.).

as a prudent and careful parent itself it should not have permitted him to participate in the sport.[17]

Lack of Supervision

Whether the absence of supervision by a teacher constitutes conduct falling below the required standard of care will depend upon all of the circumstances. Courts recognize that teachers cannot be at all places at all times. As a general rule, the absence of supervision by a teacher becomes a relevant part of the negligence inquiry where it can be shown that the presence of the teacher might have prevented the accident.[18]

After-Hours and Extra-Curricular Activities

The potential liability of a school is not limited to activities which take place on school premises during school hours. The school continues to owe a duty of care to its students during field trips off school premises and during extra-curricular activities on school premises after normal hours. The "careful and prudent parent" standard of care would apply in these circumstances.[19]

Cases may arise where a student remains on school property after school hours and does not engage in a school-related activity. For example, a parent may drop off a child early in the morning before the school opens, or pick up the child late in the afternoon after the school has closed. A school must clearly communicate to parents the opening and closing times of the school. It is not reasonable for parents to assume that a school will provide supervision to a child after the designated school hours. Nonetheless, even after school hours, the school owes a general duty of care to any person who comes on to school premises. As mentioned above, the *Occupiers' Liability Act* would require a school to ensure that any person entering school premises is reasonably safe while on the premises.[20] Schools owe an obligation to their younger students to avoid sending them into situations of danger off school property. Thus, if a child is stranded at school due to an emergency, or must unexpectedly go home early, the school must make appropriate arrangements in the circumstances to ensure that the young child will travel safely home.[21]

---

[17] *Supra*, at p. 15 of judgment.
[18] Brown and Zuker, *op. cit.*, footnote 12, at pp. 62-4; *Mainville v. Ottawa Board of Education* (1990), 75 O.R. (2d) 315 (Dist. Ct.) — snowball fight; *Hentze (Guardian ad Litem of) v. Board of School Trustees District No. 72* (1994), 80 W.A.C. 241 (B.C.C.A.) — schoolyard rough housing not properly supervised.
[19] *Moddejonge v. Huron County Board of Education* (1972), 25 D.L.R. (3d) 661, [1972] 2 O.R. 437 (H.C.J.).
[20] Brown and Zuker, *op. cit.*, footnote 12, at p. 71.
[21] *Ibid.*, at pp. 71-2.

A school must also ensure that the drop-off and pick-up zones for children are located in safe areas and, depending upon the age of the students, properly supervised.[22]

Transportation of Pupils

Where a school provides transportation to and from school for its students, or transportation on school trips, the school owes a duty of care to the students to ensure that they travel safely.[23] Where a school owns the vehicles which provide the transportation, the school assumes full responsibility of ensuring the safety of the vehicles and the competence of the drivers of the vehicles. Where a school contracts out its transportation requirements to an independent transportation company, the legal problems may become more complex. A school may not be responsible for the negligence of an independent contractor hired to transport students.[24] To the extent that the school insists that the transportation company follow specific school policies and procedures, the school will be viewed as controlling the activities of the transportation company. Yet even at the other end of the spectrum, where the school simply hires an independent contractor to transport its students, a school may not escape liability in the event of an accident. At a minimum, a school must make appropriate inquiries to ensure that any transportation company which it hires can provide service in a safe and competent manner.[25]

Causation

Even where a plaintiff can show that a school owed him a duty of care and fell below the required standard of care, the plaintiff must still demonstrate that the school's breach of the standard of care caused the plaintiff's injuries. Courts often refer to this requirement of causation as the "but for" test: but for the negligence of the school or its teacher, the injury to the student would not have occurred. If this "but for" test is met, then the plaintiff has established a sufficient causal relationship between the school's conduct and his injuries to find the school liable in negligence. Some courts have added a gloss to the "but for" test, concluding that it is sufficient for a plaintiff to show that the negligent act *contributed* to the injury.

Even where a plaintiff can establish this direct causal link, the plaintiff must still satisfy the courts that the defendant's conduct was the "proximate cause" of the injury. The requirement of proximate cause is a form of judicial

---

[22] *Germschied v. Richardson* (1987), 7 A.C.W.S. (3d) 162 (B.C.S.C.).
[23] *Mattinson v. Wonnacott* (1975), 59 D.L.R. (3d) 18, 8 O.R. (2d) 654 (H.C.J.).
[24] *Baldwin v. Erin District High School Board* (1961), 29 D.L.R. (2d) 290, [1961] O.R. 687 (C.A.).
[25] For a more detailed discussion and references to several helpful cases see Anthony Brown and Marvin Zuker, *Education Law* (Toronto: Carswell, 1994) at pp. 69-70.

safety valve which prevents defendants from being held liable for injuries which are too remote, or beyond the horizon of reasonable foreseeability, and the requirement circumscribes potential liability to circumstances which are predictable or reasonably foreseeable. An illustration of the operation of the proximate cause requirement was a case in which an outdoor education instructor permitted a small number of students to go swimming in a reservoir, one of whom was a non-swimmer. Although the instructor told the students that there was a drop-off under the water and instructed them not to go beyond that point, the drop-off line was irregular and not indicated by buoys. A breeze pushed the non-swimmer beyond the drop-off line and another student drowned coming to his rescue. The court found the instructor liable for the death of the student who came to his fellow student's rescue as this was a foreseeable response to the emergency which had been created through the instructor's negligence.[26]

LIABILITY OF A SCHOOL FOR NEGLIGENT ACTS OF ITS TEACHERS

The principle of "vicarious liability" makes a school legally responsible for the acts of its employees which are done in the course of their employment. If a teacher is negligent, he or she is personally liable in damages to the injured student; if the teacher's negligent act occurred during the normal course of a teacher's employment with the school, then the school will be vicariously liable for the teacher's negligence.[27] While an injured student may sue both the teacher and the school for damages for the injuries caused, in practice it is usually the school, with access to greater financial resources, which becomes the primary defendant in a lawsuit.

It should come as no surprise that courts consider a broad range of activities to fall within the "normal course of employment" of a teacher. As long as a teacher was engaged in conduct related to his duties as a teacher, a court most likely will find that the teacher was acting in the normal course of employment and the school will be vicariously liable for the teacher's negligence. There may be instances, however, where a teacher involves pupils in activities which have nothing to do with the school or authorized extra-curricular activities and, in such cases, the teachers may be held personally liable for any injury incurred by the pupils and the school may escape vicarious liability.[28]

In order to minimize the risk of negligence claims, a school should take several basic precautions. First, a school should ensure that teachers are ade-

---

[26] *Moddejonge v. Huron County Board of Education, supra,* footnote 19.
[27] *Beauparlant v. Appleby Separate School Board,* [1955] 4 D.L.R. 558, [1955] O.W.N. 286 (H.C.J.).
[28] *Supra.*

quately screened in the hiring process to ensure that they are competent, qualified and capable of properly supervising their students. Further, the school should develop a clear and consistent supervisory policy for students which is clearly communicated to its staff and monitored by the school principal. Finally, a school should include as part of its periodic review of teachers' performance the ability of teachers to properly supervise their students and their adherence to the school's supervisory policies.

THE LEGAL EFFECT OF CONSENT FORMS AND RELEASES

A school should ensure that it obtains a written consent from a student's parents or guardian permitting the student to participate in unusual or inherently dangerous activities on school premises, or in activities which take place off school premises. The consent form should clearly describe the activity for which the parent's consent is sought in order to secure the parent's informed, voluntary consent to his or her child's participation in the specified activity. In order to ensure that written consents are obtained for all unusual, dangerous or off-school activities, the school should develop a written policy requiring its teachers to use a standard form of consent tailored to the specific circumstances. A school should seek legal advice when drafting parental consent forms.

A consent form will not automatically relieve the school, or its teachers, from liability in the event that a child suffers an injury in the course of an activity,[29] but it will enable a school to argue that the parent was aware of the risks normally inherent in the specified activity and agreed to the participation of his or her child in the activity. In this sense, a written consent serves as an additional piece of evidence demonstrating that a school, and its teachers, met the required standard of care.

A consent form differs significantly from a release or waiver of liability signed by a parent. Often, consent forms for field trips or other activities will include language whereby the parent releases, or excuses, the school and its teachers from any liability for an injury which might be caused to his child during the activity. Schools must appreciate that these releases or waivers have little, if any, legal effect. As a general principle of law, a parent cannot waive a child's legal right to sue for negligence. Consequently, even where a parent has signed a waiver of liability, if a child is injured in the school activity, the child may still bring an action against the school and its teachers for negligence.

---

[29] *Thomas v. Hamilton (City) Board of Education* (1994), 20 O.R. (3d) 598, 85 O.A.C. 161 at pp. 177-8 (C.A.).

CONTRIBUTORY NEGLIGENCE

In any lawsuit against a school for negligence, it is open to the school to assert that the student contributed to his or her own injuries. Every person has a duty to act with reasonable care for his own safety, and students are no exception to that rule. Where a court finds that a student contributed to his or her own injuries, a school will not escape liability, but the court will apportion responsibility between the school and the student.

There are many cases where students have been found contributorily negligent for injuries they suffered at school.[30] Whether a student's conduct constitutes contributory negligence depends upon a variety of considerations: the age of the student, whether the student ignored warnings and whether the student should have realized that he or she was not sufficiently trained, fit or knowledgeable, to do the activity.[31]

Where a court cannot determine the degrees of fault as between a student and a school, the Ontario *Negligence Act*[32] provides that the two parties will be deemed to be equally at fault or negligent.

OCCUPIERS' LIABILITY ACT

As mentioned, the *Occupiers' Liability Act* provides that any occupier of premises owes a duty to take such care "as in all the circumstances of the case is reasonable to see that persons entering on the premises, and the property brought on the premises by those persons are reasonably safe while on the premises".[33] While the Act applies to any person who enters onto school premises, including students, it is likely that the standard of "reasonably safe" set forth in the Act does not replace the higher standard of care of a "careful and prudent parent" owed by a school and its teachers to their pupils.[34]

The *Occupiers' Liability Act* imposes obligations on the school for any visitors to the premises whether during or after school hours. Many schools

---

[30] *Scott v. Dunphy* (1989), 98 N.B.R. (2d) 339 (Q.B.) — student using a defective stick to push wood through a jointer; *Germschied v. Richardson, supra*, footnote 22.
[31] Brown and Zuker, *op. cit.*, footnote 25, at p. 75.
[32] R.S.O. 1990, c. N.1, s. 4.
[33] *Occupiers' Liability Act*, s. 3(1).
[34] Eric Roher, *An Educator's Guide to Violence in Schools* (Aurora: Aurora Professional Press, 1997) at p. 35. In fact in *Cropp v. Potashville School Unit No. 25* (1977), 81 D.L.R. (3d) 115, [1977] 6 W.W.R. 267 (Sask. Q.B.), the court held that the duty of care owed by a school to its students was higher than that owed by an occupier to invitees as students are required to attend school. A contrary principle was stated in *Portelance v. Board of School Trustees of Roman Catholic Separate School for School Section No. 5 Grantham (Township)* (1962), 32 D.L.R. (2d) 337, [1962] O.R. 365 (C.A.).

allow community organizations to rent their gym or other facilities after school hours to carry on a variety of activities. The statute imposes on a school a duty of care for such visitors to ensure that they are reasonably safe while on the premises. If, for example, a school fails to turn on its outside parking lot lights for people attending an evening event at the school, a school may be responsible for a person who falls and is injured as a result of the absence of lighting.[35]

The *Occupiers' Liability Act* creates two exceptions to the duty of care owed by an occupier of premises which would apply to schools. First, the duty of care does not apply in respect of risks willingly assumed by a person who enters on the premises.[36] In such a case, the occupier simply owes a duty to the person not to create a danger with the deliberate intent of doing harm or damage to the person. The Supreme Court of Canada has narrowly interpreted this exception and has held that it is only available where the occupier of the premises can prove that the person who came onto the property assumed both the physical and legal risks of the occupier's failure to provide a reasonably safe environment. As Justice Iacobucci stated in that case: "Rare may be the case where a visitor who enters on premises will fully know of and accept the risks resulting from the occupier's noncompliance with the statute."[37]

In addition, the general duty of care of an occupier of premises does not apply to a person who is on the premises with the intention of committing, or in the commission of, a criminal act.[38] The occupier, however, still owes a duty to the person not to create a danger with the deliberate intent of doing harm.

---

[35] *Marchand v. School District No. 40 (New Westminster)* (1997), 76 A.C.W.S. (3d) 323 (B.C.S.C.).
[36] *Occupiers' Liability Act*, s. 4(1).
[37] *Waldick v. Malcolm* (1991), 83 D.L.R. (4th) 114, [1991] 2 S.C.R. 456 at p. 479.
[38] *Occupiers' Liability Act*, s. 4(2).

11
Miscellaneous Statutory Obligations

IMMUNIZATION OF STUDENTS

Obligations on Parents of Pupils

The *Immunization of School Pupils Act*[1] requires the parent of a pupil, including an independent school pupil, to cause the pupil to complete the prescribed program of immunization in relation to each of the diseases designated by the Act,[2] which are diphtheria, tetanus, poliomyelitis, measles, mumps and rubella.[3] The regulation under the Act sets out the schedule of immunization for a child with which a parent must comply. If a parent fails to ensure that a pupil receives the required immunization shots, the parent is guilty of an offence and on conviction is liable to a fine of not more than $1,000.[4]

The Act creates two exemptions from the general duty of a parent to ensure a child receives all the specified immunization shots. First, a physician may exempt a pupil from any immunization requirement where there is evidence of existing immunity from the disease, or where the immunization would be detrimental to the child's health. The physician must specify the length of exemption for the student and give reasons for the exemption.[5] The physician also must file a statement of medical exemption with the proper medical officer of health.

Second, a parent may file with the proper medical officer of health a statement of conscience or religious belief to exempt a child from a program of immunization.[6] In the statement of conscience or religious belief the parent must swear under oath that the requirements of the Act conflict with his or her sincerely held convictions based on religion or conscience.[7]

---

[1] R.S.O. 1990, c. I.1.
[2] Section 3(1).
[3] R.R.O. 1990, Reg. 645 (as amended by O. Reg. 299/96).
[4] *Immunization of School Pupils Act*, s. 4.
[5] Section 3(2), and R.R.O. 1990, Reg. 645, Form 1.
[6] Section 3(3).
[7] Regulation 645, Form 2.

Obligations on Independent Schools

The Act imposes three legal obligations on all schools, including independent schools. First, a medical officer of health by a written order may require a person who operates an independent school in the area served by him to suspend from attendance at the school a pupil named in the order.[8] A medical officer of health may make such an order where he has not received a statement signed by a physician showing that a child has completed a prescribed program of immunization, a physician's statement of exemption, or a parental statement of conscience or religious belief in respect of the pupil. If a medical officer of health does not receive any of those statements, and is not satisfied that the pupil has commenced and will complete the prescribed program of immunization, he may issue the order of suspension which may be for a period of 20 school days.[9] In order to be valid, an order by a medical officer of health must include written reasons for the order.[10] Although an order is only valid for 20 days, the medical officer of health may make repeated orders in respect of a pupil where the circumstances for making the order continue to exist.[11]

As a second obligation, a person who operates an independent school may be required to exclude from the school the pupil named in an order made by a medical officer of health where the officer is of the opinion that there is an outbreak or an immediate risk of an outbreak of a designated disease in the school, and the medical officer of health has not received a statement of immunization or a statement of medical exemption.[12] The order must include written reasons for the making of the order[13] and the order remains in force until rescinded in writing by the medical officer of health.[14] Where the medical officer of health is of the opinion that there is an outbreak or an immediate risk of an outbreak of a designated disease, a statement of exemption for conscientious or religious reasons by a parent does *not* exempt a pupil from such an order. In fact, the statement of conscience or religious belief which must be signed by the parent contains an acknowledgment by the parent that a pupil may be excluded from a school if there is an outbreak or an immediate risk of an outbreak of a designated disease unless a statement of immunization or statement of medical exemption has been provided to the medical officer of health.[15]

Finally, the Act imposes on an independent school obligations relating to the transfer of pupils. Where a pupil transfers from an independent school, the

---

[8] *Immunization of School Pupils Act*, s. 6(1).
[9] Section 7.
[10] Section 8(2).
[11] Section 8(3).
[12] Section 12(1) and (2).
[13] Section 12(7).
[14] Section 12(3).
[15] Regulation 645, Form 2.

person who operates the school must give notice of the transfer in prescribed form to the medical officer of health serving the area in which the school is located.[16] The prescribed notice requires the school to list the names, sex, dates of birth and grades of the pupils who have transferred, and also to identify the school or school board to which the pupils have transferred.[17]

Right to a Hearing

Where a medical officer of health makes an order to a school either to suspend or exclude a pupil, he must notify the parents concerned that they are entitled to request a hearing into the matter. A parent is entitled to a hearing if he delivers a request for a hearing to the medical officer of health and to the person who operates the independent school within 15 days after the notice is served on the parent.[18] From the school's perspective, it is important to note that the Act clearly provides that an order made by the medical officer of health takes effect when it is served on the school notwithstanding the fact that a parent might require a hearing into the matter.[19] Accordingly, if a parent notifies an independent school that he or she intends to request a hearing into the suspension or exclusion order, the school must continue with the suspension or exclusion of the pupil until notified to the contrary by the medical officer of health or the Health Protection Appeal Board.

CHILD AND FAMILY SERVICES ACT

Duty of the Public to Report

The *Child and Family Services Act*[20] establishes a mechanism to ensure that any child in need of protection can be brought under the care of a child welfare agency and taken to a place of safety. The Act sets out a number of circumstances where a child is in need of protection, including situations where: the child has suffered physical harm inflicted by the person having charge of the child, the child has been sexually molested or exploited by the person having charge of the child or the child requires medical treatment to cure physical harm and the child's parent refuses to provide or consent to such treatment.[21] The Act imposes an obligation on all persons who believe on reasonable grounds that a child is or may be in need of protection to forthwith report the belief and the information on which it is based to a child welfare

---

[16] *Immunization of School Pupils Act*, s. 14(1).
[17] Regulation 645, Form 3.
[18] *Immunization of School Pupils Act*, s. 15(1) and (2).
[19] Section 15(7).
[20] R.S.O. 1990, c. C.11.
[21] Section 37(2)(a), (c) and (e).

society.[22] This obligation to report applies to all citizens, including teachers and principals.

Duty of Teachers and School Principals to Report Abuse

The *Child and Family Services Act* places an additional obligation to report on teachers or school principals. Where a teacher or principal in the course of his professional or official duties has reasonable grounds to suspect that a child is or may be suffering or may have suffered abuse, he must forthwith report the suspicion and the information on which it is based to a child welfare society.[23] The Act defines "to suffer abuse" as applying to the following circumstances in respect of a child where:[24]

   (i) the child has suffered physical harm, inflicted by the person having charge of the child or caused by that person's failure to care and provide for or supervise and protect the child adequately;
   (ii) the child has been sexually molested or sexually exploited, by the person having charge of the child or by another person, or the person having charge of the child knows or should know of the possibility of sexual molestation or sexual exploitation and fails to protect the child;
   (iii) the child requires medical treatment to cure, prevent or alleviate physical harm or suffering and the child's parent or the person having charge of the child does not provide, or refuses or is unavailable or unable to consent to, the treatment;
   (iv) the child has suffered emotional harm, demonstrated by severe anxiety, depression, withdrawal or self-destructive or aggressive behaviour, and the child's parent or the person having charge of the child does not provide, or refuses or is unavailable or unable to consent to, services or treatment to remedy or alleviate the harm; or
   (v) the child suffers from a mental, emotional or developmental condition that, if not remedied, could seriously impair the child's development and the child's parent or the person having charge of the child does not provide, or refuses or is unavailable or unable to consent to, treatment to remedy or alleviate the condition.[25]

Where a teacher or principal has reasonable grounds to suspect that a child is, or may be, suffering abuse in any of these circumstances, the *Child and Family Services Act* requires him to "forthwith" report the suspicion and the information on which it is based to a child welfare society.

---

[22] Section 72(2).
[23] Section 72(3).
[24] Section 72(1).
[25] Section 37(2), (a), (c), (e), (f) and (h).

Miscellaneous Statutory Obligations 161

The Act recognizes that sometimes the information obtained by a teacher or principal which gives rise to such a suspicion will be imparted in confidential circumstances. Nevertheless, the Act specifically provides that the reporting obligation applies even though the information reported may be confidential or privileged.[26] The Act goes on to provide protection for any person making a report based on confidential information by prohibiting the institution of any legal action against a person who complies with the statute's reporting obligations unless the person acts maliciously or without reasonable grounds for the belief or suspicion.[27]

The Regulation Made Under the *Teaching Profession Act* requires a member of the Ontario Teachers' Federation to "concern himself with the welfare of his pupils while they are under his care".[28] It has been suggested that these duties may be interpreted to include the duty to report suspicions of child abuse.[29] Amendments to the *Teaching Profession Act*[30] introduced by Bill 160 limit membership in the Ontario Teachers' Federation to teachers who are members of the Ontario College of Teachers and are employed by a board as a teacher.[31] As a result, the duties imposed by the Regulation Made Under the *Teaching Profession Act* likely do not apply to independent school teachers. The same holds true of the statutory obligations contained in section 18(1)(b) of the Regulation Made Under the *Teaching Profession Act* requiring a teacher who makes an "adverse report" against a colleague, such as a report disclosing allegations of suspected child abuse, to furnish a colleague with a written statement of the report within three days after making the report.

The obligation to report suspicions of abuse "forthwith" was considered by the court in the case of *R. v. Girard*[32] where the court stated that the meaning of "forthwith" depended on the nature of the allegation and the circumstances of the case. In the *Girard* case, allegations by a grade 4 student of inappropriate touching by a teacher were reported by the school principal immediately to his superintendent. The board of education then began an investigatory process, interviewing all of the students involved and the teacher against whom the accusations were made. The teacher was suspended from classroom duties during the investigation. Seven days after the initial complaint, the board contacted the police and reported the allegations of sexual abuse. The court dismissed charges brought against the principal and superintendent of failing to report the child abuse forthwith, concluding that it was only five days into the

---

[26] Section 72(7).
[27] *Ibid.*
[28] Regulation Made Under the *Teaching Profession Act*, s. 14(f).
[29] Eric M. Roher, *An Educator's Guide to Violence in Schools* (Aurora: Aurora Professional Press, 1997) at p. 165.
[30] R.S.O. 1990, c. T.2.
[31] *Education Quality Improvement Act, 1997*, S.O. 1997, c. 31, s. 180(2).
[32] Unreported decision, January 20, 1993, Ont. Ct. (Prov. Div.).

investigation that the school authorities reasonably could have concluded that they had a suspicion that the touching was not merely of a friendly type. Although the court noted that the suspicion should have been reported two days earlier than it was, and there was a breach of a statutory duty, the court did not consider the breach sufficiently serious to warrant conviction.[33]

In the *Girard* case, the allegations of abuse were made against a teacher, and the school authority took immediate steps to remove the teacher from contact with the complainant. Where a student raises a concern about possible abuse at home, the school is faced with the prospect of returning a student at the end of the school day to a potentially abusive environment. Under such circumstances where the school does not have control over the alleged offender, the requirement to "forthwith" report suspicions of child abuse probably requires a school to contact the police the day on which they learn of the complaint.

Offence for Failing to Report Suspected Abuse

A principal or teacher who fails to report forthwith suspicions that a child is or may be suffering or may have suffered child abuse is guilty of an offence and on conviction is liable to a fine of not more than $1,000.[34] In addition, a director, officer or employee of an independent school corporation who authorizes, permits or concurs in such a contravention, is also guilty of an offence.[35]

OCCUPATIONAL HEALTH AND SAFETY ACT

General Obligations

The Ontario *Occupational Health and Safety Act*[36] ("OHSA"), creates a comprehensive regime designed to ensure the safety of employees in the workplace. A school falls within the definition of "workplace" under this Act. The OHSA applies to all persons who are employed as teachers as defined in the *Education Act* which means that it applies to any member of the Ontario College of Teachers.[37]

Although it is beyond the scope of this book to review in detail the requirements of the *Occupational Health and Safety Act*, its general principles can readily be stated.[38] Under the Act, every employer must ensure that the

---

[33] For a full summary of the case, see Roher, *op. cit.*, footnote 29, at pp. 167-8.
[34] *Child and Family Services Act*, s. 85(1)(b).
[35] *Ibid.*
[36] R.S.O. 1990, c. O.1.
[37] Teachers, O. Reg. 191/84, s. 2
[38] For a detailed guide to the Act, see Norman A. Keith, *Ontario Health and Safety Law* (Aurora: Canada Law Book, 1997) (April 1998, looseleaf).

measures and procedures prescribed by the regulations are carried out in the workplace and that workers are provided with prescribed equipment, material and protective devices.[39] These general obligations of the employer require an employer to provide information and instruction to a worker to protect the health or safety of the worker, acquaint a worker with any hazard in the workplace and in the handling, storage, use and disposal of any biological, chemical or physical agent, and to take every precaution reasonable in the circumstances for the protection of a worker.[40] Employers must also keep and maintain accurate records of the handling, storage, use and disposal of biological, chemical or physical agents.[41] For their part, workers must work in compliance with the provisions of the OHSA and its regulations, use or wear the equipment and protective devices required by an employer, and report the absence of, or defect in any equipment or protective device which may endanger the worker or fellow workers.[42]

The OHSA requires that a joint health and safety committee be established at any workplace at which 20 or more workers are regularly employed.[43] The committee must consist of at least two persons for a workplace of fewer than 50 workers, or at least four persons for a workplace where 50 or more workers are regularly employed. At least half the members of the committee must be workers employed at the workplace who do not exercise managerial functions. Regulations under the OHSA treat a public school principal or vice-principal as a person exercising managerial functions.[44] The members of a committee who represent workers are to be selected by the workers. The joint health and safety committee possesses the power to identify situations that may be a source of danger or hazard to workers, make recommendations to the employer for the improvement of the health and safety of workers, as well as obtain information from the employer respecting the identification of existing hazards of materials, processes or equipment.[45] The OHSA goes into considerable detail describing the operations of a joint health and safety committee and the obligations of employers to respond to concerns voiced by the committee. Regulations under the OHSA provide that an employer of teachers that establishes and maintains one joint health and safety committee for all its teachers is deemed to have complied with its obligation to establish a joint health and safety committee with respect to all its teachers.[46]

---

[39] *Occupational Health and Safety Act*, s. 25(1) ("OHSA").
[40] Section 25(2).
[41] Section 26.
[42] Section 28(1).
[43] Section 9(2).
[44] Teachers, O. Reg. 191/84, s. 3(1).
[45] OHSA, s. 9(18).
[46] Teachers, s. 3(2).

Part V of the OHSA sets out the right of a worker to refuse to work, or do particular work, where the worker believes that any equipment the worker is to use is likely to endanger himself, or another worker, or that the physical condition of the workplace is likely to endanger himself.[47] However, regulations made under the OHSA stipulate that a worker's right to refuse work does not apply to a teacher "where the circumstances are such that the life, health or safety of a pupil is in imminent jeopardy".[48]

The OHSA gives government inspectors broad powers to enter and inspect workplaces.[49] Where an inspector finds that a provision of the Act or its regulations are being contravened, he may issue an order to the employer requiring remedial work to be undertaken within a specified period.[50] The provincial director under the *Ontario Health and Safety Act* is given the power to enforce orders made by inspectors, and employers enjoy rights of appeal from orders of inspectors. The OHSA makes it an offence for any person to contravene or fail to comply with a provision of the Act or an order of an inspector, and the penalties on conviction can be significant: a fine of not more than $25,000, or imprisonment for a term of not more than 12 months. If a corporation is convicted of an offence for failing to comply, the maximum fine which may be imposed on the corporation is $500,000.[51]

The OHSA imposes on owners of a workplace the obligation to ensure that the workplace complies with the Act and its regulations,[52] as well as placing on every director and officer of a corporation the duty to take reasonable care to ensure that the corporation complies with the Act and regulations.[53]

Workplace Hazardous Materials Information System (WHMIS)

One aspect of the Occupational Health and Safety regime in Ontario which bears directly on the operation of schools is the requirement to comply with the Workplace Hazardous Materials Information System (WHMIS)[54] established under the OHSA. WHMIS is a national program of hazardous materials labelling, card-style information, instruction, training and general health and safety awareness. It is the "right-to-know program" in Canadian workplaces for hazardous materials.[55] The WHMIS system designates "controlled products" as

---

[47] OHSA, s. 43(3).
[48] Teachers, s. 3(3).
[49] OHSA, s. 54.
[50] Section 57.
[51] Section 66(2).
[52] Section 29(1).
[53] Section 32.
[54] R.R.O. 1990, Reg. 860.
[55] Norman A. Keith, *Ontario Health and Safety Law* (Aurora: Canada Law Book, 1997) at p. 6-1 (April 1998, looseleaf).

hazardous materials.[56] Controlled products include compressed gas, flammable and combustible material, oxidizing material, poisonous and infectious material, corrosive material and dangerously reactive material.[57]

The WHMIS regulation imposes several obligations on employers to ensure the safety of workers who handle or are exposed to hazardous materials. An employer must ensure that every controlled product not in a container, and every container of a controlled product, received from a supplier is labelled with a supplier label.[58] A supplier label must disclose the information about the product required by the Federal *Hazardous Products Act*, and display one of the uniform hazard symbols which must be affixed to any hazardous material used in Canada. No supplier label is required in a controlled product which originates from a laboratory supply house, is intended solely for use in the laboratory and is packaged in a container in a quantity less than 10 kilograms. However, under those circumstances the supplier must affix a label to the container which identifies the product, indicates that a material safety data sheet for the product is available and discloses the risk phrases, precautionary measures and first-aid measures applicable to the controlled product.[59]

The OHSA also requires an employer who receives a controlled product from a supplier for use in the workplace to obtain a supplier material safety data sheet for the product, and ensure that updated material safety data sheets are obtained every three years.[60]

Since it is the obligation of the employer to ensure that any hazardous materials which enter the workplace comply with the provisions of the WHMIS regulation, any school which brings hazardous biological, chemical or physical agents into the school, whether for educational or operational purposes, must ensure that the products comply with the labelling requirements of the regulation.

In addition, the WHMIS regulation requires an employer to ensure that a worker who works with, or in proximity to, a controlled product is informed about all hazard information received from the supplier concerning the controlled product, as well as any further hazard information of which the employer is, or ought to be, aware of concerning its use, storage and handling.[61] An employer must ensure that a worker is instructed in the contents required on a supplier label, procedures for the safe use, storage, handling and disposal of a controlled product, and the procedures to be followed in case of emergency involving a controlled product.[62]

---

[56] R.R.O. 1990, Reg. 860, s. 2. A "controlled product" means a product or material included in a class listed in Schedule II to the *Hazardous Products Act* (Canada).
[57] Keith, *op. cit.*, footnote 55, at p. 6-9.
[58] R.R.O. 1990, Reg. 860, s. 8(1).
[59] Section 13.
[60] Section 17.
[61] Section 6(1).
[62] Section 7.

FIRE CODE

The *Fire Protection and Prevention Act, 1997*[63] establishes standards and procedures to ensure that premises are protected against fires or explosions. The detailed standards are set out in the Fire Code,[64] many parts of which apply to schools, including independent schools. Every school should conduct a fire safety audit to ensure it complies with the provisions of the Fire Code. School administration should pay careful attention to several aspects of the Fire Code: flame resistance requirements for interior drapes and decorative materials, fire department access to buildings,[65] the ventilation of commercial cooking equipment,[66] the maximum occupancy limits for assembly rooms which vary for classrooms, school shops and school laboratories,[67] locking mechanisms for exit doors,[68] and a requirement that fire drills be held three times in each of the fall and spring school terms.[69] For the purposes of determining the number of fire extinguishers required in a building, the Fire Code classifies the activities in a building as light hazard, ordinary hazard and extra hazard occupancies. A school may contain rooms which fall into each category — classrooms fall into light hazard, shop areas into ordinary hazard, and auto repair shops into extra hazard occupancies. The number of fire extinguishers varies according to each hazard level and a school must be aware of the specific requirements for each area of its building.[70]

A person who contravenes the provisions of the *Fire Protection and Prevention Act, 1997* and the Fire Code is guilty of an offence. The penalties are significant:[71] in the case of an individual, a fine of up to $25,000 or imprisonment for up to one year; for a corporation, a fine of up to $50,000; and for a director or officer of a corporation who knows the corporation is violating or has violated the Fire Code, a fine of up to $25,000 or imprisonment for up to one year.

---

[63] S.O. 1997, c. 4.
[64] O. Reg. 388/97.
[65] Section 2.5.
[66] Section 2.6.1.12.
[67] Section 2.7.1.4.
[68] Section 2.7.2.2.
[69] Section 2.8.3.2.
[70] Sections 6.2.5 and 6.2.6.
[71] *Fire Protection and Prevention Act, 1997*, s. 28.

Appendix "A"

Relevant Sections of the Ontario Education Act

1(1) **Definitions.**— In this Act and the regulations, except where otherwise provided in the Act or regulations,

. . . . .

"private school" means an institution at which instruction is provided at any time between the hours of 9 a.m. and 4 p.m. on any school day for five or more pupils who are of or over compulsory school age in any of the subjects of the elementary or secondary school courses of study and that is not a school as defined in this section;

. . . . .

8(1) **Powers of Minister.**— The Minister may,
1. **diplomas and certificates.**— name the diplomas and certificates that are to be granted to pupils and prescribe their form and the conditions under which they are to be granted;

. . . . .

3.1 **reviews of effectiveness.**— conduct reviews of classroom practices and the effectiveness of educational programs and require a board or a private school inspected under subsection 16(7) to participate in the reviews and to provide information to the Minister for that purpose in such form as the Minister may prescribe;

. . . . .

16(1) **Intention to operate private school.**— No private school shall be operated in Ontario unless notice of intention to operate the private school has been submitted in accordance with this section.

(2) **Idem.**— Every private school shall submit annually to the Ministry on or before the 1st day of September a notice of intention to operate a private school.

(3) **Idem.**— A notice of intention to operate a private school shall be in such form and shall include such particulars as the Minister may require.

(4) **Offence to operate private school without filing notice of intent to operate.**— Every person concerned in the management of a private school that is operated in contravention of subsection (1) is guilty of an offence and on conviction is liable to a fine of not more than $50 for every day such school is so operated.

(5) **Return.**— The principal, headmaster, headmistress or person in charge of a private school shall make a return to the Ministry furnishing such statistical information regarding enrolment, staff, courses of study and other information as and when required by the Minister, and any such person who fails to make such return within sixty days of the request of the Minister is guilty of an offence and on conviction is liable to a fine of not more than $200.

(6) **Inspection of school.**— The Minister may direct one or more supervisory officers to inspect a private school, in which case each such supervisory officer may enter the school at all reasonable hours and conduct an inspection of the school and any records or documents relating thereto, and every person who prevents or obstructs or attempts to prevent or obstruct any such entry or inspection is guilty of an offence and on conviction is liable to a fine of not more than $500.

(7) **Inspection on request.**— The Minister may, on the request of any person operating a private school, provide for inspection of the school in respect of the standard of instruction in the subjects leading to the Ontario secondary school diploma, the secondary school graduation diploma and to the secondary school honour graduation diploma, and may determine and charge a fee for such inspection.

(8) **Inspection of teachers.**— The Minister may, on the request of a person operating a private school or of a person in charge of a conservation authority school or field centre, provide for the inspection of a teacher in such school or centre who requires the recommendation of a supervisory officer for certification purposes.

(8.1) **Agreements re tests.**— The Minister may enter into agreements with a person operating,
- (a) a private school;
- (b) a school provided by a band, the council of a band or an education authority where the band, the counsel of the band or the education authority is authorized by the Crown in right of Canada to provide education for Indians; or
- (c) a school provided by the Crown in right of Canada,

about administering tests to pupils enrolled in the school, marking the tests and reporting the results of the tests.

(8.2) **Same.**— Without limiting the generality of subsection (8.1), an agreement may provide for the charging of fees by the Minister to a person operating a school described in subsection (8.1).

(9) **Offence for false statement.**— Every person who knowingly makes a false statement in a notice of intention to operate a private school or an information return under this section is guilty of an offence and on conviction is liable to a fine of not more than $500.

. . . . .

21(1) **Compulsory attendance.**— Unless excused under this section,
(a) every child who attains the age of six years on or before the first school day in September in any year shall attend an elementary or secondary school on every school day from the first school day in September in that year until the child attains the age of sixteen years; and
(b) every child who attains the age of six years after the first school day in September in any year shall attend an elementary or secondary school on every school day from the first school day in September in the next succeeding year until the last school day in June in the year in which the child attains the age of sixteen years.

(2) **When attendance excused.**— A child is excused from attendance at school if,
(a) the child is receiving satisfactory instruction at home or elsewhere;

. . . . .

30(1) **Liability of parent or guardian.**— A parent or guardian of a child of compulsory school age who neglects or refuses to cause the child to attend school is, unless the child is legally excused from attendance, guilty of an offence and on conviction is liable to a fine of not more than $200.

Appendix "B"

Associations of Independent Schools in Ontario

Conference of Independent Schools (CIS)
Box 1502
St. Catharines, Ontario L2R 7S9
Tel: (905) 688-4866   Fax: (905) 688-5778
Executive Director: Ms. Janet Lewis

Canadian Educational Standards Institute (CESI)
3 Elm Avenue, Suite 201
Toronto, Ontario M4W 1M8
Tel: (416) 964-2544   Fax: (416) 964-2543
Executive Director: Solette N. Gelberg

Ontario Alliance of Christian Schools (OACSS)
617 Highway 53 East
Ancaster, Ontario L9G 3K9
Tel: (905) 648-2100   Fax: (905) 648-2110
Executive Director: Dr. Adrian Guldemond

Ontario Federation of Independent Schools (OFIS)
2199 Regency Terrace
Ottawa, Ontario K2C 1H2
Tel: (613) 596-4013   Fax: (613) 596-4971
President: Elaine Hopkins

Board of Jewish Education of the U.J.A. Federation
of Greater Toronto
4600 Bathurst St., Suite 232
Willowdale, Ontario M2R 3V3
Tel: (416) 633-7770   Fax: (416) 633-7535
Executive Director: Rabbi Dr. Jeremiah Unterman

Association of Christian Schools (ACSI)
1 Wenden Court, R.R. #2
Minesing, Ontario L0L 1Y0
Tel: (705) 729-7344   Fax: (705) 728-4404
Executive Director: Mr. Mark Kennedy

Rehoboth Christian School Societies (RCSS)
43 Main Street East
Box 220
Norwich, Ontario N0J 1P0
Tel: (519) 863-2403   Fax: (519) 863-3984
Executive Director: Mr. Martien C. Vanderspek

Non-Aligned Schools
Tel: (905) 844-0372   Fax: (905) 844-9369
Ms. Audrey Hadfield

Waldorf Schools
9100 Bathurst Street, #1
Thornhill, Ontario L4J 8C7
Tel: (905) 881-1611   Fax: (905) 881-6710
Mr. Ed Edelstein

Forum of Independent School Association (Ontario) FISA(O)
Box 63023, University Plaza
34 Plaza Drive
Dundas, Ontario L9H 5Y3
Chair: Mr. Mark Kennedy

Appendix "C"

Applications for Incorporation

SAMPLE OBJECTS OF EXISTING INDEPENDENT SCHOOLS

De La Salle College "Oaklands"

The objects for which the corporation is incorporated are:

(a) to establish and maintain a day school for the education of boys and girls in all academic subjects authorized for study by the Corporation;

(b) to maintain such standards and grades of education and to provide such lectures, classes, exhibitions, meetings, conferences, educational and sporting facilities, equipment, literature, supplies and instruction for pupils, as are deemed by the Corporation to be necessary or desirable.

Hawthorn School for Girls

The objects for which the corporation is incorporated are:

> To establish and carry on a school where students may obtain a sound primary or secondary classical, mathematical, technical and general education; and to provide for the delivery and holding of lectures, exhibitions, public meetings, classes and conferences, calculated directly or indirectly to advance the cause of education, whether general, professional or technical.

The Toronto French School

(a) To establish and maintain in Metropolitan Toronto, in the said County of York, a school, college, academy or other educational institution to give instruction in English and French equivalent to that given in kindergarten and from Grades I to XIII both inclusive in a public or sepa-

rate school and for such other additional educational instruction as the directors may deem meet;
(b) To enter into any arrangement with any authorities, federal, provincial, municipal, local or otherwise, including agreements for affiliation with any other school, college or university or board of education that may seem conducive to the Corporation's objects or any of them and to obtain from any such authority any rights, privileges and concessions which the Corporation may think it desirable to obtain and to carry out, exercise and comply with any such arrangements, rights, privileges and concessions;
(c) To take by gift, devise, lease or purchase and to hold real and personal property including all such lands, buildings, hereditaments and possessions as may from time to time be acquired or erected by the Corporation, and to use or occupy for the purposes of the Corporation, including any preparatory or academic department, and for residences of the principals, deans, directors, professors, lecturers, students and officers of the Corporation and to accept on behalf of the Corporation or any department thereof, including any preparatory department, any gift, devise or bequest of any property real or personal and to invest the proceeds thereof or the income therefrom in acquiring and maintaining a school or college for the purpose of teaching students and others and to fix the fees of students or others seeking academic training in such college; and
(d) To establish and support or aid in the establishment and support of associations, institutions, funds, scholarships, endowments and conveniences calculated to benefit the Corporation, its employees or ex-employees or the dependants in connection with such person or its scholars or students, and to grant pensions and allowances and to make payments towards insurance and to subscribe or guarantee money for educative objects or purposes.

The Toronto Waldorf School

(a) To establish maintain and operate in the Province of Ontario non-denominational schools to educate children at the nursery, kindergarten, elementary and secondary school level through a curriculum covering the sciences, the humanities and the arts, according to principles of education developed in Waldorf Schools since 1919;

Toronto District Christian High School

(i) To establish, maintain a school or schools for Christian secondary education in accordance with the basis and purpose of the Corporation, and to do and perform all things incidental thereto.

(ii) The basis of this Corporation is the infallible Word of God (the Holy Bible) as interpreted by the Belgic Confession, the Heidelberg Catechism, the Canons of Durdt, the Westminister Confession and the Westminister Catechisms.

(iii) The purpose of the Corporation is the establishment and maintenance of a school or schools for Christian secondary education in the Municipality of Metropolitan Toronto or adjacent areas, and the promotion of Christian instruction by way of school education, distinctively Reformed in emphasis and character, in accordance with the basis of the Corporation.

Appendix "D"

Applications for Incorporation

SPECIAL PROVISIONS OF EXISTING INDEPENDENT SCHOOLS

De La Salle College "Oaklands"

The special provisions are:

(a) The Corporation shall be carried on without the purpose of gain for members and any profits or other accretions to the Corporation shall be used in promoting its objects.
(b) The Corporation shall be subject to the *Charities Accounting Act* and the *Charitable Gifts Act*.
(c) The Directors shall serve as such without remuneration and no Directors shall directly or indirectly receive any profit from his/her position as such, provided that Directors may be paid reasonable expenses incurred by them in the performance of their duties.
(d) The borrowing power of the Corporation pursuant to any by-law passed and confirmed in accordance with section 59 of the *Corporations Act* shall be limited to borrowing money for current operating expenses, provided that the borrowing power of the Corporation shall not be so limited if it borrows on the security of real or personal property.
(e) Upon the dissolution of the Corporation and after payment of all debts and liabilities, its remaining property shall be distributed or disposed of to charitable organizations which carry on their work solely in Ontario.
(f) If it is made to appear to the satisfaction of the Minister, upon report of the Public Trustee, that the Corporation has failed to comply with any of the provisions of the *Charities Accounting Act* or the *Charitable Gifts Act*, the Minister may authorize an inquiry for the purpose of determining whether or not there is sufficient cause for the Lieutenant Governor to make an Order under subsection 317(1) of the *Corpora-*

tions Act to cancel the Letters Patent of the Corporation and declare it to be dissolved.

(g) For the above objects, and as incidental and ancillary thereto, to exercise any of the powers as prescribed by the *Corporations Act*, or by any other statutes or laws from time to time applicable, except where such power is contrary to the statutes or common law relating to charities, and in particular, without limiting the generality of the foregoing:

POWER TO ARRANGE WITH GOVERNMENT AUTHORITIES

(i) To enter into any arrangements with any authority, whether Federal, Provincial, Municipal, Local or otherwise, and including agreements for the affiliation or federation with any other school, college or university, that may seem conducive to any or all of the Corporation's objects, and to obtain from any such authority the rights and privileges which the Corporation may think it desirable to obtain, and to carry out, exercise or comply with any such arrangements, rights and privileges.

POWER TO RECEIVE GOVERNMENT SUPPORT

(ii) Subject to the *Charities Accounting Act* and the *Charitable Gifts Act*, to receive, acquire, accept and hold government or municipal grants or aid of any kind, and in furtherance of the objects of the Corporation, to expend or invest same in such manner as the Corporation may from time to time determine.

POWER TO ACCUMULATE

(iii) To accumulate from time to time part of the fund or funds of the Corporation and income therefrom subject to any statutes or laws from time to time applicable.

POWER TO INVEST

(iv) To invest and re-invest the funds of the Corporation in such manner as determined by the Directors, and in making such investments, the Directors shall not be limited to investments authorized by law for trustees, provided such investments are reasonable, prudent and sagacious under the circumstances and do not constitute, either directly or indirectly, a conflict of interest.

POWER TO SOLICIT DONATIONS AND GRANTS

(v) To solicit and receive donations, bequests, legacies and grants, and to enter into agreements, contracts and undertakings incidental thereto.

POWER TO RECEIVE PERSONAL PROPERTY

(vi) To acquire by purchase, contract, donation, legacy, gift, grant, bequest or otherwise, any personal property and to enter into and carry out any agreements, contracts or undertakings incidental thereto, and to sell, dispose of and convey the same, or any part thereof, as may be considered advisable.

POWER TO HOLD AND DISPOSE OF REAL PROPERTY

(vii) To acquire by purchase, lease, devise, gift or otherwise, real property, and to hold such real property or interest therein necessary for the actual use and occupation of the Corporation or for carrying on its charitable undertaking, and, when no longer so necessary, to sell, dispose of and convey the same or any part thereof.

POWER TO HIRE

(viii) To employ and pay such assistants, clerks, agents, representatives and employees, and to procure, equip and maintain such offices and other facilities and to incur such reasonable expenses, as may be necessary, provided that the Corporation shall not pay any remuneration to a Director in any capacity whatsoever.

POWER TO CO-OPERATE WITH OTHER CHARITABLE ORGANIZATION

(ix) To co-operate, liaise, and contract with other charitable organizations, institutions or agencies which carry on similar objects to that of the Corporation.

POWER TO PARTICIPATE IN THE REORGANIZATION OF A COMPANY

(x) To take up proportions of any increased capital of a company or corporation in which the Corporation may at any time hold shares or obligations, to purchase any additional shares or obligations in such company or corporation; to join in any plan for the reconstruction or reorganization or for the sale of assets of any company or corporation, or part thereof; to enter into any pooling or other agreement in connection with the shares or obligations of a company or corporation held by the Corporation; and to give consent to the creation of any mortgage, lien or indebtedness of any company or corporation whose shares or obligations are held by the Corporation; provided, however, that all of the foregoing is subject to the provisions of the *Charitable Gifts Act*.

POWER TO SUE AND COMPROMISE CLAIMS

(xi) To demand and compel payment of all sums of money and claims to any real or personal property in which the Corporation may have an interest and to compromise any such claims, and generally to sue and be sued in its corporate name.

POWER TO ISSUE CHEQUES
(xii) To draw, make, accept, endorse, execute and issue cheques and other negotiable or transferable instruments.
POWER TO PAY COSTS OF INCORPORATION
(xiii) To pay all costs and expenses of, or incidental to, the incorporation.

Hawthorn School for Girls

The special provisions are:

(a) persons may be admitted to membership in the Corporation by a resolution of the board of directors on such terms and conditions as shall be specified in such resolution provided, however, that no such resolution shall be effective until it has been confirmed by the members of the Corporation;

(b) the Corporation shall be carried on without the purpose of gain for its members and any profits or other accretions to the Corporation shall be used in promoting it objects;

(c) the directors shall serve as such without remuneration, and no directors shall directly or indirectly receive any profit from the position as such; provided that a director may be paid reasonable expenses incurred by him or her in the performance of director's duties;

(d) the borrowing power of the Corporation pursuant to any by-law passed and confirmed in accordance with section 59 of the *Corporations Act* shall be limited to borrowing money for current operating expenses, provided that the borrowing power of the Corporation shall not be so limited if it borrows on the security of real or personal property;

(e) upon the dissolution of the Corporation and after the payment of all debts and liabilities, its remaining property shall be distributed or disposed of to or among such one of more exclusively charitable organizations which carries on its work, or carry on their work, solely in Canada as the directors of the Corporation in their discretion select;

(f) the Corporation shall be subject to the *Charities Accounting Act* and the *Charitable Gifts Act*; and

(g) if it is made to appear to the satisfaction of the Minister, upon report of the Public Trustee, that the Corporation has failed to comply with the provisions of the *Charities Accounting Act* or the *Charitable Gifts Act*, the Minister may authorize an inquiry for the purpose of determining whether or not there is sufficient cause for the Lieutenant-Governor, in his discretion, to make an order under section 317(1) of the *Corporations Act* to cancel the Letters Patent of the Corporation and declare it to be dissolved.

For the further attainment of the objects aforesaid, the powers of the Corporation are:

(a) in furtherance of the aforesaid objects to establish, create, administer, maintain and dispense a fund or funds either of money in the Corporation or its warnings and from donations, gifts, legacies, devises and contributions from the public;

(b) the Corporation may raise funds by any means whatsoever and acquire or lease by means of solicitation and donation or by any other means whatsoever any kind of real or personal property;

(c) the Corporation may acquire, own and use real estate for the purposes of actual use or occupation for the charitable purpose and may convey or otherwise dispose of such real estate; and

(d) the Corporation may print and publish literature.

Toronto District Christian High School

(c) And to further provide the following special provisions to the Letters Patent:

(i) The membership of the Corporation shall consist of all persons who indicate their agreement with the basis and purpose of the Corporation as hereinbefore described, and who meet the conditions for membership as contained in the by-laws of the Corporation.

(ii) The Board of Directors shall consist of not less than twelve (12) directors who shall be elected or appointed in accordance with the by-laws of the Corporation and who shall serve as such without remuneration, and no director shall directly or indirectly receive any profit from his position as such; provided that a director may be paid reasonable expenses incurred by him in the performance of his duties.

(iii) That upon the dissolution of the Corporation and after the payment of all debts and liabilities, its remaining property shall be distributed or disposed of to charitable organizations which carry on their work solely in Ontario in the furtherance of Christian education causes.

(iv) That no application for a change to the Letters Patent of the Corporation with reference to the basis and purpose of the Corporation shall be made unless approved in writing by the entire membership of the Corporation of record and any application for a change to the Letters Patent of the Corporation other than as aforesaid shall not be made unless approved by two-thirds of the members present at a meeting of members called for that purpose.

(v) The directors of the Corporation shall be elected and shall retire in rotation in the following manner, that is to say, at the first meeting of members for the election of directors, four directors shall be elected to hold office for a term of three years from the date of their election or until the third annual meeting of members after such date, whichever first occurs, four for a term of two years from the date of their election or until the second annual meeting, whichever first occurs, and four for a term of one year from the date of their election or until the next annual meeting after such date, whichever first occurs, and thereafter at each annual meeting directors shall be elected to fill the positions of those directors whose term of office has expired and each director so elected shall hold office for a term of three years or until the third annual meeting after his election, whichever first occurs.

Appendix "E"

Notice of Intention to Operate under the Education Act

Appendix "F"

September Report, 1997 — Private School

Appendix "G"

Private School Manual: Information for Inspected Private Secondary Schools*

PREFACE

This document has been designed to provide a central source of information and references to the legislation, forms and practices related to **inspected private secondary schools**.

This document is not intended to be an official source. The pertinent legislation, guidelines and policy statements are to be referred to for specific requirements.

It will be revised as changes to the legislation, forms and practices are made and as additional information is requested by the users of this manual. The Ministry of Education and Training welcomes comments.

Thanks are extended to Association of Christian Schools International, Conference of Independent Schools, Ontario Council of Independent Schools, Ontario Federation of Independent Schools, as well as Education Directors, principals and teachers of First Nations private secondary schools in Northwestern Ontario, for their comments.

Section 3
SOURCES OF INFORMATION/MATERIALS

1. To request educational office material (OSR folders, Ontario Student Transcript forms, Office Record Cards, etc.):

    THE GUIDANCE CENTRE
    712 GORDON BAKER ROAD
    TORONTO, ON M2H 3R7
    TELEPHONE: 416-502-1262
    FAX: 416-502-1101

---

* August, 1997 excerpts. Reproduced with permission.

184   An Educator's Guide to Independent Schools

2. To order curriculum materials (guidelines, regulations, etc.):
    PUBLICATIONS ONTARIO
    50 GROSVENOR STREET
    TORONTO, ON M7A 1N8
    TELEPHONE: (416) 326-5300
                1-800-668-9938
    FAX: 416-326-5317

3. Ministry of Education and Training website includes the List of Private Schools in Ontario, Curricular 14 [Circular 14], List of Common Course Codes, policy documents, Ontario Curriculum: grades 1-8 in Language and Mathematics, and other information useful to inspected private secondary schools. All of these materials may be down loaded. The site is updated regularly. It is found at:

    http://www.edu.gov.on.ca

4. Ontario College of Teachers website includes information about registration, fees, membership services and general information.

    http://www.oct.on.ca
    Ontario College of Teachers
    121 Bloor Street East
    6th floor
    Toronto, Ontario M4W 3M5
    TELEPHONE: (416) 961-8800
                1-888-534-2222
    FAX: 416-961-8822

Section 7
ONTARIO STUDENT RECORDS
AND
ONTARIO STUDENT TRANSCRIPTS

Section 22 of the Notice of Intention to Operate a Private School states that by requesting inspection of the secondary program, the principal agrees to adopt the Ontario Student Transcript Common Course Coding. The Ontario Student Transcript is a component of the Ontario Student Record.

[Refer to the *Ontario Student Record Guideline, 1989*]

ONTARIO STUDENT RECORDS (OSRs)

The OSR is the record of a student's educational progress through school. It is privileged for the information and use of supervisory officers and the principal and teachers of the school for the improvement of instruction of the student.

Duty of a Principal
— to establish, maintain, retain, transfer and dispose of a record for each student enrolled in the school;
— to ensure that the materials in the OSR comply with the policies of the OSR guideline;
— to ensure the security of the OSR;
— to ensure that all persons involved with the OSR are aware of the need for confidentiality.

Report Cards
— a report card shall be completed and filed in the OSR for each student who has been enrolled in the school for more than six weeks;
— the report card shall be the original or an exact copy;
— the report card for Grade 10 to OAC courses shall indicate the common course code and title of the course;
— the report card for Grade 10 to OAC courses shall indicate the value of the credits assigned to the course, or, for courses for which credits are not awarded, the words "non-credit course".

Student Record of Accumulated Instruction in French or Native as a Second Language
— an individual record of accumulated instruction in French or Native as a Second Language shall be established and maintained for each student enrolled in such a course.
— the card must be maintained in the OSR.
— see Sections 3.6 and 3.7 of the guideline for more information.

Transfer to a Private School
— Before a principal transfers an original OSR to an inspected or to a non-inspected private school in Ontario, the principal shall have received:
  — a written request for the information from the receiving private school, in which the private school agrees to accept responsibility for the OSR and to maintain, retain, transfer, and dispose of the OSR in accordance with the OSR guideline;

— a written statement, signed by the adult student or the parent(s) or guardian(s) of a student who is not an adult, indicating consent to the transfer.

Transfer to an Education Institution Outside Ontario

— an original OSR cannot be transferred outside of Ontario.
— only an exact copy of the OSR may be transferred after receiving a written request of the principal from the educational institution.
— a written statement, signed by the adult student or the parent(s) or guardian(s) of a student who is not an adult, indicating consent to the transfer.

Retention, Storage and Destruction of the OSR

The following components of the OSR shall be retained for five (5) years after a student retires from school:

— report cards;
— record of instruction in French or Native as a Second Language.

The following components of the OSR shall be retained for fifty-five (55) years after a student retires from school:

— the OSR folder
— the OST
— the office index card (see OSR guideline)

Appendix "G"

APPENDIX 1: REQUEST FOR AN OSR FROM A PRIVATE SCHOOL

> Please forward the Ontario Student Record for
>
> _____
>
> Surname   First Name   Middle Name
>
> who has enrolled in Grade _____ at
>
> Name of School _____
>
> Address _____
>
> _____
>
> This is to certify that this is a private school inspected by supervisory officials of the Ministry of Education and Training, Ontario.
>
> I hereby agree to accept responsibility for the record and to use, maintain, transfer, and dispose of the record in accordance with the guideline for the Ontario Student Record.
>
> _____   _____
>
> Principal   Date

December 1989

> ***This form must be accompanied by a written statement signed by the adult student, or parent(s) or guardian(s) of a student who is not an adult, indicating consent to transfer.**

[Refer to the *Manual for the Ontario Student Transcript, 1986*]

ONTARIO STUDENT TRANSCRIPT (OSTs)

— The OST must be completed prior to an OSSD or a Certificate of Education being granted.
— The OST for Grade 10 to OAC must have a listing of the proper course title, the common course code, the credit value, the achievement level and an indication if the credit is compulsory.

— An official OST will be issued to any student who requires a transcript in order to enrol in an Ontario secondary school credit course, regardless of his/her last day of attendance at the school.
— See the OST manual for more information.

SCHOOL CLOSURES

When a private school closes, the principal must:
1. prepare an alphabetical list of all OSRs;
2. ensure that each OSR is complete, including the language record card and office record card;
3. submit all OSRs, in alphabetical order to the Ministry of Education and Training, Record Management Unit, Ministry of Education and Training, 7th Floor Mowat Block, 900 Bay Street, Toronto, Ontario, M7A 1L2;
4. provide a list of all OSRs which have been forwarded to another school. Include the student's name, grade, year and school to which it was forwarded.

Appendix "H"
Private School Inspection Report

Appendix "I"

Revenue Canada Information Circular 75-23*

September 29, 1975

Tuition Fees and Charitable Donations Paid to Privately Supported Secular and Religious Schools

1. Tuition fees paid to an educational institution in Canada are deductible by the student in accordance with subsection 60(f) of the *Income Tax Act*. Such fees are not considered charitable donations and official receipts designed for charitable donations may not be issued for such tuition fees even though the educational institution may be a registered Canadian charitable organization as defined in paragraph 110(8)(c) of the Act.

2. The purpose of this circular is to explain two exceptions to the above rule where a portion or all of an amount paid to a school, other than a post-secondary institution or a designated educational institution (see Appendix A), may be considered as a donation. The two types of such schools which give rise to these special circumstances are:

   (a) those which teach exclusively religion, and
   (b) those which operate in a dual capacity providing both secular (academic) and religious education.

Religious Schools

3. If such a school teaches exclusively religion and thereby operates solely for the advancement of religion, payments for students attending that school are not considered to be tuition fees but will be considered as valid donations and, providing the school is a registered Canadian charitable organization, official receipts for charitable donations may be issued for such payments.

---

* Reproduced with permission.

Secular Schools

4. The provisions of the Income Tax Act do not permit a deduction, as a charitable donation, of an amount paid to a school for academic tuition, whether the amount was paid for set fees or was a voluntary contribution. A gift, to be allowable within the concept of paragraph 110(1)(a) of the Act, must be a voluntary transference of property without consideration. The consideration here is the academic training received by the children attending the school. On the other hand religious training is not viewed as consideration for purposes of the definition of a gift.

5. School fees are normally based on the costs of operation. However, there are some schools in Canada, usually connected with a church, which do not levy set fees and operate solely through contributions of parents or guardians and other members of the church. These schools, which are subject to the inspection of provincial educational authorities, operate in a dual capacity providing both secular and religious education.

6. Under certain circumstances receipts for charitable donations may be issued for a portion of an amount paid to attend schools, other than post-secondary institutions or designated educational institutions, which operate in this dual capacity. There are two methods of calculating the donation portion of amounts paid, depending on how the school maintains its accounting records.

7. The most favourable treatment will be received where the school can and does segregate the cost of operating the secular portion of the school and the cost of providing religious training. Under this method, the net cost of operating the secular portion of the school is to be pro-rated over the number of pupils enrolled during the school year to determine a "cost per pupil" for the secular training. An official donation receipt can be issued for that portion of a payment which is in excess of the pro-rated "cost per pupil" for academic training. If a taxpayer has more than one child in attendance at the school, the amount to be deducted from his total payment, to determine the donation portion, is the "cost per pupil" for academic training multiplied by the number of his children enrolled during the school year.

8. The net cost of operating the secular portion of the school will be determined to be the total operating costs of that portion of the school for a school year (excluding capital expenditures and depreciation) less miscellaneous income, grants received and donations received from persons with no children in attendance, unless such grants or donations were designated for a capital purpose. "Cost per pupil" would be the above described cost divided by the number of students enrolled during the school year.

9. Where such a school which operates in a dual capacity does not or cannot segregate the cost of operating the secular portion of the school and the cost of providing religious training, a donation receipt can be issued only for

that part of the payment which is in excess of the net operating "cost per pupil" of the whole school for a school year. The net operating cost of the whole school in this case will be the total operating costs of the school including both secular and religious education (excluding capital expenditures and depreciation) less miscellaneous income, grants and donations from persons with no children in attendance, unless such grants or donations were designated for capital purposes. "Cost per pupil" will be the above described cost divided by the number of students enrolled during the school year. For taxpayers with more than one child in attendance, the rule in the last sentence of paragraph 7 above will apply using the "cost per pupil" of the whole school.

10. For purposes of either of the above methods, where a payment has been made to a school before December 31st of a school year and the school must issue an official donation receipt for taxation purposes before the "cost per pupil" for the school year can be determined, the school may use the "cost per pupil" of the previous school year, if the school operated in that previous year.

11. The school must be prepared to substantiate that the "cost per pupil" for a school year has been determined from the books and records of the school in accordance with the above policy.

12. A payment to such a school by a person who is neither the parents or guardians of a pupil who attends such a school and for which no benefit is derived qualifies in full as a donation.

Index

Abuse, child
    duty to report, 159-62
Accounting
    audit, 32
    books and records, 80-81
    segregation of costs, 74-5
Adler Case, 6-7, 67-8, 99-100
Admissions
    acceptance letters, 61
    application for enrolment, 60-61
    confidential information, 131
    human rights considerations, 63-6
    new students, legal contract, 58-62
    returning students, legal contract, 62-3
Assessment, exemption of schools, 82-4
Auditors, 32
Building Code, 38-9
Canadian Charter of Rights and Freedoms
    right to send children to independent schools, 4-7
Catalogue, school, 59-60
Charitable Gifts
    generally, 75-7
    receipts, 77-8
    tuition, tax treatment, 70-75
Charitable Organizations
    application for registration, 35-6
    approval of objects by Public Trustee and Guardian, 19
    directors' duties, 36-7
    directors' remuneration, 23, 36-7
    taxation, exemption, 69-70
Circular 14, 90, 96-7

Codes of Conduct
  non-teaching staff, 124-5
  teachers and principals, 117-24
College of Teachers, 111-12
Committees, directors, 28-30
Consent Forms, 153
Constitution Act, 1867
  constitutional position of independent schools, 4-7
  section 93, 4
Contracts of Instruction
  documents constituting, 58-62
  key components, 57-62
  legal capacity of parties, 58
  material changes, 62-3
  primary legal relationship with parents, 57
Corporal Punishment, 142-4
Corporations
  business and not-for-profit, 14-15
  legal benefits and disadvantages, 13-14
  non-share —
    annual filings, 32-3
    application for incorporation, 15-16
    auditors, 32
    by-laws, 20
    corporation information return, 19
    directors, 21-30
    incorporation procedure, 17-19
    membership, 20-21
    membership fees, 21
    names, 16-17
    objects, 17-18, Appendix "C"
    officers, 30
    personal liability, 33-4
    special provisions, 18-19, Appendix "D"
Defamation
  student records, 133
  teacher evaluations, 117
Diplomas, power of Minister to grant, 52
Directors
  chair, 27
  charitable organizations, additional duties, 36-7
  committees, 28-30
  conflict of interest, 23-4

Directors — *continued*
- executive committee, 26
- meetings, 25-6
- numbers, 24
- occupational health liability, 33-4
- personal liability, 33-4
- powers, 27-8
- qualifications, 22
- remuneration, 23
- standing committees, 28-30
- term of office, 25

Discipline
- corporal punishment, 142-4
- in loco parentis, 136-8
- power to discipline, 135
- procedural rules, 138-41
- searches, 142

Education Act
- certification of teachers, 11
- compulsory attendance, 9-10
- definition of private school, 9
- inspections of private schools, 10-11
- ministerial powers, 11-12
- notice of intention to operate, 10, 41-5
- offences, 11
- province-wide tests, 11-12
- sections on private school, 10-11, Appendix "A"
- September return, 10, 45

Education Quality and Accountability Office, 98-9

Elementary School, program of study, 87, 88-9

Employment
- principal, 107-9
- teachers —
  - categories of contracts, 112
  - duties, 112-13
  - length of contract, 113
  - performance reviews, 116-17
  - salaries and benefits, 114
  - termination, 114-16

Enrolment
- new students, 57-62
- returning students, 62-3

Expenditures
    charitable organizations, 79-80
    not-for-profit corporations, 78-9
    segregating costs, Information Circular 75-23, 72-5
Expulsion of Students, 138-41
Filings, corporate and tax, 81-2
Fire Code, 38-9, 166
Funding
    absence of government funding, 67-8
    charitable donations, 69
    tuition, 69
Guardians, contract of instruction with, 58
Handbook, student, 61-2
Hazardous Materials, 164-5
Health, approval of medical officer of, 38-9
Health Protection and Promotion Act, 100
Holidays, 100-101
Home Schooling, and independent schools, 54-6
Hours, course, 101
Human Rights Code
    admission of students, 63-6
    codes of conduct, 117-25
Immunization of Pupils
    exemption, 157
    parental obligation, 157
    school obligation, 132, 158-9
Independent schools
    associations, Appendix "B"
    history, 1-4
    operation of home campuses, 54-6
    overview of Ontario legislation, 9-12
    regulation by other provinces, 7-8
Injuries, liability for student
    chemistry and industrial arts classes, 149
    extra-curricular activities, 150-51
    physical education classes, 148-9
    school liability for teacher's negligence, 152-3
    sports, 149-50
    standard of care generally, 147-8
    transportation of students, 151
Inspections of Independent Schools
    elementary schools, 45-6

Inspections of Independent Schools — *continued*
   inspected secondary schools —
      conduct of inspection, 49-50
      costs, 50
      inspection reports, 50-51
      preparing for an inspection, 48-9
      private school manual, 47-8
      unsatisfactory inspections, 52-4
   inspection report, Appendix "H"
   kinds of inspections, 45-51
   NOI inspections, 45-6
   non-diploma secondary schools, 46
   purpose, 52-3
   statutory authorization, 10-11
Insurance, 84-5
Interest, overdue accounts, 80
International Bacculareate, 90-91
Joint Health and Safety Committee, 163
Lottery, 69
Meetings
   directors, 25-6
   members, 31-2
Members of School Corporation
   meetings, 31-2
   personal liability, 33-4
   qualifications, 21
Membership fees, 21
Minister of Education and Training, powers following inspection, 52-3
Minors, contracts of instruction, 58
Municipal Freedom of Information and Protection of Privacy Act, 130-31
Negligence
   causation, 151-2
   contributory negligence, 154
   duty of care, 145-7
   lack of supervision, 150
   liability of school for teacher's negligence, 152-3
   occupiers' liability, 154-5
   standard of care, 147-51
Notice of Intention to Operate, 10, Appendix "E"
   agreement to adopt Common Course Coding, 43
   annual filing, 45
   application for secondary inspection, 42-3
   approval by municipality, 43

Notice of Intention to Operate — *continued*
   content, 41-3
   initial filing, 43
   initial inspection, 43-4
   requirement to file, 41
Occupational Health and Safety, 162-4
Occupiers' Liability Act, 154-5
Officers, corporation, 30
OHIP, school health support services, 99-100
Ontario Education Numbers, 129-30
Ontario Student Record Guideline, 127-9
Ontario Student Transcript, 128
OS:IS, 90
Parents
   duty to educate, 9-10
   duty to immunize, 157-9
Premises, defective, 154-5
Principal
   application of Education Act, 105-7
   codes of conduct, 117-24
   duties, 106-7, 107-8
   employment terms, 105
   evaluation, 108-9
   membership on board of directors, 22-3, 37, 108
   role, 103-5
Private School, definition, 44, 55-6
Private School Manual, 47-8, Appendix "G"
Program of Study
   course hours, 101
   elementary school, 87, 88-9
   inspected secondary school, 87, 90-92
   non-inspected secondary school, 87, 89
Reasonable Force, 142-4
Records, student
   access to and confidentiality, 130-33
   contents, 128
   defamatory statements, 133
   Ontario Education Numbers, 129-30
   Ontario Student Record Guideline, 127-8, Appendix "G"
Refunds, tuition, 63
Release Forms, 153
Religious Education, 101-2
Report Cards, 129

Revenue Canada
    approval of charitable corporation by-laws, 17-18
    tuition, Information Circular 75-23, 72-5, Appendix "I"
Satisfactory Instruction
    court cases, 92-5
    Education Act, 92
    Private School Manual, 95-6
School Boards, co-operation agreements with, 86
School Year, 100-1
Searches, 142
Secondary School
    inspected, program of study, 87, 90-92
    non-inspected, program of study, 87, 88
September Report, 10, 45, Appendix "F"
Shapiro Report, 1-4, 11-12
Special Education, 99
Taxation
    exemption of non-profit corporation, 70
    exemption of registered charity, 69-70
    municipal taxes, exemption, 82-4
Teachers
    application of Education Act, 105-7
    codes of conduct, 117-24
    duties, generally, 106-7, 112-13
    duty to report abuse, 160-62
    employment terms, 105, 112-17
    inspection for certification, 11, 48, 109-11
    membership in College of Teachers, 111-12
    performance reviews, 116-17
    qualifications, 109
    role, 103-5
    salary and benefits, 114
    termination, 114-16
Tests, province wide, 11, 97-9
Textbooks, selection, 90, 96-7
Transcript, 128
Transportation of Students, liability, 151
Trespass to Property Act, 144
Tuition
    charitable gift, limited treatment as, 70-72, Appendix "I"
    contract to pay, 57, 61
    employee fringe benefit, 78
    refunds, 63

Vicarious Liability, student injuries, 152-3
Workplace Hazardous Material Information System (WHMIS), 164-5
Zoning, 38